A MILTON CHRONOLOGY

AUTHOR CHRONOLOGIES

General Editor: Norman Page, Emeritus Professor of Modern
English Literature, University of Nottingham

Published titles include:

J. L. Bradley
A RUSKIN CHRONOLOGY

Gordon Campbell
A MILTON CHRONOLOGY

J. R. Hammond
A ROBERT LOUIS STEVENSON CHRONOLOGY

John McDermott
A HOPKINS CHRONOLOGY

Norman Page
AN EVELYN WAUGH CHRONOLOGY

Peter Preston
A D. H. LAWRENCE CHRONOLOGY

A Milton Chronology

Gordon Campbell

Professor of Renaissance Literature
University of Leicester
President, The English Association

First published in Great Britain 1997 by
MACMILLAN PRESS LTD
Houndmills, Basingstoke, Hampshire RG21 6XS and London
Companies and representatives throughout the world

A catalogue record for this book is available from the British Library.

ISBN 0–333–63326–1

 First published in the United States of America 1997 by
ST. MARTIN'S PRESS, INC.,
Scholarly and Reference Division,
175 Fifth Avenue, New York, N.Y. 10010

ISBN 0–312–17586–8

Library of Congress Cataloging-in-Publication Data
Campbell, Gordon, 1944–
A Milton chronology / Gordon Campbell.
p.   cm.
Includes bibliographical references (p.   ) and index.
ISBN 0–312–17586–8 (cloth)
1. Milton, John, 1608–1674—Chronology.   2. Poets, English—Early
modern, 1500–1700—Chronology.   I. Title.
PR3583.C36 1997
821'.4—DC21   97–10705
                                                                         CIP

This book is printed on paper suitable for recycling and made from fully managed and sustained forest sources.

10   9   8   7   6   5   4   3   2   1
06   05   04   03   02   01   00   99   98   97

Printed and bound in Great Britain by
Antony Rowe Ltd, Chippenham, Wiltshire

Contents

General Editor's Preface

Most biographies are ill adapted to serve as works of reference – not surprisingly so, since the biographer is likely to regard his function as the devising of a continuous and readable narrative, with excursions into interpretation and speculation, rather than a bald recital of facts. There are times, however, when anyone reading for business or pleasure needs to check a point quickly or to obtain a rapid overview of part of an author's life or career; and at such moments turning over the pages of a biography can be a time-consuming and frustrating occupation. The present series of volumes aims at providing a means whereby the chronological facts of an author's life and career, rather than needing to be prised out of the narrative in which they are (if they appear at all) securely embedded, can be seen at a glance. Moreover, whereas biographies are often, and quite understandably, vague over matters of fact (since it makes for tediousness to be forever enumerating details of dates and places), a chronology can be precise whenever it is possible to be precise.

Thanks to the survival, sometimes in very large quantities, of letters, diaries, notebooks and other documents, as well as to thoroughly researched biographies and bibliographies, this material now exists in abundance for many major authors. In the case of, for example, Dickens, we can often ascertain what he was doing in each month and week, and almost on each day, of his prodigiously active working life; and the student of, say, *David Copperfield* is likely to find it fascinating as well as useful to know just when Dickens was at work on each part of that novel, what other literary enterprises he was engaged in at the same time, whom he was meeting, what places he was visiting, and what were the relevant circumstances of his personal and professional life. Such a chronology is not, of course, a substitute for a biography; but its arrangement, in combination with its index, makes it a much more convenient tool for this kind of purpose; and it may be acceptable as a form of 'alternative' biography, with its own distinctive advantages as well as its obvious limitations.

Since information relating to an author's early years is usually scanty and chronologically imprecise, the opening section of some volumes in this series groups together the years of childhood and adolescence. Thereafter each year, and usually each month, is dealt with separately. Information not readily assignable to a specific month or day is given as a general note under the relevant year or month. The first entry for each month carries an indication of the day of the week, so that when necessary this can be readily calculated for other dates. Each volume also contains a bibliography of the principal sources of information. In the chronology itself, the sources of many of the more specific items, including quotations, are identified, in order that the reader who wishes to do so may consult the original contexts.

NORMAN PAGE

Preface

Milton scholarship is a cumulative enterprise, and any scholar who seeks to see further than his predecessors is conscious that he must construct his vantage point on the work of others. I have erected my chronological edifice on the foundations laid by three scholars. The first scholar systematically to collect the documents associated with the life of Milton was David Masson, and the fruits of his labours are enshrined in the seven weighty volumes of the life of Milton that he published between 1859 and 1894. The second scholar is J. Milton French, whose five-volume edition of the *Life Records of John Milton* (1949–58) supplemented Masson in many areas (especially that of legal records) and presented the documents in a chronological format that makes it the single most important model for this volume; I differ from French in many points of dating and interpretation, and the scholarship of the past 40 years has enabled me to add many documents that he overlooked, but such differences should be construed as a tribute to a distinguished Miltonist rather than a slighting of his remarkable scholarship. The third scholar is William Riley Parker, whose two-volume life of Milton (1968) I have recently been privileged to supplement in a revised edition (1996); Parker took legal documents on trust from French, but his command of parish registers enabled him to add many new documents to the corpus of Milton material.

French published his research on *Milton in Chancery* in 1939, but thereafter the war intervened and he had to rely, *faute de mieux*, on photographs and on transcriptions made by others. Similarly, Parker drafted his biography during the war (he had completed a draft by 1946), and thereafter conducted much of his research by relentless correspondence, the most important product of which is his world-wide survey of surviving copies of Milton's publications. The scholarly authority that characterises the pages of French and Parker can lead scholars to rely too much on material that is being reported at second hand. It is clear, for example, that neither French nor Parker examined the records of the Company of Goldsmiths, and so references to Milton's dealings with the Company have been overlooked. Indeed, an unreported entry in the

Company's records dated 3 July 1656 may imply that the Milton family lived at the Red Rose in Bread Street as well as, or rather than, the smaller Spread Eagle in which Milton's father conducted his business. Could the poet have been born in the Red Rose? John Aubrey thought so, but later decided that he must have been born in the Spread Eagle.

Refining and adding substantially to the research of Masson, French and Parker is no small undertaking; the two scholars who have managed to do so are John Shawcross and the late Leo Miller. Shawcross's exacting bibliographical researches and Miller's untiring pursuit of the Miltonic state papers in the chancelleries of Europe have produced much of the new material in this volume; these scholars have also contributed to it in a more personal way, by urging me, when I was a novice, to examine the manuscripts myself. This has not always been a straightforward task, because many of the manuscripts have been elusive (and some continue to elude me), but the attempt to see as many as possible has been salutary as well as fruitful, in part because I have been able to find scores of manuscripts that have changed hands or been lost amidst the millions of documents in the Public Record Office, but also because the process has led me to many documents that have not previously been examined by students of Milton. In searching for manuscripts I have often found myself dogging the heels of Peter Beal, whose bibliography of the Milton manuscripts has resolved many problems, including the authorship of the anonymous life of Milton, which can now be said with confidence to be the work of Cyriack Skinner. In the case of the State Papers, I have often been grateful for the labours of Robert Fallon in that difficult soil. I have tried to examine as many manuscripts and printed sources as possible, but when I have been unable to do so, I give a reference to French's *Life Records* (abbreviated as *LR*), in which many of the documents that I cite are printed *in extenso*. Legal documents, which were French's particular forte, have remained a mystery to most students of Milton, because there is no accessible guide to the complex system of courts that dispensed justice for centuries until they were swallowed up in the reforms of the late nineteenth century. I have therefore appended a Glossary of Legal Terms in which I describe those aspects of the legal system of Stuart England that must be elucidated if the large corpus of legal documents associated with Milton is to be understood. The reference in my text to PRO C228, for example, will take the curious reader to the appropriate entry in the Bibliography, which explains that the file contains Chancery proceedings on the Statute Staple, Petty Bag Office. The Glossary of Legal Terms identifies Chancery, Statute Staple and Petty Bag Office.

Many colleagues have come to my aid as I have assembled this volume: Stephen Bamforth, Peter Beal, Cedric Brown, Charles Burnett, Edward Chaney, Thomas Corns, Hans-Jürgen Diller, Robert Fallon, Roy Flannagan, Neil Forsyth, John Gough, Neil Harris, Stella Lanham, John Law, Peter Lindenbaum, Peter Mack, Deborah Madsen, Jeremy Maule, Robin White, Paul Sellin, John Shawcross, Nicholas von Maltzahn and Henry Woudhuysen have all given generously of their time and expertise, and I am pleased to acknowledge their assistance. I am also grateful for the assistance of a host of archivists and librarians: J. A. Bayford (Deputy Clerk, Merchant Taylors' Company), David Beasley (Worshipful Company of Goldsmiths), Henry Button (Christ's College, Cambridge), Judith Crawford (Hartlib Collection, Sheffield), Peter Durrant (Berkshire Record Office), Kate Harris (Longleat), Aideen Ireland (National Archives, Ireland), David McKitterick (Trinity College, Cambridge), Ian Murray (Inner Temple), Bernard Nurse (Society of Antiquaries), Palle Ringsted (Royal Library, Copenhagen), Moortheeswari Madhava Rao (Fort Museum, Madras), Raymond Refaussé (Representative Church Body Library, Dublin), Robert Yorke (College of Arms) and the large number of colleagues in the Bodleian, the British Library, Cambridge University Library and, most of all, the Public Record Office, who have helped me to find elusive documents. I am conscious that this is the last research that I shall be able to conduct in Great Russell Street and Chancery Lane, and I can but hope that the imminent move of the British Library to St Pancras and the Public Record Office to Kew will not result in a reduction of the expert services that have been available to generations of readers.

A substantial layer of the palimpsest that underlies this book was drafted at the bedside of my son Stuart as he recovered in hospital from a serious road traffic accident. I should like to dedicate this book to him in tribute to the courage and cheerful irony that he evinced as he travelled and travailed along the road to recovery.

GORDON CAMPBELL
Leicester

List of Abbreviations

ADB	*Allgemeine Deutsche Biographie* (56 vols)
BL	British Library
DBF	*Dictionnaire de Biographie Française* (19 vols to date, A–Laglenne)
DBI	*Dizionario Biografico degli Italiani* (45 vols to date, A–Federigo)
DBL	*Dansk Biografisk Leksikon, 1537–1814* (19 vols)
DNB	*Dictionary of National Biography* (68 vols)
EF	*Epistolarum Familiarum* 1674 (JM's personal letters)
LR	*The Life Records of John Milton*, (ed.) J. M. French, 5 vols (1949–58).
HMC	Royal Commission on Historical Manuscripts
NNBW	*Nieuw Nederlandsch Biografisch Woordenboek* (10 vols)
NYPL	New York Public Library
NDB	*Neue Deutsche Biographie* (17 vols to date, A–Moller)
P	John Milton, *Complete Prose Works* (8 vols, Yale University Press, 1953–82)
PCC	Prerogative Court of Canterbury
PHSR	*Publications of the Harleian Society, Registers*
PRO	Public Record Office, London
SBL	*Svenskt Biografiskt Lexikon* (27 vols to date, A–Nässtrom)
SMK	*Svenska Män och Kvinnor: Biografisk Uppslagsbok* (8 vols)
SR	*A Transcript of the Registers of the Company of Stationers, 1554–1640*, (ed.) E. Arber (5 vols, 1875–77, 1894, 1950); *A Transcript of the Registers of the Company of Stationers, 1641–1708*, (eds) G. E. B. Eyre and H. R. Plomer (3 vols, 1913–14, 1950).
W	John Milton, *Works* (18 vols, Columbia University Press, 1931–38)

Introduction

The construction of chronologies for seventeenth-century literary figures is a perilous undertaking. It is often remarked, for example, that Shakespeare and Cervantes died on the same day. That statement is true inasmuch as both are believed to have died on 23 April 1616, but in fact Cervantes died ten days before Shakespeare: the Gregorian calendar in use in Spain was, in the seventeenth century, ten days ahead of the Julian calendar which was retained in England until 1752. Historians refer to the Julian Calendar as Old Style (O.S.) and the Gregorian as New Style (N.S.), but literary scholars often muddy the water by using O.S. and N.S. to describe the discrepancy between documents that assume that the new year begins on 25 March and those that follow the continental (and Scottish) convention of reckoning the new year from 1 January. Further confusion is generated by Latin records, because they not only use unfamiliar terms for days of the week (Dies Solis, Lunae, Martis, Mercurii, Jovis, Veneris, Saturni), but they also fix the day of the month by the Roman system of counting backwards from the three divisions of the month (*calends, nones* and *ides*) rather than by counting forwards in ordinal numbers from the beginning of each month. The chronologist must also contend with several additional calendars in use in seventeenth-century England: the regnal year used to date official documents (except for the years 1649 to 1660), the ecclesiastical calendar, which produces documents dated by saints' days and festivals, the legal chronology (related to the law terms, on which see Watson) used to date legal proceedings, the university terms and, in the acknowledgement of correspondence, the Islamic year. Several of these calendars are too technical to warrant an exposition in a volume in this series, and readers will simply have to trust my interpretation of documents dated in ways that are now unfamiliar. The Julian–Gregorian discrepancy and the uncertainty over the beginning of the year, however, need to be explained if the dating of a large number of Miltonic documents is to be understood. Milton's habit of dating Latin poems by his age also needs to be considered, because his practice in Latin seems to be inconsistent.

The Julian calendar is named after Julius Caesar, who declared the mean length of the solar year to be 365 days and six hours, and decreed that the quarter day should be accommodated by the addition of an extra day every four years; in this calendar the vernal equinox was fixed at 25 March. In fact, however, the solar year is 365 days, 5 hours, 48 minutes and 46 seconds long. The annual discrepancy of 11 minutes and 14 seconds meant that the equinox slowly retrograded towards the beginning of the Julian year, and by the time Constantine convened the Council of Nicaea in 325, the equinox had moved back to 21 March. Pope Gregory XIII effected a reform of the calendar in 1582, by which time the equinox had retrograded to 11 March. Gregory commanded that ten days be suppressed in the calendar for 1582, so that the day after 4 October became 15 October and the equinox was restored to 21 March; he proposed to prevent a recurrence of the problem by stipulating that centurial years only be leap years if they were divisible by 400.

The Gregorian calendar was adopted throughout the Catholic world, but Protestant and Orthodox countries demurred, and sometimes took several centuries to adopt the reformed calendar. Amsterdam, Leiden and The Hague, for example, changed in 1582, but Utrecht waited till 1700, Geneva till 1701, St Gallen till 1724, Britain till 1752 and Russia till 1923 (after which the anniversary of the October Revolution was celebrated in November). I know of no account in English that charts the gradual changes on the continent, which vary from province to province and canton to canton, but there are complete lists (in Italian and German) in Cappelli and Grotefend (see Bibliography). Throughout the seventeenth century the difference between Britain's Julian calendar and the Catholic Gregorian calendar was ten days; the year 1700 was a leap year in the Julian calendar but a common year in the Gregorian calendar, so the discrepancy became 11 days until 1752, when Britain moved to the Gregorian calendar by suppressing 11 days: 2 September was followed by 14 September. The discrepancy is now 13 days, so in the Russian Orthodox Church, which retains the Julian calendar, Christmas is celebrated on what the secular calendar calls 7 January.

Most of the dates in this chronology are Julian, but when there is any possibility of confusion (as in the case of correspondence with the continent) I provide a split date; the first of the two dates is always the English Julian date. Peter Heimbach wrote to Milton from The Hague (which had adopted the Gregorian calendar) on 18 December 1657. Milton replied on 18 December 1657, which was ten days later. I date Heimbach's letter 8/18 December and Milton's reply 18 December.

The second complication concerns the beginning of the year. The Roman civil year began on 1 January, but the medieval church chose to repudiate its pagan antecedents by starting the year on 25 March, the Feast of the Annunciation, the day on which Jesus was deemed to have been conceived. In England this reckoning became widespread late in the twelfth century, and it remained in use until 1752, when the new year was officially fixed at 1 January. The year beginning with the Annunciation still survives in a slightly modified form in the British tax year, which ends on 5 April, a date which accommodated the 11-day adjustment and thus ensured that rents and interest payments that had traditionally been exacted on 25 March reflected payment for a full year. In the sixteenth century most countries in Europe (including Scotland) reverted to a new year beginning on 1 January, and in Catholic countries this practice was confirmed by the Gregorian reform of 1582. In seventeenth-century England the ambiguity is often resolved by recourse to a split date (in the form 30 January 1648/49). When the date is undivided, it is usually safe to assume that the year is deemed to begin on 25 March, but there are exceptions, such as the printed almanacs, which started their year on 1 January. The year on the title pages of printed books also seems invariably to start on 1 January.

Milton used the Latin formula *anno aetatis* ('in the year of [his] age') to date ten of his poems (eight Latin and two English). Three of these poems (*Elegia II, Elegia III* and *In obitum Praesulis Eliensis*) are commemorative pieces dated *anno aetatis 17*, and as those commemorated all died in the autumn of 1626 (see the entries for 25 and 26 September and 5 October), when Milton was 17, it seems safe to assume that Milton used the phrase to mean 'at the age of 17' rather than 'in his seventeenth year'; similarly, the dating of the 'Vacation Exercise' as *anno aetatis 19* would seem to be consistent with the fact that Milton was 19 in July 1628. On the other hand, in his *History of Britain* Milton had taken a phrase in Ingulf's *Historia* to the effect that the monk Turgarus had died *completis annis vitae suae 115* to mean that he had died 'in the 115th year' of his life; this instance, however, is more likely to be a simple slip than a repudiation of the usual sense of the phrase. On one or two occasions inconsistencies are likely to be attributable to lapses in memory: *In obitum Procancellarii medici*, for example, is said by Milton to have been written *anno aetatis 16*, but the Vice-Chancellor had died when Milton was 17 (see 21 October 1628); similarly, the subject of

Milton's 'On the Death of a Fair Infant' is likely to be a child who died when Milton was 19 (see 22 January 1628), so the caption *anno aetatis 17*, which Milton added in 1673, is almost certainly an error. In the other four instances there is no corroborative evidence for dating, but the dating of *Elegia IV* as *anno aetatis 18* is consistent with the most likely date (see 26 March 1627), the dating of *In quintum Novembris* as *anno aetatis 17* may be correct (see 5 November 1626), and the dating of *Elegia V* as *anno aetatis 20* is certainly possible (see headnote to 1629). Finally, *Elegia VII* is dated *anno aetatis undevigesimo*. This unique use of a Latin ordinal number is puzzling, but I suspect that the Latin should be taken literally and must therefore mean 'in his nineteenth year' rather than 'at the age of 19' (see 25 May 1627). The evidence is not sufficiently conclusive to offer decisive assistance with Milton's use in Sonnet 7 of the ordinal adjective in the phrase 'three and twentieth year'.

Some of Milton's works cannot be dated by recourse to external evidence, but the absence of evidence seems not to preclude judgements that are confident to the point of unreasoned passion. The most obvious case in point is *Samson Agonistes*. The only solid evidence of the date of composition is the publication of the printed version in 1671. Milton's nephew Edward Phillips commented that the date of composition 'cannot certainly be concluded' but this warning has not inhibited scholars who argue with missionary zeal for one date or another. A few scholars, led by Milton's biographer W. R. Parker, have contended that *Samson* was begun in 1646 or 1647, and then taken up again in 1652 or 1653 (Parker, 1996, 903–17). Other scholars subscribe to the view of A. S. P. Woodhouse (1949) that *Samson* was written in the months after the Restoration in May 1660. The arguments of Parker and Woodhouse are advanced with considerable ingenuity, but most scholars continue to defend the traditional date of 1667–69. The most eloquent articulation of this position is that of Lady Radzinowicz, who marshals a huge array of evidence based on Milton's changing stylistic practices, his thematic and intellectual concerns, and what seem to be autobiographical and historical references (Radzinowicz, 1978, 387–407); more recently, Thomas Corns (1990, 116–17) has undertaken an analysis of type-token ratios that seems to suggest that *Samson* was written at approximately the same time as *Paradise Regained* and Blair Worden has advanced compelling contextual arguments for a slightly earlier date *c.*1663–65 (Worden, in MacLean (1995), 111–36). Learned speculation about the date is harmless unless it becomes dogmatic, and the debate will doubtless continue indefinitely unless decisive documentary evidence is found. My own perpetually tentative position is that formulated by Henry Todd in his edition of 1801, which is that *Samson* 'furnishes some internal proofs of its having been composed at different periods'.

The central spine of this chronology is the documentary evidence of Milton's life. The decision about what to include and what to exclude has not always been straightforward. I have included a considerable amount of information about Milton's family, but have resisted the temptation to weave into this account allusions to the hundreds of documents that refer to matters such as Milton's father-in-law Richard Powell's complex financial dealings and Milton's brother Christopher's various Chancery suits. I have also eschewed the notion of a 'life and times' volume that records matters such as the birth of writers who were later to become famous and the painting of pictures that Milton would never see, and have instead attempted to look at the world that Milton inhabited through his eyes. In the entries documenting the early years of his life, for example, I have concentrated on the activities of his father's business, which was conducted in a shop in the family home on Bread Street. Similarly, I assume that in the autumn of 1623, 14-year-old Milton was more interested in the collapse of a nearby secret Catholic chapel than in the brideless return of Prince Charles from Spain or the death of the composer William Byrd. My assumption, which is admittedly arbitrary, is that Milton began to develop an interest in the wider world when he went up to Cambridge, and it is at that point in the chronology that I begin to intersperse brief comments on national and international events of which Milton is likely to have been aware. The one obvious exception to my resolution to ignore international affairs before 1625 is my summary account of the Thirty Years' War, which I place at the moment of its inception in the Defenestration of Prague on 13/23 May 1618. There are a few other points at which it has seemed sensible to abandon my attempt to use an imagined Milton as the focaliser of this volume: Milton could not, for example, have been aware of the births of his future wives, nor could he have known that he was being discussed in the private correspondence of the period. I have listed printed allusions to Milton and his works when they first occur, but have not recorded subsequent editions which simply repeat allusions; complete lists can be found in John

Shawcross's *Bibliography* (1984), which also lists variant editions of Milton's works in scrupulous detail, and provides details of advertisements for Milton's works, which I do not include unless they constitute evidence of the date of publication or, in the post-Restoration period, of the extent to which he is tolerated.

The construction of a documentary chronology of a seventeenth-century poet would seem to be an improbable scholarly exercise to those who are unaware of the vast amount of material that survives from the seventeenth century. There are thousands of references in hundreds of documents that enable the student of Milton to assemble the skeleton of his life, and scholars are constantly finding new material in manuscripts and in printed sources. Manuscripts are often precisely dated, but printed books are usually only dated by year. Sometimes the *Stationers' Register* helps to narrow a date, but in the mid-seventeenth century the most substantial help is afforded by Milton's friend George Thomason, who amassed a collection of some 22,255 publications (now bound in 2,008 volumes) between 1640 and 1663; the collection is now in the British Library. In the spring of 1641 Thomason began to write the date on which he received each publication on the title page. Sometimes this was the day of publication, but the pattern of his dating suggests that this was not always the case: he seems to have purchased books two or three times a week rather than daily, so a day on which five or six books are dated is often followed by one on which he seems not to have bought any books. Not all of the books are dated, but Thomason's own ten-volume catalogue often enables the scholar to infer dates, because the books are listed in order of acquisition; these catalogues are not widely known because, although they have long been visible through glass in the North Library, they are catalogued as books rather than manuscripts, and do not appear either in the British Library's catalogue of manuscripts or in the microfilm edition of the Thomason collection. Neither Thomason's inscriptions on title-pages nor his catalogues are infallible, and on occasion his dates can lead scholars astray, but Thomason's dates nonetheless ease the task of the chronologist to an extent that is unparalleled elsewhere in early modern Europe.

Many of the seventeenth-century documents that mention Milton are legal records, and these records are organised according to court. Details of some of these courts are set out in the Glossary of Legal Terms. Broadly speaking, there were four types of courts in early seventeenth-century England: prerogative courts, common law courts, ecclesiastical courts and Vice-Admiralty courts. Prerogative courts were courts of equity through which monarchs exercised their prerogative and discretionary powers. The main court of equity, and the only one to survive until the Restoration, was the Court of Chancery; courts of equity with specialised jurisdictions included the Court of Star Chamber, which dealt with offences against public order, the Court of High Commission, which dealt with ecclesiastical affairs arising from the Reformation, and the Court of Requests, a small claims court. Under James I these courts became closely associated with the Royal prerogative, and in the reign of Charles I were increasingly opposed by common lawyers. Common law courts formed a hierarchy ranging from the King's Bench, which travelled with the King, through the Court of Common Pleas, which met in Westminster, to local magistrates' and manorial courts. Thirdly, there was a national system of ecclesiastical courts that was in certain areas of jurisdiction in competition with the Court of High Commission. At a provincial level, the court of the Archbishop of Canterbury was the Court of Arches and the court of the Archbishop of York was the Chancery Court of York; the lower courts, at diocesan level, were consistory courts. The jurisdiction of ecclesiastical courts was criminal, civil and administrative. The criminal jurisdiction was abolished in 1641 but restored in 1661; the civil jurisdiction included marriage, divorce (that is, judicial separation), legitimacy and probate; the administrative jurisdiction included matters such as ordination and consecration. The vast testamentary jurisdiction of the ecclesiastical courts was discharged through the Prerogative Court of Canterbury and the Prerogative Court of York. Finally, a network of Vice-Admiralty Courts exercised jurisdiction up to high-water marks on coasts and first bridges on rivers.

In quiet moments scholars sometimes reflect on how the subjects of their enquiries would have felt had they known that their daily lives would be the subject of investigation several centuries later. The student of Milton is offered a hint in Milton's own enthusiasm for chronologies. On 24 March 1657, for example, the sightless Milton wrote to a correspondent in Paris asking that he attempt to secure six books for him: one was an historical account of Constantinople, and the other five were chronologies.

A Milton Chronology

December

9 (Friday) JM is born in Bread Street, London, probably at the Spread Eagle but possibly at the Red Rose. JM's family Bible records in his hand that 'John Milton was born the 9th of December 1608 die Veneris [that is, Friday] half an howr after 6 in the morning' (BL Add MS 32,310). The date and time are confirmed in JM's horoscope, which was cast some time after the publication of *Eikonoklastes* in October 1649; the horoscope is in the Bodleian (Ashmole MS 436, part I, fol. 119); see Rusche.

JM's father, also called John Milton, is a professional scrivener (in practice a notary and money-lender) and an amateur composer who had published a madrigal in Thomas Morley's *Triumphs of Oriana* in 1601.

JM's paternal grandfather was Richard Milton, of Stanton St John, a village in Oxfordshire less than a mile from Forest Hill, later the home of the first wife of the poet (see June 1642). Richard's father Henry, also of Stanton St John, had died early in 1559, leaving an estate of £6.19s to his wife Agnes, his children Isabel and Richard and other relations named Roland and Alice Milton (Oxfordshire Archives, Wills 182/236); Agnes Milton's will was signed on 9 March 1561 and proved on 14 June 1561 (Oxfordshire Archives, Wills 184/2). Richard Milton was a recusant, and was excommunicated on 11 May 1582 (Bodleian MS O.A.P. Oxon.e.11, fol. 182v); he was convicted of recusancy on 13 July 1601 (PRO E377/29d/10). Richard disinherited his son John (Skinner, in Darbishire, p. 18), who moved to London and became an apprentice scrivener in about 1583; he was admitted to the Company of Scriveners on 27 February 1599/1600 (Guildhall MS 5370, p. 162). Shortly thereafter he married Sara Jeffrey; their first child died in infancy, and was buried on 12 May 1601 (Parish Register, All Hallows). Their second child was Anne, whose date and place of birth are unknown (see 22 November 1623 for her marriage). Sara Jeffrey, JM's mother, was the elder daughter of Paul Jeffrey, a merchant-tailor who had died in 1583, and his wife Ellen, who lived with the Miltons in Bread Street from 1602 (or earlier) until her death in February 1611. On JM's father's business dealings before 1610 see *LR*, V, 165–94.

December
20 JM is baptised at All Hallows Church, Bread Street (Parish Register); on the same day JM's father witnesses a receipt signed by Richard Scudamore (Dulwich College Muniment 503).

1609

December
9 (Saturday) JM's first birthday.

1610

In this year JM's father is taxed six shillings, apparently on holdings valued at £6 (PRO E179/146/470).

January
9 (Tuesday) Oliver Lowe, servant to JM's father, is buried (Parish Register, All Hallows).

December
9 (Sunday) JM's second birthday.

1611

February
26 (Tuesday) Ellen Jeffrey, JM's maternal grandmother, is buried (Parish Register, All Hallows).

December
9 (Monday) JM's third birthday.

1612

JM's father becomes acquainted with the mercer William Hurt; the date is an inference from the fact that on 14 September 1632, JM's

father testified that he had known Hurt 'these xx years or thereabouts' (PRO C24/587/46).

April
16 (Thursday) JM's father arranges loan by William Rogers to
    John Drabull, Thomas Humfreys and Francis Michell (PRO
    C24/596/33).

May
15 (Friday) JM's father deposes in Chancery suit brought against
    him by William Symonds over a loan to a Mr Scryven (PRO
    C24/377/60).

July
15 (Wednesday) JM's sister Sara is baptised (Parish Register, All
    Hallows).

August
6   (Thursday) JM's sister Sara is buried (Parish Register, All
    Hallows).

December
9   (Wednesday) JM's fourth birthday.

1613

November
19 (Friday) JM's father deposes in Harvey–Jones suit (PRO C24/
    386/44).

December
9   (Thursday) JM's fifth birthday.

1614

Sir William Leighton's *The Teares Or Lamentacions Of A Sorrowfull
Soule* is published. The collection includes four musical settings by
JM's father. The same four songs survive in undated manuscripts
related to *The Teares* in BL Roy. App. 63 and in the Royal College of

Music (MS 1940); there is a manuscript copy of a German translation of one of the songs, 'Thou God of might' in the Nationalbibliothek, Vienna (MS 19287). In this year JM's father probably takes
as apprentices William Bower and Richard Milton, son of Thomas
Milton of Cheltenham; apprenticeship normally lasted seven years,
and both were freed in 1621 (Bodleian MS Rawl Miscell. 51, fol. 29).

January
30   (Sunday) JM's sister Tabitha is baptised (Parish Register, All
     Hallows).

December
 9   (Friday) JM's sixth birthday.

1615

JM enters St Paul's School at an unknown date between 1615 and
1621; the early records of the school were lost along with the school
buildings in the fire of 1666, and the only record of his attendance
is the entry admitting JM to Christ's College (see 12 February 1625).
The evidence for dating is mixed. JM's nephew Edward Phillips
says that JM 'was entered into the first rudiments of learning'
(Darbishire, p: 53), and JM's brother Christopher told John Aubrey
that JM 'went to school when he was very young' (Darbishire,
p. 10); these remarks suggest an early date. On the other hand,
Edward Phillips says that JM was sent to St Paul's 'together with
his brother'; if 'together' implies 'at the same time', then it seems
unlikely that JM would have entered much before December 1622,
when Christopher had his seventh birthday. In the *Defensio Secunda*
JM speaks of studying till midnight 'from the age of twelve', and
Christopher clearly associates this evening study with JM's attendance at school; JM became twelve on 9 December 1620. JM's
friendship with Charles Diodati, which was said by JM in *Epitaphium Damonis* to have dated from boyhood (*a pueritia*), must have
developed at St Paul's well before Diodati matriculated at Oxford
on 7 February 1623. On JM at St Paul's see Clark.

March
 2   (Thursday) Shortly before this date JM's father writes a six-line
     poem in praise of John Lane's continuation of Chaucer's

'Squire's Tale' (Bodleian MS Douce 170, fol. 4v); the volume contains a manuscript licence for printing dated 2 March 1614 (i.e. 1615) and signed 'John Taverner'.

April
24 (Monday) JM's father is appointed as an Assistant (one of 11) of the Stationers' Company (Guildhall MS 5370, p. 279); his name is substituted for that of Robert Woodforde, which is deleted. The date is sometimes said in error to be 14 April.

August
3 (Thursday) JM's sister Tabitha is buried (Parish Register, All Hallows).
5 JM's father witnesses (with Richard Stock) the will (proved 16 August) of neighbour Ralph Hamor, who dies 8 August and is buried 22 August (PROB 11/126/78).
14 JM's father attends a meeting of the Court of Assistants of the Stationers' Company and signs a document concerning precedence (Guildhall MS 5370, p. 279).

November
24(?) (Friday) JM's brother Christopher is born. Some thirty years later (before August 1646) JM is to write in his family Bible that 'Christofer Milton was born on Friday about a month before Christmass at 5 in the morning 1615' (BL Add MS 32,310). JM's vague phrase seems to point to 24 November, but could refer to 17 November or 1 December.

December
2 (Saturday) William Bold, described (in Latin) as 'servant to John Milton, scrivener', witnesses a bond (BL MS Cart. Harl. 112.D.19); see 27 June 1616.
3 JM's brother Christopher is baptised (Parish Register, All Hallows).
4 JM's father witnesses a release in the house of Sir Baptist Hicks in Cheapside; see 21 May 1619.
9 JM's seventh birthday.

1616

Music by JM's father is included in two manuscript collections now in the BL. One collection, containing ten of JM's father's songs, was compiled by Thomas Myriell, who is probably the man of the same name who was later to officiate at the wedding of JM's sister Anne to Edward Phillips; this collection, entitled *Tristitiae Remedium*, survives in six parts in BL Add MSS 29, 372-29,377. The other collection, BL Add MS 29,427, is undated, but clearly related to *Tristitiae Remedium*; it contains the alto part of eight of JM's father's songs. The songs are sometimes said to have been collected in the Myriell manuscript now in the Bibliothèque Royale in Brussels (MS II 4109 Fétis 3095), but none of the 99 attributed songs is JM's father's, and the only unattributed song ('Complaine with tears') is unlikely to be his. In this year JM's father also arranges the loan by William (later Sir William) Campion to Philip Pitts; see 6 March 1622.

June
27   (Thursday) Thomas Shelley pays bond (signed on 2 December 1615) at the shop of JM's father (BL Cart. Harl. 112.D.19).

December
 9   (Monday) JM's eighth birthday.

1617

Thomas Bower is engaged as 'servant' (i.e. apprentice) to JM's father; the date is an inference from the deposition of 3 May 1631, in which Bower is said to have been JM's servant for eight years and his partner for six years.

January
28   (Tuesday) Company of Scriveners receives a royal charter (Guildhall MS 8716; PRO C66/2093/5).

July
13   (Sunday) John Lane's 'The Corrected historie of Sir Gwy, Earle of Warwick', which contains a commendatory sonnet by JM's father, is licensed to be printed; it nonetheless remains unprinted until 1888, but survives in manuscript (BL Harleian MS 5243).

October
16   (Thursday) JM's family home in Bread Street is surveyed. The survey, together with floor plans, survives in the library of

Eton College (MS Records 16), which owned the house (see Blakiston); the transcription in *LR*, I, 14–19 is inaccurate in many details.

28 JM's uncle William Truelove signs his will, and dies before 7 May 1618, when his will was proved (PROB 11/131/41); the puzzling reference ('23 Ayloffe') given in *LR* I 126 and Parker (1996), 701 would seem to refer to a will proved in 1518, when an Ayloffe compiled the register, rather than 1618.

December
9 (Tuesday) JM's ninth birthday.

1618

JM's portrait is painted by an unknown artist, traditionally said to be Cornelius Janssen. The painting is now in the Pierpont Morgan Library in New York (see Miller, 1976*a*).

January
24 (Saturday) At some point in Hilary Term (24 January–12 February) Edward Lord Zouche acquires a final quitclaim on the Manor of Hartley Wintney in Hampshire. In subsequent dealings with Edward Topsell relating to this property, JM's father was a signatory on one or more deeds. A bundle of ten deeds relating to these transactions was sold at Sotheby's on 20 November 1973 (Lot 83); the present location of the documents is unknown.

May
13/23 (Wednesday) The Defenestration of Prague, in which Protestant noblemen throw Roman Catholic governors out of the windows of the Hradcin Palace, inaugurates the Thirty Years' War, a series of wars that begins in the Austrian Monarchy, spreads to the Holy Roman Empire (Germany) and eventually encompasses most of continental Europe. The fighting may be distinguished into five phases: first, the Bohemian War (1618–20), in which the Emperor Ferdinand II, with the assistance of Spanish finance and troops, Bavarian Catholics and the Papacy, defeated the Bohemian Protestants led by Frederick V, elector palatine of the Rhine and king of Bohemia;

second, the Palatinate War (1621–23), in which a Bavarian army under Tilly and Spanish troops under Spinola conquered the Upper Palatinate, and Spain and Holland renewed the Eighty Years' War, which had been suspended for 12 years; third, the Danish War (1624–29), in which the army of Wallenstein, the commander-in-chief of the Emperor, defeated an anti-Habsburg coalition led by Christian IV of Denmark; fourth, the Swedish War, in which Gustavus II Adolphus, King of Sweden, conquered most of Germany except for Bavaria and defeated Wallenstein at the cost of his own life; fifth, the Franco-Habsburg War (1635–48), a pan-European war in which the French fought the Spanish in France, Italy, Spain and (with Swedish assistance) along the Rhine, the Dutch fought the Spanish in the southern Netherlands, the Swedes reconquered north Germany and repeatedly invaded Bohemia and Moravia, the Danes fought the Swedes in the second Swedish–Danish War and the French and Swedish armies fought their way through Bavaria and Bohemia to Vienna, which was saved by news of the Treaty of Westphalia (14/24 October 1648), which concluded the Thirty Years' War, though France and Spain remained at war until November 1659.

October
7   (Wednesday) JM's father deposes in Leeds–Knolles suit (PRO C24/456/84). The document records that he had been acquainted with Sir Thomas Leeds 'for the space of many years' and the late John King 'for divers years'.

December
9   (Wednesday) JM's tenth birthday.

1619

JM's widow told Aubrey that in 1619 JM 'was ten years old, as by his picture, and was then a poet'. The picture may be the portrait in the Pierpont Morgan Library; no poetry survives from this period. Aubrey adds over these lines that 'his schoolmaster was a puritan in Essex, who cut his hair short' (Darbishire, 2). JM became ten in 1618, so the date and the age are inconsistent. The schoolmaster may have been Thomas Young, who is known to have taught JM, but he had lived in Suffolk, not Essex. The phrase 'school master ... in Essex' (not 'from Essex') may suggest that JM attended a school in Essex, where his mother had relatives. In *Reason of Church Government* (1641) JM was to say that he was taught from his 'first years' by 'sundry masters and teachers both at home and at the schools'. Another of his teachers may have been Patrick Young, who was at this time Prebendary and Treasurer of St Paul's Cathedral (see 29 May 1651).

On 26 September 1631 Richard Sherratt, haberdasher, testified to the effect that he had known Milton (that is, JM's father) for 'some twelve years or thereabouts' (PRO C24/574/40); the acquaintance may therefore have begun in 1619.

February
9   (Monday) JM may have accompanied his parents to the wedding of Hester Jeffrey, a relative of his mother, and William Blackborough (Parish Register, St Peter's Cornhill); JM often visited Blackborough in the early 1640s, and may later have witnessed his will (see 11 April 1645).

March
2   (Tuesday) Queen Anne dies of dropsy.

May
21   (Friday) JM's father deposes in Gott–Hicks suit (PRO C24/461/55).

December
9   (Thursday) JM's eleventh birthday.

1620

In this year JM's father invests money for John Downer and John Cotton; the date is an inference from the deposition of 3 May 1631.

January
24   (Monday) On or shortly after this date Richard Powell, JM's future father-in-law, buys Wheatley from Sir George Simeon (PRO CP 25/2 Oxon); the document is dated Hilary term (that is, 24 January–12 February), 17 James I.

May

2 (Tuesday) JM's father is named in will of William Priestley, merchant tailor (PRO PROB 11/135/39); see 30 May.

6 JM's father arranges William Rowley–John Jeffrey indenture (PRO C2 James I/W21/45).

18 JM's father arranges loan by John Cotton to Sir William Sandys; the bond is lost, but the date is recorded in Bower's schedule of Cotton's bonds (see 25 November 1630) and in Cotton's bill (see 28 May 1636).

23 JM's father deposes in Warwick–Searle suit (PRO C24/467/97).

30 William Priestley (see 2 May) is buried (Parish Register, All Hallows).

July

4 (Tuesday) JM's father is appointed as one of the four trustees of the Blackfriars Playhouse. The other trustees are Henry Hodge and Robert Hunt (both brewers) and Edward Raymond (see 9 February 1622). The original documents are lost, but details are recorded in legal action of 1640 (PRO E112/221/1215; E125/27 fols. 199–200); see Berry.

November

19 (Sunday) JM's father arranges loan by John Cotton to a Mr Charnock; the bond is lost, but the date is recorded in Bower's schedule of Cotton's bonds (see 25 November 1630) and in Cotton's bill (see 28 May 1636).

December

1 (or 10) (Friday or Sunday) JM's father arranges loan by John Cotton to the judge Robert Heath; the bond is lost. Bower's schedule (see 25 November 1620) gives the date as 1 December, but Cotton's bill (see 28 May 1636) gives the date as 10 December. Heath had just been returned to Parliament, and was to be knighted on 28 January 1621.

9 JM's twelfth birthday.

1621

Thomas Ravenscroft's *The Whole Book of Psalms* is published; it contains six musical settings by JM's father. The musicianship of

JM's father is praised in a poem by John Lane (BL Reg. 17 B xv, fol 179v; Trinity College Cambridge MS O.ii.68 fol 187).

April
6 (Friday) William Bower, JM's father's apprentice, is made free of the Company of Scriveners (Guildhall MS 5370, p. 210).

May
13 (Sunday) JM's father arranges loan by John Cotton to Mr 'Lea' (Leigh?); the bond is lost, but the date is recorded in Bower's schedule of Cotton's bonds (see 25 November 1630) and in Cotton's bill (see 28 May 1636); cf 30 November 1624.
25 JM's father and John Lane buy property near the north end of Gray's Inn Lane from Dr Leonard Poe (PRO C54/2477/34), on whom see DNB.

September
20 (Thursday) Richard Milton, apprentice to JM's father, is made free of the Company of Scriveners (Guildhall MS 5370, p. 211).

October
2 (Tuesday) JM's future father-in-law Richard Powell acquires Forest Hill from Edmund Brome (PRO SP 23/109, pp. 517–21). The lease is scheduled to extend for 20 years at an annual rent of £5. The date is recorded in John Reading's report of 1 January 1651, which also records that the lease expired on 1 November 1641.
31 Richard Powell is appointed as tax-collector (PRO E179/289/31, m.2).

December
9 (Sunday) JM's thirteenth birthday.

1622

In this year JM's father is appointed (for the second time) as an Assistant in the Scriveners' Company (Bodleian MS Rawlinson 51, fol 29); it may be during this year that he offers to buy Scroops Court property from John Cochin; the date is a guess based on the deposition of 9 April 1630.

January
Richard Powell is assessed in Forest Hill (PRO E179/289/31, m.2).

February
9   (Saturday) JM's father lends £50 to Edward Raymond (PRO C2 James I/A6/35).

March
6   (Wednesday) JM's father deposes in Freere suit (PRO C24/486/28).

April
3   (Wednesday) JM's father and John Lane sell most of the property acquired on 25 May 1621 to James Kent (PRO C54/2525/m.32).

August
JM's father receives interest and continues bond of Edward Raymond. Some time in the next few months JM's father demands repayment and threatens court action (PRO C2 James I/A6/35).

November
28   (Thursday) JM's father arranges loan of £100 by John Cotton to a Mr Carrent; the bond is lost, but the date is recorded in Bower's schedule of Cotton's bonds (see 25 November 1630) and in Cotton's bill (see 28 May 1636).

December
9   (Monday) JM's fourteenth birthday.

1623

January
23   (Thursday) On or shortly after this date JM's father enters court action against Raymond and Ayloffe (PRO C2 James I A6/35); the court action was initiated during Hilary Term (23 January–12 February).

February
7   (Friday) JM's friend Charles Diodati matriculates at Trinity College Oxford, aged 13 (Oxford University Matriculation Register, p. 126).

March

26 (Wednesday) JM's father brings action against Raymond in the Lord Mayor's Court and secures a judgement (PRO C2 James I/A6/35).

May

17 (Saturday) JM's father arranges loan by John Cotton to Sir Richard Molyneux (later Viscount Maryborough; see DNB); the bond is lost, but the date is recorded in Bower's schedule of Cotton's bonds (see 25 November 1630) and in Cotton's bill (see 28 May 1636).

21 JM's father arranges loan by John Cotton to a Mr Bannester; the bond is lost, but the date is recorded in Bower's schedule of Cotton's bonds (see 25 November 1630) and in Cotton's bill (see 28 May 1636).

26 Thomas Bower and John Hutton, apprentices of JM's father, witness an indenture as 'servants to John Milton Sr' (PRO SP 14/145/36).

June

11 (Wednesday) JM's father deposes in Edward Bold–Sir Francis Leeke suit (PRO C24/499/15).

24 JM's father receives £10 quarterly payment (due on Midsummer Day) from Edward Raymond, who dies shortly thereafter (PRO C2 James I/A6/35).

July

4 (Friday) JM's father arranges bond from Edward Ewer and John Palmer to Sir Peter Temple, his father Sir Thomas Temple and Sir John Lenthall (Huntington Library MS); on the same day he arranges a bond from Robert Hassard and George Sheres to Sir Peter Temple (Huntington Library MS).

21 Richard Powell buys the manor of Forest Hill (PRO SP 23/109/517, p. 521).

September

1 (Monday) A licence is issued to Edward Brome to sell Forest Hill to Richard Powell, who is not named (PRO C66/2318/40).

25 JM's father deposes in Thomas Williams–Thomas Powlett suit (PRO C24/501/99).

October

8 (Wednesday) JM's father deposes in Robert Walthewe (Walten?)–George Sheres suit (PRO C24/501/105).

9 On or shortly after this date the final conveyance ('concord of fine') for the sale of Forest Hill to Richard Powell is drawn up (PRO CP25/2/340); the conveyance is dated Michaelmas term (i.e. 9 October–28 November) 21 James I.

November

15 (Saturday) A secret Catholic chapel near JM's home collapses, killing at least 90 people. JM's friend Alexander Gill composes Latin verses in vindictive celebration of this event; there is an English version of this poem in the Bodleian (MS Ashmole 36, 37). Gill's comparison of the collapse of the chapel to Samson's destruction of the temple may have influenced the conclusion of JM's *Samson Agonistes* (see Miller, 1990*a*).

22 JM's sister Anne marries Edward Phillips (Parish Register, St Stephen, Walbrook). The rector, who conducted the wedding, is Thomas Myriell, apparently the musical friend of JM's and Anne's father.

27 JM and his mother Sara witness the marriage settlement of his sister Anne and Edward Phillips. This is JM's earliest recorded signature and Sara's only recorded signature; the manuscript is in the Pierpont Morgan Library (MA 953). On the same day JM's father arranges a loan by John Cotton to a Mr Chetwood; the bond is lost, but the date is recorded in Bower's schedule of Cotton's bonds (see 25 November 1630) and in Cotton's bill (see 28 May 1636).

December

9 (Tuesday) JM's fifteenth birthday. Some time in the course of the next year JM composes his paraphrases of Psalms 114 and 136, which he was later to say 'were done by the author at fifteen years old'.

1624

In this year and possibly earlier JM writes several times to his tutor Thomas Young. The letters are lost, but in his letter of 26 March 1627 JM apologises for not having written for more than three years and acknowledges Young's complaint that the letters were few in number and short in length. Early in this year JM's father sues Edward Raymond's estate and (with John Lane) sues James Ayloffe (see 10 May).

March
2 (Tuesday) JM's father and his apprentice John Hutton witness Margaret Webber–James Cooper bond (Corporation of London Records Office, Historical Papers 1/11).

April
18 (Sunday) JM's father arranges Sir George Peckham–Samuel Burton–William Smith bond; the bond is lost, but the date is recorded in Burton's bill of 10 May 1626.

May
1 (Sunday) James Ayloffe brings action against JM's father (PRO C2 James I/A6/35).
10 JM's father answers James Ayloffe's bill; his attorney is Edmund Breres (PRO C2 James I/A6/35).
11 JM's father arranges loan by John Cotton to a Mr Erdiswick; the bond is lost, but the date is recorded in Bower's schedule of Cotton's bonds (see 25 November 1630) and in Cotton's bill (see 28 May 1636).

June
29 (Tuesday) James Hodgkinson and Thomas Bower, JM's father's apprentices, are admitted to the Company of Scriveners (Guildhall MS 5370, p. 215).

July
26 (Monday) JM's father signs audit of Scriveners' Company (see Clarke); the Account Book has been lost in the twentieth century, and the annual catalogue of the Company (Bodleian MS Rawlinson 51) does not record that JM's father acted as auditor in 1624, but there is no reason to doubt that he did sign the accounts on this date.

November
JM's father arranges loan by Rose Downer to Sir Francis Leigh (PRO C2 Charles I/D39/47), the nephew of John Egerton, Earl of

Bridgwater, in whose honour JM's *Comus* was to be performed on 29
September 1634. Mrs Downer was the widow of John Downer, a
tallow-chandler who had died earlier in 1624. Mrs Downer continued her late husband's practice of lending money through JM's
father. This loan to Sir Francis Leigh and a subsequent loan to Sir
Fulke Greville were called in early in June 1628, but Thomas Bower,
by then JM's father's partner, persuaded her to reinvest this money
(and more) with the scriveners. Mrs Downer repeatedly tried to
recover £50 lent to Matthew Ewens, and on 26 April 1631 she sued
the scriveners in Chancery.

30   (Tuesday) JM's father arranges loan by John Cotton to Sir
      Francis Leigh; the bond is lost, but the date is recorded in
      Bower's schedule of Cotton's bonds (see 25 November 1630)
      and in Cotton's bill (see 28 May 1636).

December
JM is likely to have finished his education at St Paul's in this month.
Works composed by JM during his schooldays include the epigram
Philosophus ad regem, the *Apologus De Rustico et Hero* (a fable in
imitation of Mantuan) and two poems (*Carmina Elegiaca* and *Ignavus
satrapam*) and a prose theme on early rising which are written on a
single leaf now in the Harry Ranson Humanities Research Center in
Austin, Texas, shelf-mark 'Pre-1700 Manuscript 127'; the manuscript
is claimed to be an autograph, but the handwriting does not resemble mature examples of JM's hand such as the supplicat of 1629.

9   (Thursday) JM's sixteenth birthday.

1625

JM's father is appointed a Steward in the Stationers' Company (Bodleian MS Rawlinson 51, fol. 29); it is probably in this year that JM's
father takes Thomas Bower as a partner (PRO C2 Charles I/D39/47).

January
13   (Thursday) Lent Term at Cambridge begins. JM may arrive in
      Cambridge in time for the start of term, but he is not formally
      admitted until 12 February.
16   JM's nephew John Phillips is baptised (Parish Register, St Martin
      in the Fields). This John Phillips died on 15 March 1629; his
      better-known namesake was probably born in October 1631.

24 Mary Powell (later JM's first wife) is baptised (Parish Register, Forest Hill).

February
12 (Saturday) JM is admitted to Christ's College, Cambridge, as a minor pensioner (a status below that of 'fellow-commoner', or 'greater pensioner', but above that of 'sizar') under William Chappell (Christ's College Admission Book); the admissions register records that JM had studied under Alexander Gill at St Paul's School and that he paid ten shillings for admission.
26 A freak high tide on the Thames destroys property close to Bread Street and claims many lives.

March
27 (Sunday) King James dies.
30 King Charles is proclaimed at the market-cross in Cambridge.

April
8 (Friday) Lent Term at Cambridge ends.
9 JM presents himself with six other new undergraduates (including Robert Pory, JM's contemporary at St Paul's) to John Tabor, the University Registrary, and formally matriculates at University of Cambridge (Cambridge University Matriculation Book, unnumbered pages).
13/23 Maurice, Prince of Orange, dies after failing to lift the siege of Breda; he may be one of the 'lost princes of Belgia' of JM's *Elegia* III, 12.
14 JM's father arranges loan by John Cotton to a Mr Bold; the bond is lost, but the date is recorded in Bower's schedule of Cotton's bonds (see 25 November 1630) and in Cotton's bill (see 28 May 1636).
20 John Stock, Rector of All Hallows, Bread Street (JM's London church) dies, and is succeeded on 22 April by Samuel Purchas (author of the *Pilgrims*, which JM is later to read).

May
1/11 (Sunday) King Charles is married by proxy to the French princess Henrietta Maria.
7 King James is buried in Westminster Abbey. Members of Cambridge University assemble at 9.00 a.m. in academic dress and process to St Mary's to hear memorial sermons.

June

5/15 (Sunday) Breda (Netherlands) falls to Spanish forces under Ambrogio Spinola after a siege of 11 months. Those killed in operations related to the defence of Breda included Henry de Vere, Earl of Oxford, and Sir Walter Devereux, who may be the 'heroes of Belgia' of JM's *Elegia* III, 11.

18   The First Parliament of Charles I is convened in Westminster. Parliament attacks Buckingham, votes tonnage and poundage for one year only, refuses to grant money for the war against Spain, criticises the Roman Catholic leanings of the King, and levies a tax on tobacco.

July

8   (Friday) Easter Term at Cambridge ends. A plague epidemic causes thousands of deaths in London, but Cambridge is not yet infected, so it is possible that JM remains in College for part of the long vacation; many other undergraduates do so.

10   An undergraduate who had drowned in the Cam is buried in Grantchester.

August

1   (Monday) All public gatherings at the University are discontinued because of the onset of plague in Cambridge; JM presumably leaves Cambridge and joins his family at a retreat in the country. On the same day Parliament adjourns from Westminster to Oxford because of the plague.

12   King Charles dissolves Parliament.

October

8   (Saturday) The Duke of Buckingham leads an English expedition to Cádiz; the expedition subsequently fails to capture the city and the Spanish treasure fleet, and returns empty-handed.

10   Michaelmas Term at Cambridge begins.

November

30/9 December (Wednesday) Treaty of the Hague commits England, the Palatinate and the United Provinces to offering financial support to King Christian IV of Denmark in his campaign in Lower Saxony (see 27 August 1627).

December
9 (Friday) JM's seventeenth birthday.
10 JM's friend Charles Diodati receives his B.A. at Oxford.
16 Michaelmas Term at Cambridge ends.

1626

In this year Richard Powell, JM's future father-in-law, obtains a lease on a freehold in Wheatley from All Souls College (Bodleian Wood 515 (16), pp. 2–3).

January
12 (Thursday) JM's niece Anne Phillips, daughter of Edward and Anne, is baptised (Parish Register, St Martin in the Fields).
13 Lent Term at Cambridge begins.

February
2 (Thursday) Charles I is crowned at Westminster Abbey. Over the course of the next five years he raises £173,537 by invoking an act of 1227 which allowed the king to fine all men worth more than £40 a year who had failed to attend his coronation to be knighted.
6/16 The Second Parliament of Charles I is convened; on the same day the Treaty of La Rochelle is signed by Richelieu and the Huguenot rebels.
23/5 March Treaty of Monzón is signed by France and Spain, guaranteeing provision for Catholic worship in the Protestant canton of Grisons. On the same day the impeachment of the Duke of Buckingham begins.

March
31 (Friday) Lent Term at Cambridge ends.

April
JM may compose *Elegia* I (To Charles Diodati) in the first half of this month, when he is in London and expecting to return shortly to Cambridge.
15/25 (Saturday) Wallenstein defeats Mansfeld at the Battle of the Bridge of Dessau on the Elbe.

19   Easter Term at Cambridge begins.

May
10   (Wednesday) JM's father is sued by Dr Samuel Burton (PRO
      Req. 2/387; Parker, 1996, p. 737); the documents of the suit are
      PRO CP40/2137, m.3030. On the same day King Charles impri-
      sons Sir Dudley Digges and Sir John Eliot for organising the
      impeachment of Buckingham.
24   JM's father arranges loan by John Cotton to a Mr Veale; the
      bond is lost, but the date is recorded in Bower's schedule of
      Cotton's bonds (see 25 November 1630) and in Cotton's bill
      (see 28 May 1636).

June
6/16 (Tuesday) Christian of Brunswick dies in Wolfenbüttel; he
      may be the 'venerable brother' (*frater verendus*) of JM's *Elegia
      III*, 1.
  9   Edward King ('Lycidas') is admitted to Christ's College
      (Admissions Book).
 15   King Charles dissolves Parliament, refusing to grant the
      request of Parliament that Buckingham be dismissed.
 21   JM's father arranges loan by John Cotton to a Mr Clopton; the
      bond is lost, but the date is recorded in Bower's schedule of
      Cotton's bonds (see 25 November 1630) and in Cotton's bill
      (see 28 May 1636).
 23   A book consisting of three theological treatises is found in the
      maw of a codfish in Cambridge market, provoking both witty
      and grave responses within the University; the treatises are
      reprinted in 1627 as *Vox Piscis* ('The Voice of the Fish'). In 1638
      the incident was to be recalled in John Pullen's commemor-
      ative poem for Edward King.
 27   JM's father receives injunction from Court of Requests (PRO
      Req 1/32, p. 966).
 28   JM's father appears in court to answer Burton (PRO, Req 1/
      111, part 2, fol. 6).

July
  6   (Thursday) Edward King matriculates at University of Cam-
      bridge (Matriculation Book, unnumbered pages).
  7   Easter Term at Cambridge ends.
26/5 August Tilly captures Göttingen.

August

In this month JM's father collects Mrs Rose Downer's money from Sir Francis Leigh and reinvests it with Sir Fulke Greville (PRO C2 Charles I/D39/47); see June 1628.

7 (Monday) JM's father arranges loan by John Cotton to Sir Kenelm Digby; the bond is lost, but the date is recorded in Bower's schedule of Cotton's bonds (see 25 November 1630) and in Cotton's bill (see 28 May 1636).

17/27 The Catholic League under Tilly defeats Christian IV of Denmark at Lutter (north-west Germany); Christian subsequently abandons northern Germany to the League.

September

25 (Monday) Lancelot Andrewes, the distinguished scholar and divine, dies (funeral 11 November). JM subsequently writes *Elegia Tertia, In Obitum Praesulis Wintoniensis* ('Elegy 3, On the Death of the Bishop of Winchester'). In 1645 JM adds his age, *anno aetatis 17* ('at the age of 17'); if his recollection is accurate, this poem and the following poems in commemoration of Ridding and Felton must have been written before his 18th birthday on 9 December. On the order of the poems written in September and October, see Parker (1996), p. 111, and Miller (1980*b*).

26 Richard Ridding, University Beadle, dies. JM subsequently writes *Elegia Secunda, In Obitum Praeconis Academici Cantabrigiensis* ('Elegy Two, On the death of the Beadle of the University of Cambridge'). In 1645 JM adds his age, *anno aetatis 17* ('at the age of 17').

October

5 (Thursday) Nicholas Felton, Bishop of Ely (1619–26), dies. JM subsequently writes *In Obitum Praesulis Eliensis* ('On the Death of the Bishop of Ely'). In 1645 JM adds his age, *anno aetatis 17* ('at the age of 17').

10 Michaelmas Term at Cambridge begins.

21 John Gostlin, Master of Caius College (1619–26), Regius Professor of Physic (1623–25) and Vice-Chancellor (1625–26) dies. JM subsequently writes *In Obitum Procancellarii Medici* ('On the Death of the Vice-Chancellor, a Physician'). JM's recollection of his age (added in 1645) as *anno aetatis 16* ('at the age of 16') must be an error; he was 17.

November

5   (Sunday) Anniversary of Gunpowder Plot, by which date JM
     must have completed *In quintum Novembris* ('On the fifth of
     November'), which, according to JM's note in 1645, was written
     anno aetatis 17 ('at the age of 17'). Scholars who believe that JM's
     poem is indebted to Phineas Fletcher's *Locustae*, which was
     printed in Cambridge in 1627, either assume that JM saw
     Fletcher's poem in manuscript or argue that JM's recollection
     of his age was wrong and that his poem should be dated 1627.
     JM's four epigrams on the Gunpowder Plot (*In Proditionem
     Bombardicam*) and a fifth on the inventor of gunpowder (*In
     inventorem Bombardae*) are presumably contributions to
     academic celebrations of Guy Fawkes Day. The second of the
     Gunpowder poems refers to King James as deceased (line 5), so
     it could not have been written before 1625. The Gunpowder
     poems may have been written in successive years or in a single
     creative burst; the poem in praise of the inventor of gunpowder
     may be part of the sequence (if it is intended ironically), but may
     be an unconnected poem that JM intended as a simple
     encomium.

7   JM's father arranges loan by John Cotton to Lord Strange; the
     bond is lost, but the date is recorded in Bower's schedule of
     Cotton's bonds (see 25 November 1630) and in Cotton's bill
     (see 28 May 1636).

15   JM's father appears in court to answer Burton's bill of 10 May
     (PRO Req 1/111, part 2, fol. 10^v; his answer is filed as Req 2/387).

18   JM's father arranges loan by John Cotton to Sir William Norris;
     the bond is lost, but the date is recorded in Bower's schedule
     of Cotton's bonds (see 25 November 1630) and in Cotton's bill
     (see 28 May 1636).

29   Dr Daniel Featley, who is later to attack JM in print, is appointed
     rector of All Hallows. On the same day Ernst von Mansfeld dies;
     he may be the glorious leader (*clarus dux*) of JM's *Elegia* III, 9.

December

9   (Saturday) JM's eighteenth birthday.

10/20 Emperor Ferdinand II signs the Treaty of Pressburg with
     Bethlen Gábor, the Calvinist Prince of Transylvania and King
     of Hungary, who is poised to take Vienna.

12   JM's father arranges loan to Sir Francis Leigh and a Mr
     Rodney; the bond is lost, but the date is recorded in Bower's

schedule of Cotton's bonds (see 25 November 1630) and in Cotton's bill (see 28 May 1636).

16   Michaelmas Term at Cambridge ends.
19   JM's father arranges loan by John Cotton to Sir George Horsey; the bond is lost, but the date is recorded in Bower's schedule of Cotton's bonds (see 25 November 1630) and in Cotton's bill (see 28 May 1636); cf 5 July 1627.

1627

January
England and France drift into an undeclared war.
13   (Saturday) Lent Term at Cambridge begins. JM may have delivered Prolusion 4 during this term. On the dates of the prolusions see Shawcross (1965*b*) and Miller (1980*a*).

March
Five knights are imprisoned for failing to pay the forced loan demanded by Charles I.
17   (Saturday) Lent Term at Cambridge ends.
26   JM writes from London to Thomas Young in Hamburg. In *EF* the letter (No. 1) is mistakenly dated 26 March 1625 (Parker, 1938). In the letter JM promises a companion poem, which must be *Elegia IV*. JM dates the poem *anno aetatis 18*, which confirms that the year must be 1627, when JM was 18; lines 33–8 place the composition of the poem between the vernal equinox (11 March in the Julian calendar) and the beginning of the ancient festival of Chloris on 28 April.

April
4   (Wednesday) Easter Term at Cambridge begins. This is likely to be the term in which JM quarrels with his tutor, William Chappell, and is rusticated (see Miller, 1980*a*). Documents signed by JM in London on 25 May and 11 June suggest that he was absent for a substantial part of the term. JM may have delivered Prolusion 3 during this term.

May
25   (Friday) JM is in London, where he signs (along with his father) an indenture recording the purchase of property in St Martin

in the Fields from Anthony and Johane Rudd (PRO C54/2715/
20). JM is described as 'John Milton the younger of the University of Cambridge'. JM's presence in London this month
makes it probable that it was on this visit that he composed
Elegia VII. JM was later to date the poem *anno aetatis undevigesimo,* and this unique use of a Latin ordinal number makes it
likely that it means 'in his nineteenth year', i.e. 1627, rather
than 'at the age of 19', which is what *anno aetatis 19,* JM's usual
formulation, would have meant.

JM and his father were to sell the house to its tenant Sir
Matthew Lyster on 15 April 1638, but it may have been used as
a second home by the Milton family or occupied by the Phil-
lipses; see Clavering and Shawcross (1960).

June
11 (Monday) JM's father lends Richard Powell (JM's future
     father-in-law) £300, receiving as security a staple bond for
     £500 made payable to his son JM; the loan, at eight per cent,
     would earn £24 interest annually, payable on or about 12 June
     and 12 December every year (PRO C152/61); the statute staple
     is recorded the same day, and the record mentions JM (PRO
     LC 4/56). Powell was to service the debt for 17 years before
     defaulting on 12 June 1644. JM signs the agreement in London,
     which may imply a protracted absence from Cambridge.
14 Concord of Fine between the Rudds, JM and JM's father con-
     cerning the property in St Martin in the Fields (PRO CP 24/3/4).
23 JM's father buys property near Covent Garden from Anne
     Westrawe (PRO C54/2715/19; Parker, 1995, p. 734).

July
 5 (Thursday) JM's father arranges another loan by John Cotton
     to Sir George Horsey; the bond is lost, but the date is recorded
     in Bower's schedule of Cotton's bonds (see 25 November 1630)
     and in Cotton's bill (see 28 May 1636); cf 19 December 1626.
 6 Easter Term at Cambridge ends.
10/20 Buckingham's expeditionary force of 6,000 lands on the
     Ile de Ré with a view to liberating the Huguenots in nearby
     La Rochelle.

August
1/10 (Wednesday) Richelieu besieges La Rochelle.

September

On a day between 18 September and 25 October JM's father is apparently appointed to serve as a Warden of the Scriveners' Company (Bodleian MS Rawlinson D.51, fol. 29); there is an asterisk after his name for which no explanation is given, but it may indicate that he paid a fine in order to be released from the obligation to serve as Warden. The appointment is not confirmed in the Common Paper (Guildhall MS 5370), but entries in that manuscript enable the date to be fixed between 18 September and 25 October.

October

10 (Wednesday) Michaelmas Term at Cambridge begins.
11 JM's father arranges loan by John Cotton to a Mr Blacker; the bond is lost, but the date is recorded in Bower's schedule of Cotton's bonds (see 25 November 1630) and in Cotton's bill (see 28 May 1636).
12 Buckingham's expedition returns from the Ile de Ré, having failed to relieve the Huguenots; half of the 3,000 survivors have to be carried ashore.

November

 7 (Wednesday) JM's father arranges loan by John Cotton to William Welby; the bond is lost, but the date is recorded in Bower's schedule of Cotton's bonds (see 25 November 1630) and in Cotton's bill (see 28 May 1636).
30 JM's father arranges loan by John Cotton to a Mr Vaudray; the bond is lost, but the date is recorded in Bower's schedule of Cotton's bonds (see 25 November 1630) and in Cotton's bill (see 28 May 1636).

December

4/14 (Tuesday) Wolfenbüttel surrenders to the Imperial Army.
 9 JM's nineteenth birthday.
12 JM receives interest payment of £12 from Richard Powell.
16 Michaelmas Term at Cambridge ends.
17 JM's father arranges loan by John Cotton to a Mr Dabridgecourt; the bond is lost, but the date is recorded in Bower's schedule of Cotton's bonds (see 25 November 1630) and in Cotton's bill (see 28 May 1636).

21   JM's father arranges loan by John Cotton to a Mr Prewet; the
      bond is lost, but the date is recorded in Bower's schedule of
      Cotton's bonds (see 25 November 1630) and in Cotton's bill
      (see 28 May 1636).

1628

In this year John Hutton, apprentice to JM's father, is made free
(Bodleian MS Rawlinson D.51. fol. 29ᵛ).

January
13   (Sunday) Lent Term at Cambridge begins. JM may have
      delivered Prolusion 5 during this term; the prolusion seems to
      allude to the suppression of Isaac Dorislaus's history lectures,
      the first of which had been given on 7 and 12 December 1627.
      JM may also have delivered Prolusion 1 during this term.
16/26 Wallenstein seizes the Duchy of Mecklenburg.
22   JM's niece Anne Phillips, daughter of Edward and Anne, is
      buried (Parish Register, St Martin in the Fields); she is the most
      likely subject of JM's 'On the Death of a Fair Infant'. In the
      1673 *Poems* JM was to add the caption *'anno aetatis 17'*, which
      would place the poem between 9 December 1625 and 8
      December 1626, but it seems probable that JM misremembered
      the date; see Parker (1996), 738.

March
17   (Monday) Third Parliament of Charles I meets (till 2 March
      1629), called in order to vote funds for a second expedition to
      La Rochelle.

April
 2   (Wednesday) Katherine Woodcock, JM's future second wife, is
      baptised (Parish Register, St Dunstan in the East).
 4   Lent Term at Cambridge ends.
 9   JM's niece Elizabeth Phillips, daughter of Edward and Anne, is
      baptised (Parish Register, St Martin in the Fields).
23   Easter Term at Cambridge begins.
24   Sir Edward Coke introduces a bill that sets out Parliament's
      grievances against the King and develops into the Petition of
      Right.

May

20 (Tuesday) According to *EF*, JM writes to Alexander Gill on this date (No. 2); see 20 May 1630 for a possible redating.

29 JM's father arranges loan by John Cotton to Matthew Ewens; the bond is lost, but the date is recorded in Bower's schedule of Cotton's bonds (see 25 November 1630) and in Cotton's bill (see 28 May 1636).

June

In approximately this month JM's father arranges a loan by a Mr Bulteell to Matthew Ewens and William Keymer (PRO C2 Charles I/D39/47). He also arranges a loan (repaid in June 1630) by Rose Downer to a Mr Waring (PRO C2 Charles I/D39/47).

7 (Saturday) Charles is forced to accept the Petition of Right, which declares forced loans and arbitrary imprisonment to be illegal.

9 Rose Downer visits JM's father in Bread Street and becomes angry (PRO C2 Charles I/D39/47).

10 JM's father arranges loan by Rose Downer to Matthew Ewens and William Keymer (PRO C2 Charles I/D39/47).

11 Parliament makes Remonstrances attacking ecclesiastical ritual and Arminianism, and demands the dismissal of the Duke of Buckingham.

12 JM receives interest payment of £12 from Richard Powell.

July

2 (Wednesday) According to *EF*, on this day JM writes from Cambridge to Alexander Gill, his former teacher at St Paul's (No. 3). See 2 July 1631 for an alternative date.

3 Gustavus II of Sweden signs a defence treaty with Stralsund (in Pomerania).

4 Easter Term at Cambridge ends; on or shortly before this date JM reads an Oration, Prolusion 6 (both in Latin) and the English poem 'At a Vacation Exercise' (dated *'anno aetatis 19'*) to the members of Christ's College. The Oration records a recent visit to London; in the Prolusion JM acknowledges his college nickname, 'the Lady'. On the same day William Laud is appointed Bishop of London.

6 Wallenstein besieges Stralsund.

8 JM's friend Charles Diodati receives his MA at Oxford.

21   JM writes to Thomas Young from Cambridge (*EF* No. 4).

August
Wallenstein's army abandons the siege of Stralsund.
23   (Saturday) The Duke of Buckingham arrives in Portsmouth in order to embark for La Rochelle, and is assassinated by John Felton.

September
 1   (Sunday) JM's friend Alexander Gill, drinking with friends in the wine-cellar of Trinity College Oxford, disparages the king and proposes a toast to John Felton.
 4   Gill is arrested at St Paul's School on the order of Bishop Laud.
 6   JM's father arranges loan by John Cotton to a Mr Mort; the bond is lost, but the date is recorded in Bower's schedule of Cotton's bonds (see 25 November 1630) and in Cotton's bill (see 28 May 1636).

October
10   (Friday) Michaelmas Term at Cambridge begins.
18/28   La Rochelle surrenders after a siege of 14 months, and the political and military power of the Huguenots is broken.
22   JM's father (with his apprentices John Hutton and Henry Rothwell) witnesses Samuel Oakley–John Macy bond (Westminster Abbey Muniment 28,515).

November
 6   (Thursday) Alexander Gill is sentenced by the Court of Star Chamber to be degraded from the ministry, deprived of his university degrees, to be fined £2,000, to lose one ear in the pillory at Westminster and the other in Oxford and to be imprisoned in the Fleet Prison at the king's pleasure. Gill's father subsequently petitions the king, who grants a mitigation of the fine and a remission of the corporal punishment. Gill remains in prison for about two years, until November 1630.

December
 9   (Tuesday) JM's twentieth birthday.
12   JM receives interest payment of £12 from Richard Powell.
16   Michaelmas Term at Cambridge ends.

17   Thomas Wentworth is appointed President of the Council in
     the North.

1629

January
13   (Tuesday) Lent Term at Cambridge begins. In the course of this
     term JM supplicates for his BA (Cambridge University Archives,
     Supplicats 1627, 1628, 1629, fol. 331); the supplication is in JM's
     hand, except for the signature of John Fenwick, who received the
     supplications (supplications are often in the hand of the supplic-
     ant). Later in the year JM signs the three Articles of Religion in
     the University Subscription Book (Subs 1, p. 286).

March
 2   (Monday) The House of Commons passes resolutions deplor-
     ing religious innovators (i.e. Laudian bishops) and supporters
     of the King's tax on tonnage and poundage. The Speaker is
     ordered by the King to dissolve the House, but is held down
     while the resolutions are read and passed. The King dissolves
     Parliament, which does not meet again until 13 April 1640.
15   JM's nephew John Phillips, son of Edward and Anne, is buried
     (Parish Register, St Martin in the Fields).
19/29   The Emperor Ferdinand II issues the Edict of Restitution
     which returns church property secularised since 1555 to the
     Roman Catholic church and restricts freedom of worship.
27   Lent Term at Cambridge ends.

April
JM probably writes *Elegia V* in the spring of this year; he later dates
it *anno aetatis 20*.
 1   (Wednesday) JM's father receives licence to sell Aldersgate
     Street property to Alexander and Mary Dorington (PRO
     C66/2527/70); see 19 June.
14/24   Peace of Suze concludes war between England and France.
15   Easter Term at Cambridge begins.

May
Sonnet I ('O Nightingale') is probably written in May of 1629 or
1630. 'Song. On May Morning' resembles Sonnet 1 and Elegia V,
and was probably written at the same time.

22   (Friday) Christian IV of Denmark signs Treaty of Lübeck with
      Emperor Ferdinand, so concluding the Danish War.

June
12   (Friday) JM receives interest payment of £12 from Richard
      Powell.
18/28   Peace of Alais concludes the Huguenot rebellion.
19   JM's father appears in Chancery to acknowledge the indenture
      of sale of the Aldersgate Street property to Dorington (PRO
      C54/2803/18).
26   JM's father arranges a loan by John Cotton to a Mr Cherfield or
      Sherfield; the bond is lost, but the date is recorded in Bower's
      schedule of Cotton's bonds (see 25 November 1630) and in
      Cotton's bill (see 28 May 1636).

July
10   (Friday) Easter Term at Cambridge ends.
18   JM's father buys a Ludgate Hill property from John (later
      Sir John) Suckling and William Barrett (PRO C54/2800/7).
      Suckling did not sign the document, because he was abroad
      at the time.

September
4/14   (Friday) Frederick Henry, Stadholder of the United Pro-
      vinces, captures Bois-le-Duc ('s-Hertogenbosch, in Brabant)
      with the assistance of French troops. JM's friend Alexander
      Gill subsequently composes a celebratory poem, 'In Sylven-
      Ducis' and sends a copy to JM, which he acknowledges in *EF
      No 2* (see 20 May 1630).
25   Sweden and Poland sign Treaty of Altmark (negotiated by
      Richelieu).

October
10   (Saturday) Michaelmas Term at Cambridge begins. JM may
      have delivered Prolusion 2 during this term. His Italian
      sonnets may also have been written in this term (see Carey;
      for an opposing view see Miller (1981)).

November
15   (Sunday) JM is said to have bought and subsequently annot-
      ated the copy of Pindar (Saumur, 1620) now in the Harvard

University Library, but the handwriting is not JM's; see Kelley and Atkins (1964). Bethlen Gábor dies.

20(?) JM's father arranges another loan by John Cotton to William Welby; the bond is lost, but the date is recorded in Bower's schedule of Cotton's bonds (see 25 November 1630) and in Cotton's bill (see 28 May 1636). The exact date is missing in the schedule and partially missing in the bill, but in the latter the date ends with 'tieth' and so must be the 20th or 30th.

December

JM buys *Rime e Prose di Giovanni della Casa* (Venice, 1563) for tenpence and writes his name and the date on the title page; the margin has been torn away, and so the precise date of purchase has been lost. The volume is now in the NYPL (Rare Book Room *KB 1529), bound with Dante's *L'Amoroso Convivio* (Venice, 1529) and Benedetto Varchi's *Sonetti* (Venice, 1555); some of the marginalia in the Della Casa and the Varchi may be in JM's hand. See Kelley (1961)

9   (Wednesday) JM's twenty-first birthday.

12   JM receives interest payment of £12 from Richard Powell.

13   Charles Diodati writes to JM, who in the headnote to *Elegia VI* says that the letter was written on the Ides of December. The letter is lost, but the correspondence may be related to the second of two undated letters in Greek from Diodati to JM now in the British Library (BL Add MS 5016* fols. 5, 71).

16   Michaelmas Term at Cambridge ends.

25   JM completes 'On the Morning of Christ's Nativity'. Shortly thereafter JM writes *Elegia VI* in reply to Charles Diodati's letter of 13 December; JM's poem refers to his recently composed 'Nativity Ode'.

1630

JM composes 'On Shakespeare', which is dated '1630' in the 1645 *Poems*; the poem may have been written at any point before the end of the Julian year on 24 March 1631.

January

13   (Wednesday) Lent Term at Cambridge begins.

March
19   (Friday) Lent Term at Cambridge ends.
26   (Good Friday) JM composes 'The Passion'; the year of compo-
     sition is not certain, but the poem would seem to be a succes-
     sor to the Nativity Ode of 1629.

April
 7   (Wednesday) Easter Term at Cambridge begins.
 9   JM's father visits Exeter, where he deposes in Susanna Peck–
     Edmund Randolph suit (PRO C24/566/73).
16   JM's friend Charles Diodati matriculates at the Academy (later
     University) of Geneva ('Matricula Studiosorum', in
     Bibliothèque Publique et Universitaire de Genève, MS fr.
     141C (Inv. 345), fol. 9v).

May
In a new phase in the War of Mantuan Succession (1627–31),
Cardinal Richelieu leads an army into Italy.
12   (Wednesday) JM's father arranges loan by John Cotton to a Mr
     Marbury; the bond is lost, but the date is recorded in Bower's
     schedule of Cotton's bonds (see 25 November 1630) and in
     Cotton's bill (see 28 May 1636).
20   JM may have written to Alexander Gill from London on
     this date; the date of 20 May 1628 in *EF* (No. 2) may be an
     error as the poem seems to allude to Gill's poem on the fall of
     Bois-le-Duc in September 1629 (see Chifas). On the same day
     JM's father arranges loan by John Cotton to a Mr Reed; the bond
     is lost, but the date is recorded in Bower's schedule of Cotton's
     bonds (see 25 November 1630) and in Cotton's bill (see 28
     May 1636).

June
10   (Thursday) Edward King is appointed to a Fellowship at
     Christ's College Cambridge by Royal Mandate.
12   JM receives interest payment of £12 from Richard Powell.

July
 6   (Tuesday) Gustavus II Adolphus arrives in Pomerania and
     leads his army into Germany.
8/18 Mantua falls to a Spanish force.
 9   Easter Term at Cambridge ends.

August

JM's nephew Edward Phillips is born. No record of his birth
has been found, but JM was later to note in his family Bible (BL
Add MS 32,310) that Edward Phillips was 15 years old in August
1645.

13 (Friday) Ferdinand II dismisses Wallenstein and appoints
    Count Tilly as commander of the Imperial army.

October

10 (Sunday) Michaelmas Term at Cambridge begins. JM is likely
    to have delivered Prolusion 7 during this term. The prolusion
    refers to JM having spent the summer in the country. 1630 was
    a plague year, and the Milton family presumably moved to a
    rural bolthole.

31/10 November The 'Day of Dupes', on which Richelieu defeats
       the attempt of Marie de Medici and Michel de Marillac to
       depose him; Marie was subsequently banished and Marillac
       executed.

November

5/15 (Friday) Treaty of Madrid ends war between England and
      Spain.

25 JM's father's partner Thomas Bower signs a schedule of bonds
    for John Cotton acknowledging the receipt of Cotton's invest-
    ments, 'which are all that are due at Mr Milton's shop in Bread
    Street' (BL Cottonian Charters 1/5/4). The partners had paid
    £2,000 for bonds with a total face value of £3,600. JM's father
    had handled Cotton's investments for 40 years.

December

9 (Thursday) JM's twenty-second birthday.

12 JM receives interest payment of £12 from Richard Powell.

16 Michaelmas Term at Cambridge ends.

1631

JM is said to acquire a silver gilt watch (now in the British
Museum, Registration no. 1862, 8–1.1) inscribed 'Ioanni Miltoni,
1631'. The inscription is possibly retrospective, but probably spurious; the maker, William Bunting, was not made free of the

Company of Clockmakers until 1647, and the style is that of the 1650s. On an unknown date in 1631 JM buys (for 2s. 6d) and subsequently annotates the Paris 1559 edition of Aratus's *Phenomena;* the volume is now in the BL (C.60.1.7). On the annotations see Kelley and Atkins (1955).

January
1 (Saturday) Thomas Hobson, the University carrier, dies.
13 Lent Term at Cambridge begins. JM may have returned to Cambridge for the start of term, and could have written his two Hobson poems any time after this date, but he may have delayed his return until 15 February, when his brother was admitted.

February
10 (Thursday) JM's father and his apprentice Henry Rothwell witness indenture between Francis and John Farley (Hereford and Worcester County Record Office, K11/3232/3/23).
15 JM's brother Christopher is admitted to Christ's College under Nathaniel Tovey, paying 10 shillings for admission (Admissions Book, Christ's College); on Tovey see Campbell.
19 JM's niece Elizabeth Phillips, daughter of Edward and Anne, is buried (Parish Register, St Martin in the Fields).

March
19/29 (Saturday) Tilly destroys a Swedish force in New Brandenburg.
25 JM's father (?) rents two tenements on London Bridge (Bodleian MS Tanner 121, fol. 121^v); the 'John Milton' could be the poet or his father or another namesake. Cf 12 February 1632.

April
1 (Friday) Lent Term at Cambridge ends.
3/13 Gustavus II captures Frankfurt an der Oder.
15 Jane Savage, Marchioness of Winchester, dies.
20 Easter Term at Cambridge begins. JM's 'Epitaph on the Marchioness of Winchester' was sent 'from the banks of Came', and must therefore have been written in Cambridge during this term; there is a manuscript copy, apparently in the hand of John Walrond, Secretary to Francis, Lord Willoughby, in BL Sloane MS 1446, fols. 37–8.

26 JM's father is sued in Chancery by Rose Downer (PRO C2 Charles I/D39/47).
30 JM's father is assessed 6s. in 'an assessment made the last day of April Anno Domini 1631 for the relief of the poor of the parish of Fulham on Hammersmith side, beginning at Easter last, and to continue for a whole year' (Hammersmith and Fulham Record Office, PAF/1/212, fol. 68). 'Easter last' fell on 10 April 1631. The four collections of 1s. 6d would have fallen on the quarter-days: 24 June, 29 September, 25 December and 25 March. Four diagonal strokes across the line following the name of 'Mr Milton' record that he completed his payments.

The three entries in this document that mention JM's father (see also 24 April 1632 and 12 May 1633) were drawn to my attention in November 1996 by Jeremy Maule, who plans to prepare a paper on the subject. JM's father is not listed amongst the petitioners who proposed the founding of a chapel of ease in Hammersmith on 5 December 1629 (Hammersmith and Fulham Record Office, DD/818/56), nor is he listed in the poor relief assessment of 1630 (PAF/1/21, fols. 42–3). The assessments for 'Hammersmith side' (i.e. the chapel of ease, for which the mother church was All Saints Fulham) for 1633, 1634 and 1635 seem to be missing, but JM's father was presumably assessed during those years.

May
 3 (Tuesday) JM's father and his partner Thomas Bower answer Rose Downer's bill (PRO C2 Charles I/D39/47).
14 Mervyn Touchet, Earl of Castelhaven, is executed for sexual crimes. The view that the scandal coloured *Comus* has been advanced by Breasted (1971) and others, and resisted by Creaser (1984).
20 Magdeburg falls to Tilly's Imperial army, which kills most of the 36,000 inhabitants and burns the city, leaving only the cathedral and 140 houses standing.

June
JM may write 'Naturam non pati senium' and 'De Idea Platonica' during this month (Shawcross, 1965b).
 9/19 (Thursday) Treaty of Cherasco ends War of Mantuan Succession. There are metrical arguments supporting the view

that 'L'Allegro' and 'Il Penseroso' (which may have been written any time in the 1630s) were most likely written in the
summer of 1631 (see Oras, 1953).

12 JM receives interest payment of £12 from Richard Powell.
24 June JM's father pays poor relief of 1s. 6d (see 30 April).

July
Urbino is annexed to the Papal States.

2 (Saturday) JM may write to Alexander Gill from Cambridge on
this day (*EF* No. 3); see Shawcross 1965*b*; cf the entry for 2 July
1628.

8 Easter Term at Cambridge ends.

23 Gustavus repels an Imperial army at Werben; a second assault
on 28 July causes heavy loss of life.

August
Count Tilly invades Saxony with an army of 20,000 troops made
available by the ending of the Mantuan War of Succession.

1 (Friday) JM's father (with his apprentice Henry Rothwell) witnesses will of his son-in-law Edward Phillips (PRO PROB 11/
160/99).

25 Edward Phillips, JM's brother-in-law, is buried 'in the church
at night' (Parish Register, St Martin in the Fields).

September
11 (Sunday) Elector of Saxony signs treaty of alliance with
Gustavus II of Sweden.

17 Gustavus II's army of Swedes and Saxons defeats Tilly at the
Battle of Breitenfeld (near Leipzig).

19 Between 19 and 26 September JM's father is named (and said to
be living in Bread Street) in depositions by Olive Street, George
Broome, Francis Stacy and Richard Sheratt (PRO C24/574/40);
James Fisher, JM's father's apprentice, is absent in Ireland, but
is subsequently (28 November) summoned to testify in the
Downer–Milton suit (PRO C33/161, fol. 171). The Bread Street
address must be a vestige of earlier litigation (see 30 April).

29 JM's father pays poor relief of 1s. 6d (see 30 April).

October
JM's nephew John Phillips is born. There is no surviving record
of his birth, but JM was later to write in his family Bible that

'John Phillips is a year younger [than his brother Edward] about October' (BL Add MS 32,310). During this month Saxon troops invade Bohemia, Gustavus marches across Thuringia and Francosia towards the Rhine with a view to liberating Protestant subjects of Maximilian of Bavaria, and the Emperor commands Wallenstein to assemble an army that could defeat Sweden and Saxony.

10 (Monday) Michaelmas Term at Cambridge begins.

November
15 (Tuesday) Prague falls to a Saxon army under Armin.

December
In this month Oppenheim and Mainz fall to the army of Gustavus II.

6/16 (Tuesday) Mount Vesuvius erupts with a loss of 18,000 lives.

 9 JM may compose Sonnet 7 ('How soon hath time') close to this date, his 23rd birthday. The ordinal phrase 'my three and twentieth year' seems likely to refer to the year between his 22nd and 23rd birthdays, though JM's only other deployment of an ordinal adjective (*anno aetatis undevigesimo* in *Elegia VII*) does not offer decisive support (see 25 May 1627); see Sirluck, 781–4, and Hunter, 179–83. For an alternative date see 9 December 1632.

12 JM receives interest payment of £12 from Richard Powell.

16 Michaelmas Term at Cambridge ends.

25 JM's father pays poor relief of 1s. 6d on or shortly before this date (see 30 April).

1632

In about this year music by JM's father is collected by Thomas Myriell in manuscripts now in Christ Church Oxford (MS 44; MSS 423–8). JM's 'On Shakespeare' is published in the Second Folio of Shakespeare. At an unknown time in the 1630s, probably between 1632 and 1637, JM began to enter drafts of his poems in the notebook now known as the Trinity Manuscript (Trinity College Cambridge MS R.3.4); JM used the notebook until about 1658.

January

5   (Thursday) JM's sister Anne marries Thomas Agar at St Dunstan in the East (Parish Register); on Agar see Clavering and Shawcross (1960) and Parker (1996), pp. 807–8.

13 Lent Term at Cambridge begins. In the course of this term JM supplicates for his MA (Cambridge University Archives, Supplicats 1630, 1631, 1632, fol. 270, No. 124).

February

12 (Sunday) A fire on London Bridge destroys about 60 houses (see 25 March 1631).

March

In this month, or possibly earlier, JM's father takes a long lease on the Red Rose, a large house in Bread Street; see 20 April 1649. Gustavus II leads his army into the Palatinate, capturing Nuremberg and Donauwörth.

23 (Friday) Lent Term at Cambridge ends.

25 JM's father pays poor relief of 1s. 6d (see 30 April 1631).

April

3/13 (Tuesday) The Emperor reinstates Wallenstein as commander-in-chief, with an army of 50,000 soldiers, and orders him to expel the Saxon army from Bohemia.

4/14 Gustavus II defeats Tilly's Imperial army at the Lech; Tilly is wounded.

11 Easter Term at Cambridge begins.

20/30 Count Tilly dies of his wounds.

24 JM's father is again assessed 6s. for poor relief in Hammersmith, 'beginning at Easter last' (i.e. 1 April 1632) 'and to continue for one whole year' (Hammersmith and Fulham Record Office PAF/1/21, fol. 85). The four collections of 1s. 6d would have fallen on the quarter-days: 24 June, 29 September, 25 December and 25 March. Four diagonal strokes across the line following the name of 'Mr Milton' record that he completed his payments.

May

Elector of Saxony occupies Prague.

17 (Thursday) Gustavus II captures Munich and occupies territory south of the Danube.

June

12 JM receives interest payment of £12 from Richard Powell.

20 Chancery issues decree in Downer–Milton suit. JM's father, whose attorney is a Mr Estcott, pays £50 to Rose Downer as ordered by the court and receives her bond (PRO C33/161 fol. 704).

24 JM's father pays poor relief of 1s. 6d (see 24 April).

July

3 (Tuesday) JM signs Subscription Book, graduating as MA (Cambridge University Archives, Subscr. 1, p. 377).

6 Easter Term at Cambridge ends.

August

This seems the most likely period for JM's *Arcades* to be performed at Harefield. A performance in 1631 is unlikely because the Castlehaven scandal would have touched the Earls of Derby directly: the Earl of Castlehaven was the son-in-law of the Dowager Countess of Derby, in whose honour *Arcades* was performed. The earliest possible date for the performance would seem to be July 1632, after JM came down from Cambridge. The latest possible date would seem to be July 1634, when the family of the Earl of Bridgwater embarked on their progress through Wales; the Bridgwater family need not have been present, but the absence in the Harefield accounts of any sign of a large gathering in the summer of 1634 after the Bridgwater family left in late June seems to rule out such a date. The occasion is discussed most fully by Brown, who argues that the evidence of the family records and the Trinity manuscript points to a performance in the late summer of 1632 (Brown, 47).

September

14 (Wednesday) JM's father deposes in Huet–Baron suit, giving his address as Hammersmith. The discovery in 1949 of this document and three later Chancery Town Depositions in which JM's father gives his address as Hammersmith (see 17 April and 5 August 1634 and 8 January 1635) dispelled the 250-year-old myth that JM retired with his family to Horton after graduating from Cambridge; the precise date of the eventual move to Horton is not known, but see 12 May 1636 (PRO C24/587/46). Jeremy Maule's discovery (in 1996) of the Fulham rate books (see 30 April 1631) shifts the date of the Milton

family's move to Hammersmith back to at least the beginning of 1631.

22 JM's brother Christopher, who evidently left Cambridge with JM in July 1632, after spending five terms there, is admitted to the Inner Temple as a student of law (Inner Temple Archive Admissions Book 1571–1640, p. 593); the register describes him (in Latin) as a gentleman, and as the second son of John Milton.

29 JM's father pays poor relief of 1s. 6d (see 24 April).

October

20/30 (Saturday) Henri de Montmorency is executed for inciting rebellion in Languedoc.

November

6/16 (Tuesday) Gustavus II, supported by Armin's Saxon army, defeats Wallenstein at the Battle of Lützen, but is killed in action. On the same day Christina accedes as Queen of Sweden.

December

9 (Sunday) JM may compose Sonnet 7 ('How soon hath Time') close to this date, his 24th birthday. JM's 'Letter to an unknown friend' describes Sonnet 7 as a 'Petrarchian stanza' which he had composed 'some while since'. As this letter seems to have been written early in 1633, December 1632 seems a possible date for the sonnet (see Parker (1996), 784–7); for an alternative date see 9 December 1631. Later in the month JM may have written 'On Time' (but see Shawcross (1960) and Parker (1996) p. 761, n. 49).

12 JM receives interest payment of £12 from Richard Powell.

25 JM's father pays poor relief of 1s. 6d on or shortly before this date (see 24 April).

1633

JM probably writes his 'Letter to an unknown Friend' early in this year; the letter survives in two drafts in the Trinity manuscript. It must have been written some time after JM's graduation on 3 July 1632 and his withdrawal to the family home in Hammersmith. The unknown friend may have been Thomas Young, JM's former tutor, or John Lawson, Rector of All Hallows from 1628 to 1642. JM may have composed 'At a Solemn Music' early in the year (but see Shawcross (1960) and Parker (1996) p. 762, n. 53).

January
1 (Tuesday) JM perhaps composes 'Upon the Circumcision'. The year of composition is not certain; see Shawcross (1960) and Parker (1996), p. 762, n. 51.

February
Wallenstein invades Silesia.

March
8 (Friday) Charles I fines the City of London £50,000 for failing to honour its undertakings.
25 JM's father pays poor relief of 1s. 6d (see 24 April 1632).

April
23 (Tuesday) German Protestants in the four Circles of Franconia, Swabia and the Upper and Lower Rhine (but not Saxony) form the Heilbronn League, which is organised by Sweden and financed by France.

May
12 (Easter Sunday) JM's father signs the audit of the Hammersmith overseers' accounts (Hammersmith and Fulham Record Office, PAF/1/21 fol. 92v). Signatories to such documents had to be either Justices of the Peace or churchwardens; JM's father is not known to have been a JP, so he would seem to have been a churchwarden in the Hammersmith chapel of ease.

June
12 (Wednesday) JM receives interest payment of £12 from Richard Powell.
18 Charles I is crowned King of Scotland in Edinburgh.

July
3 (Wednesday) Thomas Wentworth is appointed Deputy of Ireland.

August
6 (Tuesday) William Laud becomes Archbishop of Canterbury, and shortly thereafter uses visitations and the Court of High Commission to enforce ceremonial practices.

October

1/11 October (Tuesday) Wallenstein defeats Swedish army at Steinau (Silesia).

9 Between this date and 28 November (i.e. during Michaelmas Term) JM's father and William Bower bring a Chancery bill against Arthur Duck, William Child and others; later in the same term their bill is answered (PRO C2 Charles I/M78/26).

18 Charles I reissues his father's 'Book of Sports', and so angers the Puritans.

21 JM is said to have bought and inscribed a copy of the *Collectanea* of John Creccelius (now in the Huntington Library) on this date and signed the title page, but the handwriting is not JM's.

23 William Juxon is elected Bishop of London.

November

The Infanta Archduchess Isabella dies in Brussels, and under the terms of the instrument of cession of 1598, the Belgic provinces pass to the direct administration of Spain, and are henceforth known as the Spanish Netherlands; a rising in Brussels is quickly suppressed.

December

9 (Monday) JM's twenty-fifth birthday.

12 JM receives interest payment of £12 from Richard Powell.

1634

JM buys Lycophron's *Alexandra* (Geneva, 1601) for thirteen shillings, and records the purchase on the flyleaf. The book is now in the Rare Book Room at University of Illinois (MS /x q821 M64/BF63+); see Fletcher and Shawcross (1989). He also buys (for 12s. 6d) and annotates Euripides, *Tragoediae quae extant* (2 vols., Geneva, 1602), now in the Bodleian Library (Don.d.27,28); see Kelley and Atkins (1961). JM's father is appointed Master of the Scriveners' Company, but the asterisk beside his name may mean that he declines the office, instead paying a fine (Bodleian MS Rawlinson D.51, fols. 29–30).

January

14/24 (Tuesday) Emperor dismisses Wallenstein and declares him to be a traitor.

February

15/25 (Saturday) Wallenstein is murdered by order of the Emperor.

17 William Prynne, who had been imprisoned in the Tower since 1 February 1633 for libelling King Charles and Henrietta Maria, is sentenced to life imprisonment, fined £5,000, expelled from Lincoln's Inn, deprived of his degree, and condemned to lose his ears in the pillory; he was pilloried on 7 and 10 May. See 14 June 1637.

April

17 (Thursday) JM's father deposes in Abdy–Dunsmore suit, giving his address as Hammersmith (PRO C24/591/2).

May

7 (Wednesday) William Prynne's ears are cut off for publishing (in 1633) *Histrio-mastix*, which is deemed to libel Queen Henrietta Maria. JM was to allude to the mutilation in the draft version of 'On the New Forcers of Conscience', though the reference could be to the second mutilation on 30 June 1637.

June

12 (Thursday) JM receives interest payment of £12 from Richard Powell.

August

5 (Tuesday) JM's father deposes in Humphreys–Drabull suit, giving his address as Hammersmith (PRO C24/596/33).

21 Richard Powell is summoned to the Heralds' office about his Coat of Arms (BL MS Harleian 1557, fol. 111).

26–27/5–6 September Battle of Nördlingen (in Swabia), in which the Swedish army of Bernhard of Saxe-Weimar is defeated with a loss of 17,000 lives by the army of Matthias Gallas.

September

29 (Wednesday) *Comus* is acted at Ludlow Castle. A presentation copy (in a scribal hand) known as the Bridgewater manuscript has been deposited in the BL (Loan 76), which also holds the five songs of Comus (Add MS 11518, in a scribal hand, and Add MS 52723, in the hand of Henry Lawes).

October

20 (Monday) Charles I issues the first writs for the collection of ship money.

November

Imperial armies recapture Württemberg and Franconia from the Swedes.

20 (Thursday) Alexander Gill writes a 75-line epithalamium for a wedding (East Sussex Record Office FRE 690) and sends a copy to JM (see Miller, 1990*a*).

December

Imperial siege of Heidelberg is lifted by a French army.

2 (Tuesday) Alexander Gill writes to JM. The letter is lost, but on 4 December JM describes it as *nudiustertius*, which means 'the day before yesterday'.

4 JM replies to Alexander Gill enclosing his recently composed translation of Psalm 114 into Greek verse (*EF* No. 5).

9 JM's twenty-sixth birthday.

12 JM receives interest payment of £12 from Richard Powell.

1635

According to Wood, JM is incorporated MA at Oxford during this year; there is no surviving evidence in the University records to corroborate Wood's contention; indeed, Aubrey had written to Wood on 29 June 1689 reporting the assertion of Edward Phillips that JM 'was never of Oxford' (Bodleian MS Wood F39 fol. 386ᵛ). JM is said to have purchased and signed a copy of the 1635 edition of Terence's *Comedies* (now in the Harvard College Library), but the signature is not JM's. Similarly, the copy of William Ames' *Conscientia* (now in the Princeton University Library) signed 'Ex libris Johannis Miltonii' may have been JM's, but the inscription is not in his hand.

January

8 (Thursday) JM's father deposes in Campion–Terrell suit, giving his address as Hammersmith (PRO C24/600/37).

March

15 (Sunday) Archbishop Laud becomes First Lord of the Treasury.

May

4   (Monday) A writ is issued in an action by JM's father and Thomas Downer against Sir Arthur Duck (PRO C33/167, fol. 635ᵛ). The case against Duck is a continuation of the Rose Downer case; see Parker (1996), p. 797, n. 73.

8   JM's father brings action against Sir Arthur Duck and others (PRO C8/39/39); the Chancery bill is in the name of Rose Downer, but was almost certainly brought by JM's father.

9/19 France declares war on Spain.

20/30 Ferdinand II and the Elector of Saxony sign the Peace of Prague; the treaty is subsequently ratified by Brandenburg and most Lutheran states. The treaty effectively ends the German civil war and for the remaining 13 years of the Thirty Years' War the conflict was sustained by France, Holland and Sweden on the one side and Spain and the Emperor on the other.

June

12   (Friday) JM receives interest payment of £12 from Richard Powell.

13   Duck and others answer JM's father's Chancery bill.

August

4   (Tuesday) Charles I issues the second writs for the collection of ship money.

September

12   (Saturday) Poland and Sweden sign the Truce of Stuhmsdorf.

30   The unnamed daughter of Henry Milton, possibly a relative of the poet, is buried in St Giles Cripplegate (Parish Register).

December

9   (Wednesday) JM's twenty-seventh birthday.

12   JM receives interest payment of £12 from Richard Powell.

1636

JM buys (for 18/-) Paris 1604 edition of Chrysostom, *Orationes LXXX* and subsequently enters textual corrections on four pages; the book is now in Ely Cathedral Library.

March

6 (Sunday) Bishop Juxon is appointed Lord Treasurer of England, thus consolidating the power of the Laudian party.

May

Cardinal Ferdinand, the Spanish Infante, invades north-eastern France.

12 (Thursday) JM's father is discharged at his own request as Assistant to the Company of Scriveners because of his 'removal to inhabit in the country' (Clarke, 1880); this entry (from records that can no longer be identified) reflects the retirement of JM's family to Horton (now in Berkshire, but until 1974 in Buckinghamshire).

28 Sir Thomas Cotton brings action against JM's father in Court of Requests (PRO Req 2/630; BL Cottonian Charters 1/5/5).

June

12 (Sunday) JM receives interest payment of £12 from Richard Powell.

July

Prince Octavio Piccolomini invades France with a Spanish army, and in August is turned back at Corbie, near Amiens.

October

4/14 (Tuesday) Swedish Army defeats the Saxons at the Battle of Wittstock.

9 Charles I issues the third writs for ship money; Lord Saye and John Hampden subsequently refuse to pay.

November

Austrian troops under Matthias Gallas abandon Burgundy to the French.

December

9 (Friday) JM's twenty-eighth birthday.

12 JM receives interest payment of £12 from Richard Powell. On the same day (12/22) Archduke Ferdinand, son of the Emperor, is elected King of the Romans.

1637

JM buys for 5/- Heraclides of Pontus's *Allegoriae in Homeri fabulas de diis* (Basel, 1544); the volume is now in the library of University of Illinois.

January
23 (Monday) A writ is issued against JM's father by the Court of Requests in the Cotton case (PRO Req 1/186 fol. 1).
27 JM's father is served with a writ of the Privy Seal in the Cotton suit (PRO Req 1/141 fol. 198).

February
 5/15 (Sunday) Ferdinand III succeeds as Holy Roman Emperor on the death of Ferdinand II.
13 An affidavit of a writ is served on JM's father in the Cotton case (PRO Req 1/141, fol. 198).
16 JM's father and Thomas Bower sue Arthur Duck in Chancery (PRO C2 Charles I/M87/26).
18 JM's father and Thomas Bower are penalised by Court of Requests in Cotton case. JM's father is fined 20 shillings, and Thomas Bower is gaoled and fined. The document recording these penalties was seen by Masson among the records of the Court of Requests, but cannot now be identified (Masson, I, 630).

March
10 (Friday) Writ issued for JM's father in Cotton case (PRO, Req. 2/360).
16 Arthur Duck and William Child answer JM's father's suit (PRO C2 Charles I/M78/26).
22 JM's father is ordered to be served with writ of *dedimus potestatem* in Cotton case (PRO Req 1/71, p. 227).

April
 1 (Saturday) Christopher Milton submits an affidavit that his (and JM's) father is too infirm to attend Court in Westminster to answer Cotton's bill; JM's father is said to be living at Horton (PRO Req 1/141, fol. 218).
 3 JM's mother Sara Milton dies in Horton; the date is entered in the Parish Register and on her gravestone. On the same day Henry Perry (Sir Thomas Cotton's attorney) writes to Sir

Thomas describing the suit against JM's father (BL Cottonian Charters 1/5/5).

6 JM's mother Sara is buried. The entry in the Parish Register adds the astronomical symbol for Jupiter after the date of death; the symbol simply means 'Thursday'. French is wrong to interpret the squiggle that follows as a 9 and the symbol for Mars (*LR* I.321); its meaning is not clear, but the figure that French interprets as 9 resembles the secretary hand abbreviation for 'con'. Edward Goodall omitted the astronomical signs for the days of the week when he prepared the Bishop's Transcript.

13 JM's father answers Sir Thomas Cotton's bill (BL Cottonian Charters 1/5/1; PRO Req 2/630).

May
French army invades Artois, which is eventually wrested from the Spanish in 1640.

June
12 (Monday) JM receives interest payment of £12 from Richard Powell.

14 William Prynne is again (see 17 February 1634) sentenced to life imprisonment, fined £5,000 and condemned to lose the stumps of his ears; he is mutilated in the pillory on 30 June. The draft of JM's 'On the New Forcers of Conscience' in the Trinity manuscript alludes to the cropping of Prynne's ears ('Crop ye as close as marginal P——'s ears').

July
23 (Sunday) The introduction of the Laudian prayer book in St Giles' Cathedral in Edinburgh causes a riot.

August
10 (Thursday) Edward King, the subject of *Lycidas*, drowns.
16 Death of Ben Jonson (see Phelps)

September
The first entries in JM's Commonplace Book (BL Add MS 36,354) are probably made at about this time (Shawcross, 1993); in the autumn of 1637 JM seems gradually to have abandoned his early habit of using a Greek ϵ in favour of an Italian e, and this transition allows a tentative dating of JM's entries from 28 works, which may

be dated between September 1637 and the end of 1638. Citations in the early part of this period, in which only Greek ϵ is used in the initial entries, are those to the following: Eusebius, *Historia Ecclesiastica* and *Vita Constantini*; Socrates Scholasticus, *Historia Ecclesiastica*; the anonymous *Historia Miscella* (which JM seems to cite in the 1603 edition of the *Historia Romana* of Paulus Diaconus); Procopius, *De Bello Persico* (that is, the first two books of his *History of the Wars of Justinian*; JM's citations are taken from the Augsburg edition of 1607); Sulpicius Severus, *Historia Sacra* (which seems to be cited from the Elzevir edition published in Leiden in 1635); Evagrius, *Historia Ecclesiastica*; Sigonius, *De Occidentali Imperio* and *De Regno Italiae*; Gregoras Nicephoras, *Historia Byzantina*; Cantacuzenus (the Byzantine Emperor John VI), *Historia Byzantina*; Dante, *Divina Comedia* (and the commentary of Bernardino Daniello, cited from the Venice edition of 1568) and the *Convivio* (Canzone IV, on Nobility); Prudentius, *Peristephanon* ('Crowns of Martyrdom'); Boccaccio, *Vita di Dante*; Ariosto, *Orlando Furioso*; Clement of Alexandria, *Stromata* and *Paedagogus*; Cyprian, *De Habitu Virginum* and *Epistolae* (including pseudo-Cyprian on public shows, which is sometimes listed as a separate work); Ignatius, *Epistolae* (apparently cited from the Geneva edition of 1623); Tertullian, *De Spectaculis, De Jejuniis* and *Apologetica*; Justin Martyr, *Tryphon and Apologia pro Christianis*; Cedrenus, *Compendium Historiarum.*

30/10 October (Saturday) Breda falls to a Dutch army under Frederick Henry.

November

JM writes *Lycidas*, which is dated 'Novemb: 1637' in Trinity manuscript.

2 (Thursday) JM writes to Charles Diodati from London. In *EF* this letter (No. 6) is dated 2 September and its sequel (No. 7) 23 September. These dates conflict with the internal evidence of both the first letter (which refers to the onset of autumn as an event in the past) and the second letter (which tells Diodati to hurry because winter is imminent). It seems likely that JM dated the letters '2.ix.1637' and '23.ix.1637', and that the printer of the 1674 edition took the Roman numerals to refer to the ninth month of the year beginning in January (i.e. September) rather than the ninth month of the year beginning in March (i.e. November).

23   JM writes again to Charles Diodati from London.
26   JM's brother Christopher is 'restored into commons' by the Inner Temple (Inderwick, II, 239). Christopher had recently married Thomasine Walker, and they were living in Horton with Christopher's and JM's aged father. During term-time Christopher took up residence ('commons') in the Inner Temple.

December
 9   (Saturday) JM's twenty-ninth birthday.
12   JM receives interest payment of £12 from Richard Powell.

1638

JM's *A Masque Presented at Ludlow Castle, 1634* is published; the volume is dated 1637, but was probably published early in 1638. The copy in the Carl H. Pforzheimer Library has nine corrections in JM's hand. On the changes that JM made to the text between 1634 and 1637, see Brown (1985), 132–52. Later in the year *Lycidas* is printed in *Justa Edouardo King naufrago* part ii (*Obsequies to the memory of Mr Edward King*). At least two copies contain corrections in JM's hand: one in the BL (C.21.c.42) contains five corrections and insertions, apparently taken from a lost copy and remounted in another copy; one in the Cambridge University Library (Add MS 154) contains 14 corrections and insertions; a third copy, which was said by A. W. Pollard to contain two corrections in JM's hand, was offered for sale in W. H. Robinson's catalogue (No. 65, 1938, item 80); its present location is unknown. JM is said to have read and annotated a copy of Gildas, *De Excidio Britanniae* (Heidelberg, 1587), now in the Harvard College Library, but JM did not ordinarily write in minuscules, and in any case the annotations are transcriptions of the printed marginalia in Josseline's edition of 1558 (see Davies).

February
 1   (Thursday) JM lends £150 to Sir John Cope and others and takes a bond for repayment. The original bond is lost, but its conditions can be inferred from JM's suit against the Copes of 16 June 1654. The interest of £12 a year (i.e. eight per cent) was payable quarterly, apparently on 3 February, 3 May, 3 August and 3 November. JM's bill of 1654 implies that interest

payments were made until November 1641. On the same day the Court of Requests dismisses the Cotton–Milton suit (BL Cottonian Charters 1/5/5; the copy in the records of the Court of Requests has not been found).

19 Charles issues a proclamation defending the Scottish prayer book, and in effect declaring war.

March

JM may write *Ad Patrem* this month (Shawcross, 1993), but it has been variously dated from 1631 to 1645.

1 (Wednesday) The Scottish National Covenant is signed by the clergy of Edinburgh.
3 Bernhard of Saxe-Weimar captures Rheinfelden from the Imperial army.

April

Henry Lawes sends letter and passport (giving permission to leave the country) to JM; the passport has since disappeared. JM may have written the couplet 'Fix here' on the verso of the letter (BL Add MS 36,354). JM meets Sir Henry Wotton at Eton College.

6 (Friday) JM writes to Sir Henry Wotton enclosing a 'dainty peece of entertainment', possibly *Comus*; the letter is lost.
13 Wotton replies to JM from Eton College. The letter was first published in JM's 1645 *Poems*. The manuscript version in the BL (Add MS 28,637) appears to be an eighteenth-century copy based on the lost original rather than on the printed text.
15 JM completes sale of land in St Martin-in-the-Fields to Sir Mathew Lyster (PRO CP25/2/458, 14 Charles I E); see 25 May 1627.
18 John Lilburne, who had earlier refused to take the oath in the Court of Star Chamber, is whipped from the Fleet to Palace Yard, where he is pilloried.

May

JM leaves England for a tour of the continent that lasts approximately 15 months. It is not known whether he carried his Commonplace Book with him, and this uncertainty compounds the already considerable problems associated with dating his recorded reading (which is in any case only a partial record of his reading). There are a few days during this period when his whereabouts are known from surviving documents, but for the most part it is easier to order his movements than to date them. JM was to provide a loose chronology in *Defensio Secunda*, but the figures that he provides for the length of stay in each city are rounded off and presented with an eye to their symmetry. JM travelled from London to Paris, where he met the ambassador of King Charles, John Scudamore, Viscount Sligo; in 1654 JM recalled this meeting in *Defensio Secunda*, but misremembered Viscount Sligo's Christian name as Thomas. Sligo, later to become a prominent Royalist, is said by Clarendon to have 'furnished his own chapel in his house [in Paris] with such ornaments (as candles upon the communion table, and the like) as gave great offence and umbrage to those of the Reformation'. Sligo arranged for JM to meet Hugo Grotius, the Dutch scholar, jurist and theologian who was living in Paris as the ambassador to France of Queen Christina of Sweden; there is no mention of JM in the Grotius–Scudamore correspondence (BL Add MS 11,044 pp. 91ff). JM travelled from Paris to Nice and Genoa, and thence by ship to Livorno. He then travelled via Pisa to Florence, which he probably reached in mid-June 1638.

  3   (Thursday) JM receives £3 interest on Cope bond. If he has
       already left for Italy, payment will be received by his agent,
       probably his father.

June
JM arrives in Florence. During this period he participates in the meetings of at least two Florentine academies and becomes acquainted with the learned men of the city, several of whom compose tributes to JM which he is later to print in his 1645 *Poemata*. Among those whom JM mentions having met on one or both of his two visits to Florence are Agostino Coltellini (see *DBI*), the young lawyer who had recently founded the academy known as the Apatisti ('the Indifferent Ones') and Carlo Dati (see *DBI*), the academy's 18-year-old Secretary. Dati subsequently wrote to JM on at least four occasions; three of the letters were lost, but JM received the fourth and replied on 20 April 1647 (q.v.). JM also met the President of the Apatisti, Benedetto Fioretti, the scholarly grammarian and student of poetry, and other members such as Pietro Frescobaldi, Antonio Francini (who addressed an ode to JM) and Valerio Chimentelli (see *DBI*), all of whom are mentioned by JM in *Defensio Secunda*. JM also visited the Svogliati (literally 'the will-less') Academy on several occasions, and his visits are recorded in the minutes. Among Svogliati members (many of

whom also belonged to other academies) whom JM is known to have met are Jacopo Gaddi, the founder, Vincenzo Galilei, the illegitimate son of Galileo, Antonio Malatesti, the poet, and the scholar Benedetto Buonmattei (see 31 August). In September 1637 Malatesti had composed an erotic sonnet sequence entitled 'La Tina' at his villa at Triano. In the course of one of JM's visits to Florence, Malatesti dedicated the poems to 'the great English poet John Milton of London'. The poems seem not to have been published at the time, but the manuscript was discovered on a London bookstall in 1750 and was subsequently published (the edition bears no date); the manuscript has since disappeared. JM sent cordial greetings to Malatesti in his letter to Dati of 20 April 1647. JM also visited Galileo, either in his house at Arcetri or at Vincenzo Galilei's house on the Costa San Giorgio, where Galileo was staying for medical treatment (Harris). JM's mention of the visit in *Areopagitica* (1644) is the only evidence that it occurred. On the tradition that JM visited Vallombrosa, see the essays by Chaney (who thinks the tradition spurious) and Harris (who thinks a visit possible in the summer, but not in the autumn, when the leaves were falling) in Di Cesare. JM's purchases of books published in Florence (which need not have been bought there) included Giovanni Villani's *Croniche Fiorentine* (which JM later used when teaching Italian to his nephews) and Guicciardini's *Historia d'Italia*, as well as the books whose imprimaturs he was to cite in *Areopagitica*: Bernardo Davanzati's *Scisma d'Inghilterra* (probably the Florence edition of 1638; see Shullenburger, in Di Cesare) and Galileo's *Dialogo... sopra i due Massimi Sistemi del Mondo Tolemaico e Copernicano*; if JM purchased the *Dialogo* in Italy, he must have done so clandestinely, because it had been banned since 1633. On the imprimaturs see Miller (1971). In the same month in England, Charles I sends the Marquis of Hamilton as his special commissioner to Scotland in an unsuccessful attempt to secure the renunciation of the Covenant.

28/8 July (Thursday) An unnamed English man of letters (*letterato Inglese*) who desires to become a member of the Svogliati Academy, possibly JM, attends a meeting of the Academy (Biblioteca Nazionale, Florence, Magliabechiana MS, Cl. IX, cod. 60, fol. 46^v); the Academy's meetings were held on Thursdays in the Gaddi family's new *palazzo* (now the Hotel Astoria) in Via del Giglio, not, as is often said, in the old *Palazzo di Piazza Madonna*; the census of 1632 places 'Iacopo

Gaddi e fratelli' in Via del Giglio (Biblioteca Nazionale, MS Palatina E.B. 15,2, Striscia 1406).

July

5/15   (Thursday) An unnamed person, possibly JM, is elected to membership of the Svogliati (Biblioteca Nazionale, Florence, Magliabechiana MS, Cl. IX, cod. 60, fol. 47; see Harris). The Academy subsequently met on 19/29 July (fol. 47), 26 July/5 August (fol. 47), 3/13 August (fol. 47ᵛ), two additional unspecified dates, presumably in August (fol. 47ᵛ), 23 August/2 September (fol. 47ᵛ) and 30 August/9 September (fol. 48), but there is no list of those present until the meeting of 31 August/ 9 September, so JM may have attended any or all of these meetings.

August

Bernhard of Saxe-Weimar besieges Breisach.

3   (Friday) JM's agent, probably his father, receives £3 interest on Cope bond.

27   JM's friend Charles Diodati is buried (Parish Register St Anne Blackfriars, London).

31/10 September   JM writes to Benedetto Buonmattei (see *DBI*) proposing additions to his forthcoming *Della Lingua Toscana* (*EF* No. 8); JM's suggestions were ignored.

September

6/16   (Thursday) JM reads an unidentified Latin poem in hexameters to Svogliati Academy; the academicians thought the poem *molto erudita* (Biblioteca Nazionale, Florence, Magliabechiana MS, Cl. IX, cod. 60, fol. 48).

9   Charles I issues a declaration withdrawing the canons and liturgy for Scotland and undertaking to call a General Assembly and a Parliament.

October

JM travels from Florence to Rome via Siena. He seems to have stayed in Rome for about two months. Among those whom JM is known to have met on one or both of his two visits to Rome are Lukas Holste and Cardinal Francesco Barberini (see February 1639), the young prodigy Alessandro Cherubini, the Roman poet Giovanni Salzilli, to whom JM addressed his *Ad Salsillam* (see

Haan, in Di Cesare pp. 526–31 and Freeman) and (if they met in Rome) the poet known as Selvaggi, whose couplet in imitation of Propertius JM is to print in his 1645 *Poemata*. Selvaggi has been convincingly identified as Matthew Savage (Matteo Selvaggio), the alias of the English Benedictine David Codner, who was closely associated with the family of Jane Savage, Marchioness of Winchester, whose death JM had commemorated in the spring of 1631. Codner's Italian was so proficient that he could pass himself off as a native Roman, at least to a visiting Englishman, so JM may not have known that he was English (Chaney, pp. 244–51). Among the British travellers that JM is known to have met in Rome were his fellow guests at the English College (see 20/30 October) and Thomas Gawen, the Oxford academic who was soon to convert to Catholicism (see Chaney, pp. 389–92 and Pritchard). JM's purchases of books published in Rome (but not necessarily bought there) included George Conn's *De Duplici Statu Religionis Apud Scotis*, the imprimatur of which he was later to cite in *Areopagitica* (Miller, 1971).

4/14 (Thursday) An Imperial force led by Charles of Lorraine attempts to lift the siege of Breisach and is defeated at Sennheim.

20/30 JM dines in the English College at Rome. The Pilgrim Book records the presence of JM and his unnamed servant, a 'Dr Holding of Lancaster' (actually the secular priest Henry Holden), a titled member of the Fortescue family (either Sir John or Sir Nicholas) and Patrick Carey (the 14-year-old son of Viscount Falkland). See Miller, 1979*a*, and Chaney, pp. 282–4.

November

3 (Saturday) JM's agent, probably his father, receives £3 interest on Cope bond.

21 The General Assembly of the Church of Scotland meets in Glasgow without Charles's permission.

28 The Marquis of Hamilton abolishes the Assembly, which continues to sit (till 20 December) and abolishes episcopacy.

December

JM travels to Naples in the company of an eremite friar who introduces him to Giovanni Battista Manso, to whom JM is subsequently to address his Latin poem *Mansus*; in 1645 JM printed a distich by Manso in his *Poemata*. While in Naples JM, according to his subsequent account, is warned by English merchants of a rumour that the Jesuits plan to kill him should he return to Rome; he ignores the warning (see Benet in Di Cesare, pp. 29–49).

7/17   (Friday) Breisach falls to Bernhard of Saxe-Weimar, who gains access to Germany and a fortified town on the Rhine which cuts the Spanish Road between the Netherlands and Milan.

9   JM's thirtieth birthday.

12   Richard Powell's interest payment of £12 is paid to JM's representative (possibly his father) in London.

30   JM's future (third) wife, Elizabeth Minshull, is baptised in Wistaston, Cheshire (Parish Register, Cheshire Record Office).

1639

January
JM returns to Rome and probably stays until the end of February or the beginning of March.

February
On an unknown date shortly before he leaves Rome, JM visits Lukas Holste, the German scholar and convert to Catholicism acting as secretary and librarian to Cardinal Francesco Barberini (see *DBI*), the eponymous founder of the library that remained in Palazzo Barberini until 1902, when it was acquired by Leo XIII and transferred with the original shelving into the Vatican. Holste shows JM the library and allows him to examine his notes on some Greek codices. Holste presents JM with a copy of his recently published bilingual edition of the axioms of the later Pythagoreans; the dedication of the book is dated 5 December (O.S. 25 November) 1638, which means that JM must have been given his copy on his second visit to Rome (see Miller, 'Milton and Holstenius' in Di Cesare). Holste asks JM if he would, when returning through Florence, visit the Laurentian Library to copy parts of a Medicean codex for him. JM also attends a recital given by Leonora Baroni (see *DBI*), and subsequently writes three epigrams in her honour, *Ad Leonoram Romae canentem*; it may seem mildly surprising that JM should lavish praise on a singer rumoured to be the mistress of Cardinal Rospigliosi and Cardinal Mazarin (see Byard and Haan in Di Cesare, pp. 321–4, 543–6), but there was a vogue for poems *ad*

Leonoram, and JM's contribution to this genre was a gesture directed to his Italian acquaintances rather than to the singer.

15 (Friday) The Scots appoint Alexander Leslie as their military
commander in the First Bishops' War.

17/27 JM attends an entertainment mounted by Cardinal Francesco Barberini in the vast theatre of the newly completed
Palazzo Barberini, the comic opera *Chi soffre, speri*; the libretto
had been written by Cardinal Giulio Rospigliosi (the future
Pope Clement IX), the music composed by Virgilio Mazzocchi
and Marco Marazzuoli and the stage designed by Gianlorenzo
Bernini, the papal sculptor, painter and architect who was later
to design the colonnade around the piazza in front of St
Peter's. The audience of 3,500 included Cardinal Mazarin. JM
later recorded that he was greeted at the door by the Cardinal;
this may be an accurate recollection, but another member of
the audience (Raimondo Montecuccoli, emissary of the Duke
of Modena) recalled that it was Cardinal Antonio Barberini the
younger (Francesco's brother, and nephew of the Pope; see
DBI, vi, 166–70) who greeted guests at the door, and Cardinal
Francesco instead moved among the benches to welcome
guests.

18/28 JM has a private audience with Cardinal Francesco Barberini
who was then Prime Minister of Rome and chief adviser to his
uncle Pope Urban VIII; he was also Protector of the English,
and in that capacity regularly offered hospitality and assistance to travellers.

27 King Charles issues a declaration against the Scots, accusing
them of attempting to overthrow the royal power.

March
JM travels from Rome to Florence and some time this month tries
unsuccessfully to obtain permission to copy the manuscript for
Holste. The Covenanters take Edinburgh, Dumbarton and Stirling.

3 (Sunday) JM's agent, probably his father, receives £3 interest
on Cope bond.

7/17 JM reads an unidentified Latin poem to the Svogliati Academy (Biblioteca Nazionale, Florence, Magliabechiana MS, Cl.
IX, cod. 60, fol. 52)

14/24 JM again reads Latin verses to the Svogliati Academy (Biblioteca Nazionale, Florence, Magliabechiana MS, Cl. IX, cod.
60, fol. 52^v).

19/29   JM writes from Florence to Lukas Holste in Rome; the date
is taken from the autograph in the Vatican Library (Barb. Lat.
2181, fols. 57–8^v); the version printed in *EF* (No. 9) is dated 30
March 1639.

21/31   JM attends a meeting at the Svogliati (Biblioteca Nazionale,
Florence, Magliabechiana MS, Cl. IX, cod. 60, fol. 52^v).

26   Infant son of JM's brother Christopher is buried (Horton Parish Register); the entry is followed by the astronomical sign for
Mars, which simply means Tuesday.

April

JM travels to Venice via Bologna and Ferrara, and stays for at least
a month. He ships home the collection of books that he had
amassed in his travels, including at least one case of music books
with works by Monteverdi (who was then still living in Venice),
Marenzio, Vecchi and Gesualdo. Many of the Italian books subsequently cited in JM's Commonplace Book were presumably
included in this shipment. Purchases of books published in Venice
(which may have been bought elsewhere) later cited in JM's Commonplace Book included Francesco Berni's revision of the *Orlando
Innamorato*, Boccalini's *De' Ragguagli*, Dante's *Divina Commedia* with
the *esposizione* of B. Daniello (1568), Savonarola's *Oracolo della Rino-
vazione*, Tassoni's *Pensieri*, Tasso's *Goffredo* (the pirated 1580 version
of the *Gerusalemme Liberata*) and a five-volume collected works of
Chrysostom.

14   (Easter Day) Johan Banér's Swedish army defeats Archduke
Leopold William's army near Chemnitz, and subsequently
occupies Pirna, invades Bohemia and besieges Prague.

May

JM travels from Venice to Verona and Milan (see Cinquemani in Di
Cesare, pp. 51–60), through Lombardy and the Pennine Alps (over
either the Simplon or the St Bernard Pass) to Lake Geneva and on to
Geneva, where he visits the theologian Giovanni (or Jean) Diodati,
uncle of JM's friend Charles; if he had not heard the news of
Charles's death earlier, JM may have been told in Geneva (see
Parker, 1957). The Diodati family did not then own the house
(later occupied by Byron) now known as the Villa Diodati (see
Fatio), so JM must have stayed elsewhere, not necessarily with the
family. JM's book purchases in Geneva may have included the five-
volume edition of Jacques-Auguste de Thou's *Historia sui Temporis*.

3   (Friday) JM's agent, probably his father, receives £3 interest on
    Cope bond.
24 Skirmish of Turiff opens the First Bishops' War.
28/7 June Spanish forces raise the siege of Thionville.

June
10 (Monday) JM writes in Cardoini Album in Geneva; the album
    is now in the Houghton Library in Harvard (Sumner 84, Lobby
    XI.3.43, p. 110); see Miller, s.v. Manuscripts 'Boulder'.
12 Richard Powell's interest payment of £12 is paid to JM's
    representative (possibly his father) in London.
18 Charles signs the Pacification of Berwick in order to avoid
    confronting the Scottish Army; under the terms of the treaty
    the Scots agree to disband their army and Charles undertakes
    to refer ecclesiastical affairs to a General Assembly and civil
    affairs to Parliament.

July
JM returns to England through France. His book purchases in Paris
may have included the collected works of Basil (1618) and Gregory
(1638), Philippe de Commines' *Mémoires*, Bernard de Girard's *Histoire de France* and André du Chesne's *Histoire Générale d'Angleterre,
d'Escosse, et d'Irlande*. Unless he took his Commonplace Book with
him to Italy (in which case some of these entries should be earlier),
considerations of handwriting and layout, together with a series of
references in *Of Reformation* (1641), allow various entries in the
Commonplace Book to be tentatively dated circa 1639–40: Lactan-
tius, *De Ira Dei* and *Divinae Institutiones*; Savonarola, *Tratto delle
Revelazione della Reformatione della Chiesa*; Bede, *Historia Ecclesiastica*;
William of Malmesbury, *De Gestis Regum Anglicorum*; Stow,
Annales, or a General Chronicle of England; Holinshed, *Chronicles of
England, Scotland, and Ireland*; Speed, *History of Great Britain*; Sir
Thomas Smith, *Commonwealth of England*; Aristotle, *Ethics*; Lam-
bard, *Archeion, or a Commentary upon the High Courts of Justice in
England*; André du Chesne, *Histoire Générale d'Angleterre, d'Escosse,
et d'Irlande*; Machiavelli, *Arte della Guerra*; Camden, *Annales Rerum
Anglicarum et Hibernicarum Regnante Elizabetha*; Hayward, *The Life
and Reign of King Edward the Sixth*; Sleidanus, *De Statu Religionis et
Reipublica Carolo Quinto Caesare*; Ascham, *Toxophilus*; Paulus Jovius
(Paolo Giovio), *Historia sui Temporis*; Paolo Sarpi, *Istoria del Concilio
Tridentino*; Thuanus (Jacques-Auguste de Thou), *Historia sui*

Temporis; Bernard de Girard, *Histoire de France*; Philippe de Commines, *Mémoires*, Pierre Gilles, *Histoire des Eglises Vaudoises*;
Cyprian, *De Singularitate Clericorum*; Joannes Sinibaldus, *Genean-
thropeia*; Sozomen, *Historia Ecclesiastica*.
8/18   (Monday) Bernhard of Saxe-Weimar dies of a fever, aged 35.

August
Episcopacy is abolished in Scotland.
 3   (Saturday) JM receives £3 interest on Cope bond.

September
22   (Sunday) Wentworth arrives in London from Ireland and
becomes Charles I's principal adviser.

October
11/21   (Friday) The Dutch fleet under Van Tromp violates English
territorial waters.
31   Scottish Parliament is dissolved.

November
 3   (Sunday) JM receives £3 interest on Cope bond.

December
 9   (Monday) JM's thirty-first birthday.
12   JM receives interest payment of £12 from Richard Powell.
14   JM's father witnesses Widmer–Waller indenture, which is
signed by Anne Waller and her son the poet Edmund Waller;
the document is now in the Rutgers University Library.
18/28   The army of the Duke of Longueville crosses the Rhine
from the east and occupies Alsace.

1640

JM takes lodgings at the house of Mr Russell, a tailor, in St Bride's
Churchyard near Fleet Street, and begins to educate his nephews
John and Edward Phillips; he subsequently moves to a large house
in Aldersgate and takes on additional pupils. JM's Epitaph 'On
Shakespeare' is reprinted in *Poems written by William Shakespeare,
Gentleman* and his second Hobson poem is printed in *A Banquet of
Jests*. JM publishes a private edition of *Epitaphium Damonis*, of which

only one copy is known to survive (BL C.57.d.48; see Shawcross, 1965).

January
12 (Friday) Wentworth is created Earl of Strafford.
26 JM's brother Christopher is called to the bar of the Inner Temple (Inderwick, II, 454).

February
3 (Monday) Sir Henry Vane the elder is appointed Secretary of State.
10 Joseph Hall's *Episcopacy by Divine Right* is registered (*SR* IV, 472), and published shortly thereafter; JM subsequently reads it, and answers it in *Of Prelatical Episcopacy*.

March
3 (Tuesday) JM receives £3 interest on Cope bond.
13 Charles I's Fourth Parliament, the 'Short Parliament', meets (till 5 May).

May
2/12 (Saturday) Revolt of Catalonia begins in Barcelona.
3 JM receives £3 interest on Cope bond.
5 Charles dissolves Parliament because of its refusal to vote money and its attacks on the king's ecclesiastical policies.

June
12 (Friday) JM receives interest payment of £12 from Richard Powell; on the same day JM's father's suit against Duck and Child is defeated (PRO C33/173, fol. 349).
30 (?) JM takes land in Wheatley (Oxfordshire) owned by Richard Powell, his future father-in-law (PRO SP 23/109, pp. 517–18); on the same day Powell mortgages the leased manor of Forest Hill to Sir Robert Pye for £1,400 (PRO SP 23/109, pp. 517–18).

July
The Swedish army withdraws from Bohemia.

August
3 (Monday) JM receives £3 interest on Cope bond.

11 JM's brother Christopher's daughter Sarah is baptised in Horton (Parish Register).
20 The Scottish army invades England, inaugurating the Second Bishops' War; Charles soon leaves for York.
27 Charles leads his army northwards from York to relieve Newcastle.
28 The Scottish army defeats an English force at Newburn-on-Tyne.
29 The Scottish army enters Newcastle.

September
24 (Thursday) Charles responds to pressure to call a Parliament by opening a Great Council at York, which meets for five weeks.

October
26 (Monday) Charles signs the Treaty of Ripon, ending the Second Bishops' War. The treaty was in effect a royal surrender; the Scots were to retain Northumberland and Durham, and their army was to receive £850 a day until a settlement was reached.

November
3 (Tuesday) JM receives £3 interest on Cope bond. On the same day Charles summons Parliament (the 'Long Parliament') to conclude the peace; the Parliament was to sit until 20 April 1653.

December
3/13 (Thursday) The Duke of Braganza is crowned as John IV of Portugal, and Portugal becomes an independent country after 60 years of Spanish rule.
7 The House of Commons declares Ship Money to be an illegal tax.
9 JM's thirty-second birthday.
11 Root and Branch petition to abolish episcopacy is presented to Parliament.
12 JM receives interest payment of £12 from Richard Powell.
18 Archbishop Laud is impeached.

1641

JM's father John and brother Christopher and his family move to Reading. Several entries in JM's Commonplace Book can be tentatively assigned to the period 1641–43: John Hardyng, *Chronicle;* Claudius Sesellius (Claude de Seyssel), *De Monarchia Franciae;* Buchanan, *Rerum Scoticarum Historia;* Johannes Cuspinian (Hans Spiesshaymer), *De Caesaribus atque Imperatoribus Romanis;* Samuel Purchas, *Pilgrimes;* Edmund Campion, *History of Ireland;* Edmund Spenser, *A View of the Present State of Ireland;* Francis Bacon, *A Discourse of Church Affairs;* Sir Walter Ralegh, *History of the World;* Geoffrey Chaucer, *Canterbury Tales* and *Romaunt of the Rose;* John Gower, *Confessio Amantis;* John Selden, *De Jure Naturali et Gentium;* Justinian, *Institutiones Juris Civilis;* Jean Bodin, *De Republica;* Peter Martyr (Pietro Matire of Vermigli), *In Librum Judicum;* Julius Caesar, *Commentaries.* JM is said to have acquired and signed a copy of Thomas Farnaby's *Systema Grammaticum* now in the Harvard College Library; the handwriting is not JM's.

January
13 (Wednesday) Joseph Hall's *Humble Remonstrance* is registered (*SR* I, 9).
29 Robert Baillie says in a letter written from London that Hall's *Remonstrance* has been published 'this week' (Baillie, I, 237).

March
3 (Wednesday) JM receives £3 interest on Cope bond.
20 Smectymnuus, *Answer to the Humble Remonstrance,* is registered (*SR*, I, 16) and published shortly thereafter; the tract's 'Postscript' is sometimes attributed to JM; see Shawcross (1963*b*).
22 The trial of Strafford opens.

April
12 (Monday) Joseph Hall's *Defence of the Humble Remonstrance* is registered (*SR* I, 20).
21 The House of Commons votes Bill of Attainder for the execution of Strafford.
29 JM is taxed £4 in Aldersgate (Guildhall MS 1503/5).

May
JM's *Of Reformation* is published between 12 and 31 May; the tract alludes to *The Petition of the University of Oxford,* which was presented to Parliament on 12 May, and there is a hostile reference to JM's tract in the pseudonymous *Compendious Discourse Proving Episcopacy to be of Apostolical and Consequently of Divine Institution,*

the preface to which is dated 31 May (on the pseudonym see Miller, 1960). JM's presentation copy to Thomason (BL E.208(3)) is dated 'June' by Fortescue; the tract is anonymous, and is neither registered nor licensed. There are two presentation copies in the Bodleian, one presented to the Library (4oF.56.Th) with corrections in JM's hand, and another with an illegible inscription, perhaps to 'J.H.'

2 (Sunday) Mary, daughter of Charles I, marries William, son of the Prince of Orange.

3 JM receives £3 interest on Cope bond.

10 Charles agrees to accept the Bill of Attainder.

12 Strafford is executed.

21 James Ussher's *The Judgement of Dr Rainoldes* is registered (*SR* I, 24) and published. JM subsequently reads it and answers it in *Of Prelatical Episcopacy*.

June

12 (Saturday) JM receives interest payment of £12 from Richard Powell.

July

Poll Tax levy in Aldersgate names Jane Yates as JM's servant (PRO E179/252/1(A)). Thomason buys *Of Prelatical Episcopacy* (BL E.164 (19)); the copy is undated, but Thomason writes 'by John Milton' on the title page; the tract may have been published in either June or July (see Patrick). *Animadversions* is probably published in this month. Thomason's copy (BL E.166 (11)) is undated, but Thomason writes 'written by Mr John Milton' on the title page; Fortescue dates Thomason's copy 'September', which is probably too late.

5 (Monday) The Courts of the Star Chamber and High Commission are abolished.

August

3 (Tuesday) JM receives £3 interest on Cope bond; on the same day JM and his servant are listed among tax defaulters in Aldersgate (PRO E179/252/1(F)); JM's servant owes 6d, and JM may owe the same amount.

9 The English Parliament is prorogued.

20 The Treaty of Pacification between England and Scotland ratifies the agreement of 1640.

27 JM's brother Christopher's daughter Anne is baptised in Reading (Parish Register, St Laurence).

September

JM is taxed £6 in Aldersgate between 1 and 21 September (Guildhall MS 1503/6)

October

20 (Wednesday) The English Parliament reassembles.
23 Outbreak of Irish rebellion; thousands of Ulster Protestant settlers are subsequently massacred (see 2 June 1642).
29 Richard Powell obtains a new lease on Wheatley (Bodleian Wood 515 (16), p. 3); the printed Wood document gives only the year, but the precise date is given in Sir Edward Powell's Chancery bill of 1648 (PRO C5/2/65).

November

3 (Wednesday) JM receives £3 interest on Cope bond.
9 Robert Greville, Lord Brooke, paraphrases *Of Prelatical Episcopacy* in *A Discourse Opening the Nature of That Episcopacy* (*SR*, I, 36; see Whiting).
23 The Grand Remonstrance, a statement of Parliament's stance in opposition to the authoritarian rule of Charles I, is passed in Parliament by 11 votes.

December

9 (Thursday) JM's thirty-second birthday.
12 JM receives interest payment of £12 from Richard Powell.
18 Richard Powell sublets Wheatley to Sir Edward Powell.

1642

Thomas Fuller alludes to *Of Reformation* in *The Holy State*, pp. 291–2. Early in this year JM is taxed £3. 4s; in the fragmentary undated manuscript in the Guildhall Library (MS 1503/7) the original tax is recorded as £2. 8s, but this figure has been crossed out and the higher figure added; JM's neighbours suffered a similar fate: Dr Gill's tax, for example, is raised from £1.12s to £2. 2s. In *Defensio Secunda* JM was later to record that in this period 'an unjust tax was imposed on me'.

January

JM's *Reason of Church Government* is published at the end of the month; it is the first tract to bear his name on the title-page.

Thomason's copy (BL E.137(9)), which is dated 'February' by
Fortescue, is inscribed 'ex dono Authoris' in Thomason's hand.

4   (Tuesday) Charles marches to Westminster to arrest five pro-
    minent members of the House of Commons for commun-
    icating with the Scots; the Parliamentarians successfully seek
    refuge in the Guildhall, in the City of London.
10 Charles flees with his family to Hampton Court.
24 Joseph Hall alludes to JM (without naming him) as an oppon-
    ent in *A Letter . . . to a Private Friend*, pp. 5–6.

February
23 (Wednesday) Queen Henrietta Maria flees to Holland and
    remains there for a year before returning to England.

March
25 (Friday) After this date JM's *Animadversions* is attacked
    anonymously in *A Modest Confutation*, which is sometimes
    attributed to Joseph Hall and his son Robert.

April
8   (Friday) JM's *An Apology* is published soon after this date.
    Thomason's (undated) copy is inscribed 'by Mr Milton Ex
    dono Authoris' (BL E.147 (22)).

May
A Swedish army under Tortensson defeats an Imperial army at
Schweidnitz.

June
Edward Phillips records that 'about Whitsuntide [29 May] it was,
or a little after, that he took a journey into the country, no body
about him certainly knowing the reason, or that it was any more
than a journey of recreation'. JM's destination was Forest Hill, in
Oxfordshire, and his purpose was business, not pleasure: he
planned to collect the semi-annual interest payment of £12
from Richard Powell. JM was still in London on 2 June, and may
have visited his father and his brother Christopher as he
passed through Reading, but he probably reached Forest Hill by
12 June, when the payment was due. Phillips continues to the effect
that 'after a month's stay, home he returns a married man, that went
out a bachelor, his wife being Mary the eldest daughter of Mr

Richard Powell, then a Justice of the Peace, of Forest Hill' (Darbishire, p. 63).

1 (Wednesday) Parliament presents 19 propositions to Charles I, most of which insist on a more powerful role for Parliament in affairs of state. The king's subsequent rejection of the propositions leads to the outbreak of the Civil War.

2 JM gives £4 for relief of Irish Protestants; the donation is given from his home in St Botolph's Street. The manuscript (PRO E179/252/14) is badly damaged, and the evidence strongly circumstantial rather than conclusive.

12 Richard Powell pays JM £12 in interest.

July

JM's marriage to Mary Powell probably takes place this month, but the records have not been found, and neither date nor place is known. Phillips records that 'some few of her nearest relations accompan[ied] the bride to her new habitation [i.e. Aldersgate Street] ... where the feasting was held for some days in celebration of the nuptials, and for entertainment of the bride's friends. At length they took their leave, and returning to Forest Hill, left their sister behind.' The revellers may have included Mary's parents and some of her ten brothers and sisters.

15 (Friday) Lord Strange reaches Manchester for the king, and there is a military skirmish.

August

Phillips records that 'after a month or thereabout', Mary's 'friends, possibly incited by her own desire, made earnest suit by letter, to have her company the remaining part of the summer, which was granted, on condition of her return at the time appointed, Michaelmas [29 September] or thereabouts. In the meantime came his father, and some of [JM's] disciples [i.e. pupils, including Edward and John Phillips].'

22 (Monday) Charles raises his standard at Nottingham, inaugurating the Civil War.

September

21 (Wednesday) JM is said to have written (in Italian) 'I have read this book twice' in a copy (now in private ownership in England) of Harington's translation of Ariosto's *Orlando Furioso;*

the handwriting could be JM's, but the spelling in the annotation does not reflect JM's usual practice.

23   Prince Rupert defeats a Parliamentary force under the Earl of Essex at Powicke Bridge, Worcester.

October
21   (Friday) JM's brother Christopher is recorded in the muster roll for Reading as a supporter of the Royalist cause (Berkshire Record Office, MS R/HMC XXXIX).
23   The Battle of Edgehill, the first major battle of the Civil War, is fought between parliamentarians under the Earl of Essex and royalists under Charles I and Prince Rupert; both sides claim victory. On the same day (2 November N.S.) a Swedish army under Tortensson defeats an Imperial army at the second Battle of Breitenfeld.

November
JM writes Sonnet 8 ('Captain or Colonel'). The sonnet is dated 1642 in the Trinity manuscript ; after the Battle of Edgehill the Parliamentary Army had retreated to Warwick, thus leaving the road to London open to the army of Charles, who in November advanced as far as Turnham Green, which was only a few miles from JM's house on Aldersgate Street. The poem may have been occasioned by the prospect of the fall of London, or may have been written after Charles had retreated.

12   (Saturday) Charles I, marching on London, turns back at Brentford when faced by the parliamentary army of the Earl of Essex. In a letter from William Garret of 29 May 1667, probably addressed to Sir Edward Nicholas, Garret recalls that 'upon his late Majesty's return to Oxford after Brainford [i.e. Brentford] Fight ... I did often send intelligence to your Honour at Oxford by the hands of Mr Richard Powell' (BL MS Eg. 2539, fol. 101); this Royalist Powell is JM's 22-year-old brother-in-law.

25/4 December Richelieu dies, and is succeeded as Chief Minister to Louis XIII by Cardinal Mazarin.

December
5   (Monday) Royalists capture Marlborough.
9   JM's thirty-fourth birthday.
12   JM receives interest payment of £12 from Richard Powell.
13   Parliamentary forces take Winchester.

1643

JM's father's setting of Psalm 11 is published in William Slatyer's *The Psalms of David*. John Bramhall attacks *Of Reformation* in *The Serpent Salve* (pp. 211–12). Samuel Hartlib mentions JM in *Ephemerides*: 'Mr Milton in Aldersgate Street has written many good books a great traveller and full of projects and inventions' (Hartlib 30/4/89a). JM probably writes Sonnet 9 ('Lady that in the prime') and Sonnet 10 ('To the Lady Margaret Ley') between 1643 and 1645. The Lady of Sonnet 9 is unidentified. Lady Margaret Ley, daughter of the Earl of Marlborough, lived with her husband Captain John Hobson in Aldersgate Street, and so was JM's neighbour. JM's nephew later recalled that 'this lady being a Woman of great Wit and Ingenuity, had a particular Honour for [JM], and took much delight in his Company, as likewise her husband Captain Hobson' (Darbishire, p. 64).

January
23   (Monday) Fairfax takes Leeds for Parliament.

April
16   (Sunday) Earl of Essex besieges Reading.
27   Reading falls to Parliamentary forces; JM's father and brother leave Christopher's house in Reading; JM's father moves to JM's house in Aldersgate, where he lives till his death. Christopher's family remains in Reading, but Christopher lives elsewhere (at least part of the time in Wells; see 7 November 1644) until April 1646.

May
4/14   (Thursday) Louis XIII dies and is succeeded by four-year-old Louis XIV.
8/18   Anne of Austria, the Queen Mother, is invested with supreme power in France.
13   Cromwell defeats Royalists at Grantham.
16   Stamford's Parliamentary army is defeated at Stratton.
20   Fairfax captures Wakefield from Royalists.
31   Royalist conspirators are arrested in London.

June
18   (Sunday) John Hampden is defeated and killed at Chalgrove Field.

19   Daniel Oxenbridge sends JM a copy of Boiardo's *Orlando Inna-morato*, now in the library of University of Illinois (see Miller, 1989*a*).
30   Fairfax concedes West Riding to Royalists after Battle of Atherton Moor.

July
13   (Thursday) Royalists win Battle of Roundway Down.
26   Prince Rupert captures Bristol, suffering heavy losses.
28   Cromwell captures Gainsborough.

August
 1   (Tuesday) JM publishes *The Doctrine and Discipline of Divorce* (Thomason's date; his copy is BL E.62(17)). Hartlib notes 'Milton Divortium' in *Ephemerides* (30/4/91a), presumably with reference to JM's tract, though the entry is not precisely dated.
 3   Gloucester is besieged by Royalists.

September
 5   (Tuesday) Earl of Essex relieves siege of Gloucester.
15   'First Cessation' concludes Irish rebellion.
20   Royalists are defeated at First Battle of Newbury.
25   Westminster Assembly adopts Presbyterianism by Solemn League and Covenant between England and Scotland.

November
JM gives a three-shilling donation to Samuel Hartlib as a contribution towards the construction of a mobile military defensive structure (see Raylor).
22   (Wednesday) JM's brother Christopher's goods are seized as delinquent (Joseph Hunter, BL Add MS 24501, Fol. 11, said to be taken from the Account of the Committee for Sequestration (fol. 34); the manuscript cannot now be identified).
23   English Parliamentary alliance with Scotland is confirmed in Edinburgh.

December
 8   (Friday) John Pym dies.
 9   JM's thirty-fifth birthday.
12   JM receives interest payment of £12 from Richard Powell.

1644

JM is said to own and annotate the copy of the *Epistolae* of Polycarp and Ignatius now in Ely Cathedral library, but the handwriting may not be his. Several entries in JM's Commonplace Book can be tentatively dated 1644 to 1650, after which JM was no longer able to write in his own hand: Johannes Leunclavius (Johann Löwenklau), *Juris Graeco-Romani* (which JM was soon to cite in *Tetrachordon*); John Selden, *Uxor Ebraica*; Sigismund von Herberstein, *Rerum Moscoviticarum Commentarii*; Alessandro Tassoni, *Pensieri*; Trajano Boccalini, *De' Ragguagli di Parnasso*; Jacob Philipp Tomasini, *Petrarcha Redivivus*; Francesco Berni, *Orlando Innamorato Rifatto*; Wilhelm Schickhard, *Jus Regium Hebraeorum*; Gildas, *De Excidio Britanniae*; Sir Henry Spelman, *Concilia, Decreta, Leges*; Sidney, *Arcadia*; John Guillim, *A Display of Heraldry*; Robert Ward, *Animadversions of Warre, or a Military Magazine of Rules and Instructions for the Managing of Warre*; Theodoret, *Historia Ecclesiastica*; Basil, *Homiliae: In Psalmum I; In Hexameron VIII, In Principium Proverborum*; Chrysostom, *In Genesim Homiliae*; Socrates Scholasticus, *Historia Ecclesiastica*; Gregory of Nyssa, *De Virginitate*; Guicciardini, *Historia d'Italia*; Tasso, *Gerusalemme Liberata*; Giovanni Villani, *Croniche Fiorentine* (later studied by Edward Phillips under JM's tutelage); Codinus (Georgius Curopalata), *De Officiis Magnae Ecclesiae et Aulae Constantinopolitanae*; Frontinus, *Strategmata* (later studied by Phillips); Rivetus (André Rivet), *Praelectiones in Exodi*.

January
19 (Friday) Scottish army invades England.
22 Charles I's Parliament meets at Oxford.
24 Fairfax defeats Irish Royalists at Battle of Nantwich.

February
2   (Friday) Heavily revised second edition of *Doctrine and Discipline of Divorce* is published (Thomason's date; his copy is BL E.31(5)).
26 Hezekiah Woodward echoes *Of Reformation* and *Animadversions* in *A Dialogue arguing that arch-bishops . . . are to be cut off* (Thomason's date; his copy is BL E.34 (10)).
28 A sermon preached by Thomas Young on this day seems to draw on JM's *Doctrine and Discipline of Divorce* (*Hope's Encouragement*, London, 1644, p. 32).

March

18   (Monday) Young's *Hope's Encouragement* may have been pub-
     lished on this day. Thomason had catalogued his copy (BL
     E.35(18)) on 28 February (BL C.38.h.21, vol. 2, no. 145/18),
     the day on which the sermon was delivered, but he wrote 18
     March on the title page and bound the sermon with other titles
     dated from 1 to 7 March.

28   JM's brother Christopher is fined £10 as a holder of Royalist
     property (Joseph Hunter's transcription of sequestration
     records, BL Add MS 24501, fol. 56).

May

In this month JM reads Martin Bucer's writings on divorce.

June

4   (Tuesday) *Of Education* is registered for publication (*SR* I, 117).

5   *Of Education* is published (Thomason's date; his copy is BL E.50
     (12)). A title page survives in manuscript in Hartlib's hand
     (Hartlib 14/1/4a-b), but was not used in the published version.

12   Richard Powell defaults on his interest payment of £12 to JM,
     who subsequently attempts to seize Powell's property for debt.

29   Royalists defeat Waller's Parliamentary army at Battle of
     Cropredy Bridge.

July

1   (Monday) Committee of Sequestration allows £2.14s. to Mrs
     Isabel Webber (Christopher Milton's mother-in-law) for keep-
     ing Christopher's children. The entry, and similar entries for
     9 October, November, 16 December 1644 and 17 October 1645,
     apparently derive from papers of the Committee that can no
     longer be identified in the PRO, but survive only in an illegible
     summary by Joseph Hunter (BL Add MS 24501, fol. 23).
     Hunter seems to record the name as Mrs Elijah Webster, but
     this is almost certainly a mistranscription of Isabel Webber.

2   Cromwell defeats Royalists under Prince Rupert at Battle of
     Marston Moor.

11   John Dury refers to *Of Education* in a letter to Hartlib (Hartlib
     3/2/43A-44B).

14   Queen Henrietta Maria flees to France, where she remains
     until after the Restoration.

15   JM's *Judgement of Martin Bucer* is registered (*SR* I, 122).

16 York surrenders to Parliament.
19/29 Pope Urban VIII dies.

August
6 (Tuesday) *Judgement of Martin Bucer* is published (Thomason's date; his copy is BL E.4(19)).
13 Herbert Palmer attacks *Doctrine and Discipline of Divorce* in a sermon to Parliament preached in St Margaret's Church (Westminster). Herbert Palmer condemns *Judgement of Martin Bucer* before both Houses of Parliament; his condemnation was subsequently printed in Palmer's *The Glass of God's Providence*. Thomason catalogued his copy (BL E.6(8)) under the date of 13 August 1644 and entitled it 'Herbert Palmer's Sermon on the same day' (BL C.38.h.21, Vol. 2, No. 170/8). It seems unlikely that the sermon could have been printed on the day that it was preached, but it could have been printed in advance and published on 13 August.
24 Parliament receives a petition from the Company of Stationers against unlicensed and unregistered books, including *Doctrine and Discipline of Divorce* (*Journals of the House of Commons*, III, 605–6).
26 Stationers' petition is referred by House of Commons to Committee for Printing; there is no record of the Committee's report back to the Commons.

September
1 (Sunday) Montrose defeats Covenanters at Tibbermore and enters Perth.
2 Earl of Essex escapes from Fowey by sea, and his army surrenders to Charles.
5/15 Giambattista Pamfili is elected as Pope Innocent X.
7/17 French army captures Mainz, and subsequently conquers Mannheim, Speyer, Worms and Oppenheim.
16 William Prynne attacks JM's advocacy of 'divorce at pleasure' in *Twelve Considerable Serious Questions* (Thomason's date; his copy is BL E. 257(1)).

October
9 (Wednesday) JM's brother Christopher pays £7.10s in tax on house in Ludgate Hill (Joseph Hunter's transcription, BL Add MS 24501, fol. 56).

19   Scottish army occupies Newcastle.
22   Second Battle of Newbury, the first manoeuvre-battle (as opposed to pitched battle) of the Civil War, is fought by armies led by Waller and the Earl of Manchester, and ends indecisively.
31   Anonymous *An Answer to a Book*, an attack on JM's *Doctrine and Discipline of Divorce*, is registered (*SR* I, 135).

November
Christopher Milton is fined 20s. for an unknown offence (BL Add MS 24501, fol. 56); see 1 July.
 1   (Friday) Henry Robinson alludes to JM as a divorcer in *An Answer to Mr William Prynne's Twelve Questions*. The date is given by Thomason (whose copy is BL E.275 (1)), who attributes the tract to Henry Burton.
 7   Palmer's sermon (see 13 August) is registered (*SR* I, 136) and published soon afterwards; on the same day one John Hutchins writes to JM's brother Christopher as Royal Commissioner of Excise in Wells (BL Harleian MS 6802, fols. 279–80).
12   Sir Cheney Culpepper refers to *Of Education* in a letter to Hartlib (Hartlib 13/121A–122B).
14   Henry Burton alludes to JM as a divorcer in *A Vindication of Churches*, p. 41 (Thomason's date; his copy is BL E.17(5)). On the same day the anonymous *Answer to ... Doctrine and Discipline* is licensed.
19   *An Answer to a Book Entitled The Doctrine and Discipline of Divorce* is published (Thomason's date; his copy is BL E.17(12)).
23   *Areopagitica* is published; the date is written in the presentation copy now in the Yale University Library. In a copy now apparently in private hands the price is inscribed on the title-page as 4d (see Miller, 1975a).
24   Thomason receives and dates his presentation copy of *Areopagitica* (BL E.18(9)).

December
 9   (Monday) JM's thirty-sixth birthday.
16   £2.14s paid to Mrs Webber for keeping Christopher's children (BL Add MS 24501, fols. 23, 56); see 1 July.
18   Queen Christina comes of age (18) and begins to govern Sweden.

28   JM is summoned by the Westminster Assembly to appear
     before two judges appointed by the House of Lords to answer
     charges of unregistered and unlicensed printing (*Journals of the
     House of Lords*, VII, 116; Skinner, in Darbishire, p. 24). JM's co-
     defendant, Hezekiah Woodward, is released on 31 December,
     but there is no record of the result of JM's appearance.

1645

Third and fourth editions of *Doctrine and Discipline of Divorce*
are published. At some time in this year, before the move to the
Barbican in September, JM apparently plans to marry 'one of
Dr Davis' daughters'; Phillips reports that news of this plan
reached the Powell family, and 'caused them to set all engines on
work to restore the late married woman'. JM was in the habit of
visiting his relatives William and Hester Blackborough, who lived
nearby in St Martin-le-Grand Lane. Mary Milton was brought to
the house, and JM was surprised to meet her 'making submission
and begging pardon on her knees before him' (Darbishire, pp. 66–
7). JM and Mary were reconciled, and it was agreed that Mary
would stay with Isabel Webber (Christopher Milton's widowed
mother-in-law) in St Clement's Churchyard until the Barbican
house was ready.

January
At about this time a proposal to appoint JM as Adjutant-General in
the parliamentary army of Sir William Walker is mooted, probably
by Hartlib and Colonel Hobson; the scheme was scotched by the
New Model Ordinance of 28 January.
  8   (Wednesday) Henry Woodward echoes JM's *Areopagitica* in
      Inquiries into the causes of our miseries (Thomason's date; his
      copy is BL E.24(3)).
 10   William Laud, Archbishop of Canterbury, is executed for trea-
      son.
 13   House of Lords rejects Self-Denying Ordinance.
 29   Truce is declared in civil war.

February
  2   (Sunday) Montrose defeats Covenanters at Inverlochy.

7   Daniel Featley attacks JM's divorce tracts in *Katabaptistai Katap-tustoi, The Dippers Dipt* (Thomason's date; his copy is BL E.268 (11)).
22 Negotiations at Uxbridge between Royalists and Parliamentar-ians collapse, and armistice ends.
23/5 March   Torstensson's Swedish army defeats the Imperial army at Jankow (Bohemia).

March

In Lent of 1645 (19 February/1 March–19 March/8 April) or possibly 1646 (11/21 February–21/31 March) Andrew Marvell visits Richard Flecknoe, and subsequently writes 'Flecknoe, an English priest at Rome', in which 'The last distemper of the sober brain' (line 28) imitates 'That last infirmity of noble mind' (*Lycidas* 71).

4   (Tuesday) *Tetrachordon* and *Colasterion* are published (Thoma-son's dates; his copies are BL E.271(12) and BL E.271 (11)). At an unknown point after this date JM has ten of his tracts (only *Of Education* is excluded) bound in one volume, which he inscribes and sends to Patrick Young, the King's Librarian; the volume is now in the library of Trinity College Dublin (R. dd.39).
5   Ephraim Pagitt's *Heresiography* is registered (*SR*, I, 152); see 8 May.

April

3   (Thursday) The Self-Denying Ordinance is passed by the House of Lords; all MPs except Cromwell are required to resign their commissions within 40 days.
11 JM witnesses will of William Blackborough; the Public Record Office manuscripts (PROB 10/660 and PROB 11/196/82) are both copies, so the signature could either be that of JM or of his father.

May

8   (Thursday) Ephraim Pagitt alludes to JM as divorcer in *Here-siography, or a Description of the Heretics and Sectaries of These Latter Times*. There is a brief allusion in the first edition (dated 8 May by Thomason; BL E 282(5)) and a fuller allusion in the second edition, which was published shortly thereafter.
9   Montrose is victorious at the Battle of Auldearn.

June
10 (Tuesday) Cromwell is appointed Lieutenant-General of New Model Army.
14 At Naseby a parliamentary army under Cromwell and Fairfax defeats a Royalist force commanded by Charles I and Prince Rupert.
17 Leicester falls to Cromwell.
20 John Rous buys copies of *Doctrine and Discipline of Divorce* (for two shillings) and *Areopagitica* (price faint, but apparently 10d) for the Bodleian (Library Records, Bills to 1763, b.36 no.30); the books were never catalogued (see Hampshire).
28 Carlisle falls to Parliament.

July
10 (Thursday) Cromwell wins Battle of Langport.

September
In this month or slightly later JM and Mary move to a house in Barbican; the house, which later became No. 17 Barbican, stood until 1864 or 1865, when it was demolished by the Metropolitan Railway Company; an illustration of the house is printed in the *Illustrated London News* (16 July 1864). The date of JM's move is an inference from the birth of their first child on 29 July 1646. At about this time JM begins to record births and deaths in his family Bible (BL Add MS 32,310).
10 (Wednesday) Prince Rupert surrenders Bristol to Fairfax.
13 Montrose is defeated at Philiphaugh.

October
6 (Monday) JM's *Poems in English & Latyn* is registered for publication (*SR* I, 196).
8 Basing House, the Hampshire seat of the Marquesses of Winchester, yields to a Parliamentary siege and is destroyed by fire.
17 Committee of Sequestrations allows £2.14 to Mrs Webber for keeping JM's brother Christopher's children (Hunter's transcription, in BL Add MS 24, 501). A similar entry in the Books of Sequestration of Delinquents records the amount as only 18 shillings, but is followed by the figure £13.12s, possibly the amount paid to date (see 1 July 1644).

November

William Marshall draws and engraves JM's portrait for frontispiece to *Poems*; JM composes Greek verses (*In Effigiei Ejus Sculptorem*) to accompany portrait.

12   (Wednesday) Sir Cheney Culpepper asks Hartlib about JM as a teacher and comments on the 'good sprinklings' in *Of Education*, but adds that 'there is not descending enough into particulars' (Hartlib 13/121A-122B).

24   Robert Baillie cites *Doctrine and Discipline of Divorce* in *A Dissuasive from the Errors of the Time* (Thomason's date; he wrote the date of the first impression in his copy of the second (22 January 1646)).

December

9   (Tuesday) JM's thirty-seventh birthday.

1646

In this year, or possibly later, William Sandcroft (later to become Archbishop of Canterbury) copies JM's 'Nativity Ode' and his paraphrase of Psalm 136 into an anthology (Bodleian Tanner MS 466, pp. 34–5, 60–66). In this year, or possibly early in 1647 (see Shawcross, 1963), JM composes 'On the New Forcers of Conscience'.

January

2   (Tuesday) *Poems of Mr John Milton, both English and Latin* ('1645') is published. The date is Thomason's; his copy is BL E.1126; the date on Thomason's copy is confirmed in Thomason's catalogue (C.38.h.21, Vol. 10, No. 113/34). JM's Sonnet 11 ('A Book was writ of late') and Sonnet 12 ('I did but prompt the age') are not included in the collection, and so must have been written subsequently.

22   Second impression of Baillie's *Dissuasive* is published (Thomason's date; his copy is BL E.317(5)).

February

9   (Sunday) JM composes Sonnet 13 ('To Mr Henry Lawes'); in the first of the three drafts in the Trinity manuscript the sonnet is dated 9 February 1645 (i.e. 1646).

17 John Bachiler, the licenser, dissociates himself from JM's *Doctrine and Discipline of Divorce* in a note published in John Goodwin's *Twelve Considerable Cautions* (Thomason's date; his copy is BL E.322 (31)).

26 Thomas Edwards attacks *Doctrine and Discipline of Divorce* in *Gangrena* (Thomason's date; his copy is BL E.323(2)). A letter by Robert Baillie, apparently written late in 1645, may imply that the book appeared earlier (*LR*, II, 143).

April

13 (Monday) Exeter surrenders to Fairfax. Christopher Milton, who had been living in Exeter throughout the previous winter, returns to his family in London; the birth of their son on 2 February 1647 may imply that Christopher had left Exeter before it fell.

20 Christopher Milton takes Covenant in London (PRO SP 23/187, p. 199), giving his address as Reading.

May

Lawrence Farre, servant to Sir Robert Pye, takes possession of Forest Hill 'in the month of May or beginning of June 1646' (PRO SP 23/109, p. 524). Pye and JM are later to dispute ownership of this property in the courts.

5 (Tuesday) Charles surrenders to Scots at Newark.

16 Affidavit confirms Christopher Milton's residence in Exeter for up to seven months before the surrender of the city (PRO SP 23/187, p. 201).

28 Thomas Edwards publishes *The Second Part of Gangrena*, which contains the story of Mrs Attaway, the lace-woman who was persuaded by JM's *Doctrine and Discipline of Divorce* to desert her ungodly husband and run away with another woman's husband (Thomason's date; his copy is BL E.338 (12)). The decisive influence of JM may be open to doubt, but Mrs Attaway, the preacher of Coleman Street, did run off with William Jenney, a fellow Baptist.

June

5 (Friday) Irish Catholics defeat Scots at Benburb.

16 Household goods from Richard Powell's house in Forest Hill are sold by the parliamentary sequestrators of Oxfordshire to Matthew Appletree of London for £335 (PRO SP 23/110, pp. 547–8).

24 Fall of Oxford, where the Powell family had been living. At an unknown date after the fall of Oxford JM dispatches (at the request of John Rous, Bodley's Librarian) a volume of 11 of his prose tracts, with an inscription to Rous and a list of contents, both in JM's own hand; the volume is catalogued as Bodleian 4°F.56.Th, and kept at Arch.G.e.44. He also encloses a copy of his 1645 *Poems*, which goes astray.

25 Surrender of Oxford to Parliament, which in effect concludes the First Civil War.

27 General Fairfax issues a pass allowing Richard Powell to leave Oxford (PRO SP 23/194, p. 407). The Powells move with at least five of their children into the Milton house in the Barbican, and stay until JM's father dies in March 1647.

July

7 (Tuesday) Supporters of John Lilburne (who had been imprisoned) publish *Remonstrance of Many Thousand Citizens* advocating abolition of the monarchy (Thomason's date; his copy is BL E.343(11)).

29 JM's and Mary's daughter Anne born 'on the fast at eevning about half an howre after six' (JM's Family Bible); the date and time are confirmed in Birch's transcription of Mary Milton's Bible (BL Add MS 4244 fol. 52ᵛ). The fast was a designated 'Day of Public Humiliation' (*Journals of the House of Commons*, IV, 625).

30 'Newcastle Proportions' are presented to Charles by Parliamentary Commissioners, requiring the King to accept the Covenant, abolish episcopacy, restrict Catholic freedom of worship and surrender control of the army for 20 years.

August

6 (Thursday) Richard Powell petitions to compound for his estates (PRO SP 23/194, p. 400).

7 Christopher Milton petitions to compound (PRO SP 23/187, pp. 196–7).

8 Christopher Milton takes oath of Covenant, which is recorded on an endorsement on the certificate of 20 April.

25 Christopher Milton's petition to compound is considered, and he is fined £200 'at a third' and £80 'at a tenth' (PRO SP 23/54, pp. 681–2; cf PRO SP 23/187, p. 193, which confirms the larger fine). A tenth was supposed to equal two years' rent, but was

in practice calculated at two-fifteenths of the capital value of the land, in this case £600. Thirds were also calculated on the basis of two years' rent (as in the case of Powell on 8 December); Christopher had no personal estate, and his tenancy of the Ludgate house was valued at £40 a year, hence the fine of £80. Christopher paid the £80 fine (see 24 September and 24 December), but not the £200 fine. JM seems to have intervened on his brother's behalf (Phillips, in Darbishire, p. 52).

September
3 (Friday) The anonymous author of *Little Non-such* satirises JM's *Doctrine and Discipline of Divorce* (Thomason's date; his copy is BL E.353(8)).
7 Christopher Milton's fine of £200 'at a third' and £80 'at a tenth' is confirmed (PRO SP 23/34, p. 107).
24 Christopher pays £40, half of his fine (PRO SP 23/42, p. 60).

October
17 (Tuesday) Charles offers (to his Scottish captors) to accept Presbyterianism for five years and yield control of the army for ten years; the offer is rejected.

November
21 (Saturday) Richard Powell's debts are inventoried for compounding (PRO SP 23/194, p. 403; PRO SP 23/110, p. 543).

December
4 (Friday) Richard Powell takes Covenant and Oath (PRO SP 23/194 p. 401) and states his debts under oath.
7 *The Humble Advice*, an early version of the *Confession of Faith*, alludes to JM's views on divorce, p. 41 (Thomason's date; his copy is BL E.368(3)).
8 Richard Powell's petition acted on and his fine set at £180 (SP 23/194, p. 387).
9 JM's thirty-eighth birthday.
15 JM obtains certificate on Richard Powell's bond of 11 June 1627. The endorsement on the bond is dated 15 December, but the Chancery certificate is dated 16 December (PRO LC4/200, fol. 265).
16 Katharine Thomason, wife of JM's friend George Thomason, is buried in the south aisle of St Dunstan in the West

(Parish Register). JM subsequently writes Sonnet 14 in her memory.

17 JM is mentioned in the first of six letters from John Hall to Hartlib: 'I had a loving and modest express from worthy Mr Milton[.] I desire to be informed whether you suppose him willing to entertain a constant correspondence' (Hartlib 60/14/3a-4b). The letter is dated 17 December, but no year is given; 1646 seems likely, despite the fact that the letter contains the word 'Munday' near the date (17 December fell on a Thursday). Hall was eventually employed by the Council of State (see 14 May 1649); for details of his life see Parker (1996), 931-2.

21 JM is mentioned in a second letter from John Hall to Hartlib: 'I am much ambitious of the acquaintance of Mr Milton, who is here said to be the author of that excellent discourse of Education you were pleased to impart' (Hartlib 60/14/5a-6b; the year is not given in the letter).

24 Christopher Milton pays £40, the second half of his fine (PRO SP 23/82, p. 653); payment is an inference from the tick against his name. King Charles fails in an escape attempt.

28 Thomas Edwards attacks JM in *The Third Part of Gangrena* (Thomason's date; his copy is BL E.368(5)).

30 JM witnesses will of father-in-law Richard Powell; the manuscript, which is a copy, is PRO PROB 11/199/52; there is another copy in the Bodleian (Top. Oxon. c.289, fols. 49-51).

1647

The third and fourth editions of Pagitt's *Heresiography* are published, with engraved title pages showing a 'Divorcer' casting his wife aside. JM is said to have annotated a copy of Paul Best's *Mysteries Discovered* now in the Bodleian (Pamph. 84 (39)), but the writing is not JM's. Hartlib's 'Notes about Education', which may have been written in this year, mentions 'Mr Milton's Academy' (47/9/34A), 'Removing of Mr Milton' (47/9/33A-33B), which are both cancelled, and lists JM among 'Commissioners for the Act of the Council for Schooling' (47/13/3A-4B).

January
1 (Friday) Father-in-law Richard Powell dies at JM's house in Barbican; the date is recorded in a deposition signed by his

widow Anne Powell on 27 February 1650 to the effect that 'her late Husband died neere the first day of January...at the Howse of Mr. John Milton Scituate in Barbican' (PRO SP 23/110 p. 547).

4 JM is mentioned in a third letter from John Hall to Hartlib (Hartlib 60/14/9a-10b): Hall plans to 'address' himself to Mr Milton and Mr Worsley 'next week'.

8 JM is mentioned in fourth letter from John Hall to Hartlib: Hall asks Hartlib for an introduction to JM and Mr Worsley (Hartlib 60/14/11a-12b).

19 A broadsheet *Catalogue of...sects* is published, apparently depicting JM as a divorcer (Thomason's date; his copy is BL 669.f.10 (111)).

23 JM writes a Latin ode for John Rous (*Ad Joannem Rousiam*), Bodley's Librarian, to accompany a second presentation copy of his *Poems* to replace the copy that had gone astray. The holograph is now detached from the presentation volume, and is catalogued as Bodleian MS Lat. misc. d.77, but kept at Arch.F.D.38; the book is catalogued as 8°M.168.Art, and kept at Arch.G.f.17.

30 Scots agree to hand Charles I over to Parliament for £400,000, the amount that their army is owed in back pay.

February

2 (Tuesday) JM's brother Christopher's son Thomas is baptised at St Clement Dane's Church, London (Parish Register).

7 JM is mentioned in a fifth letter from John Hall to Hartlib (Hartlib 60/14/18a-19b).

11 JM is taken to court by Sir Robert Pye over Richard Powell's property in Forest Hill (PRO C2 Charles I/P 10/15).

22 JM answers Sir Robert Pye's bill of complaint (PRO C2 Charles I/P 10/15); see the entries for 22 February 1647, 21 November 1647, 24 January 1648 and 16 June 1649.

March

15 (Monday) JM's father is buried in St Giles' Cripplegate (Parish Register); his date of death is unknown. His will is lost, but JM inherited the lease on the house in Bread Street, and kept it until it was destroyed by the Fire of London in September 1666. After the death of his father and the departure of the

Powells JM began teaching again. His pupils included Richard Barry (second Earl of Barrimore), Thomas Gardiner, Richard Heath, Richard Jones, Henry Lawrence, 'Mr Packer' (possibly Jeremie Picard), Edward and John Phillips and Cyriack Skinner.

22(?) On a 'Munday' late in March (22 or 29?) JM is mentioned in a sixth letter from John Hall to Hartlib: 'I am sorry Mr Milton dos (is?) abundare suo sensu' ('fully persuaded in his own mind', quoted from a Latin text of Romans 14.5; Hartlib 60/14/39a-40b).

April

7 (Wednesday) Edward Hyde mentions *Doctrine and Discipline of Divorce* in a letter from Jersey to Sir Edward Nicholas (Bodleian Clarendon MS 29, fol 183).

15/25 The writer of an anonymous letter (in German) in the Hartlib Papers (59/9/9) praises JM's *Areopagitica* (see Miller, 1989*b*).

20 JM writes a letter to Carlo Dati in Florence. The letter was carried to Italy by 'Bookseller James' or by 'his master'; James Allestree was the apprentice of JM's friend George Thomason. The holograph in the NYPL is dated (in Latin) 'the third day of Easter 1647'; Easter Sunday fell on 18 April, so the third day was 20 April. The date of 21 April must be wrong (though it is consonant with the date of Easter in 1674, when the letter was published).

26 JM is satirised for his divorce views in a broadside, *These Tradesmen are Preachers* (Thomason's date; his copy is BL 669.f.11 (6)).

May

18 (Tuesday) Commons votes to disband most of the army.

June

3 (Thursday) Cromwell flees from Parliament to the army at Triploe Heath.

4 Cornet Joyce seizes Charles I at Holmby House as prisoner for the army.

July

3 (Saturday) JM's poems are imitated by Robert Baron in *Erotopaignion, or the Cyprian Academy*; Fortescue dates

Thomason's copy (BL E 1147 (1)) as 'April', but Thomason catalogued it s.v. 3 July 1647 (BL C.38.h.21. Vol 2, No. 274/ 55).

16 JM obtains an extent on Powell's Oxfordshire property (PRO C 228/6).

August
2 (Monday) The army presents proposals to Charles, who rejects them.
5 Powell's Wheatley property is subjected to inquisition (PRO C 228/6).
7 The army marches into London.

September
JM moves from Barbican to High Holborn in September or October. Edward Phillips dates the move 'not long after the march of Fairfax and Cromwell through the City of London with the whole army, to quell the insurrections of Brown and Massey', which took place on 6 and 7 August. The house was smaller than the Barbican house, and 'open[ed] backwards into Lincoln's Inn Fields' (Phillips, in Darbishire, p. 68); Cyriack Skinner had been admitted to Lincoln's Inn on 31 July.

October
10 (Sunday) John Wilkins lists JM's three divorce tracts (without comment) in the second edition of *Ecclesiastes*, a bibliography of works on religious subjects (Thomason's date; his copy is BL E.356(15)).
22/1 November Carlo Dati writes to JM from Florence. The manuscript in NYPL is probably the holograph sent to JM, but could be Dati's file copy.

November
11 (Thursday) Charles escapes but is recaptured.
14 Charles is imprisoned in Carisbrooke Castle on the Isle of Wight.
20 JM takes possession of Wheatley and allows mother-in-law Anne Powell her share of income ('thirds') from the property; JM's purpose in obtaining possession is to obtain payment of the debt owed to him by Richard Powell.

December

3 (Friday) Sir Robert Pye assigns the manor of Forest Hill to his son John (PRO SP 23/109, p. 518).

9 JM's thirty-ninth birthday.

14 Fifty Presbyterians of the Sion College group sign an attack on toleration entitled *A Testimony to the Truth of Jesus Christ* which mentions *Doctrine and Discipline of Divorce* in a statement derived from *Gangroena*.

24 'Four Bills' are presented to Charles by Parliament.

26 Charles concludes 'Engagement' with Scots, agreeing to abolish episcopacy and restore Presbyterianism in exchange for a Scottish undertaking to abolish the army, call Parliament, and restore the king, if necessary by force.

28 Charles rejects 'Four Bills'.

1648

JM's Sonnet 13 ('To Mr Henry Lawes') is published in Henry and William Lawes, *Choice Psalms*. Throughout the year Agitator and Leveller disturbances sustain a debate on their republican aspirations.

January

18 (Tuesday) *A Testimony to the Truth of Jesus Christ* is published (Thomason's date; his copy is BL E.423(3)).

24 On or shortly after this date Sir Robert Pye replies to JM's answer to his Bill of Complaint (PRO C2 Charles I/P98/30). The document is dated Hilary term, 22 Charles I, which ran from 24 January to 12 February 1648.

February

11 (Friday) Parliamentary Declaration sets out the king's misdeeds.

21 Christian IV of Denmark dies and is succeeded by Frederick III.

March

3 (Friday) The anonymous author of *A True and Perfect Picture of our Present Reformation* mentions *Doctrine and Discipline of Divorce*. Thomason's copy (BL E. 43043) is simply dated 'March' by Fortescue, but in Thomason's manuscript catalogue

it is listed between two books dated 3 March 1648 (BL C.38.h.21, Vol. 4, No. 354/13).

25 JM leases property in Wheatley. During the previous winter he had received only £2.13s. in rent, but on this day he leases tithes and cottages to John Robinson for six years for an annual rent of £60, and other land and buildings to John Gadbury and Graland Page for six years for an annual rent of £20 each. Of this yearly income of £100, JM paid Anne Powell her 'terce' or 'thirds', the proportion of a man's estate to which his widow was entitled.

April
JM translates Psalms 80–88; the translations are dated 'April 1648' in JM's 1673 *Poems*.

19? (Wednesday) JM pays mother-in-law Anne Powell first instalment of thirds (£2.10s.) from Richard Powell's estate. The entry on the document (see 4 June 1656) gives the date as 19 November, but the other five dates (13 November 1648, 23 April and 20 October 1649, 10 April and 12 October 1650) imply payments at six-monthly intervals, so 19 November is probably a mistranscription for 19 April.

May
1 (Monday) Scots begin Second Civil War.

June
In an undated entry made between June and December 1648 Hartlib refers to JM in *Ephemerides*: 'Milton is not only writing a universal history of England but also an epitome of all Purchas's volumes' (Hartlib 31/22/21a). On the date of composition of JM's *History of Britain* see von Maltzahn 1991 and 1993 and Woolrych 1986 and 1993.

July
8 (Saturday) JM's Sonnet 15 is entitled in the Trinity manuscript 'On the Lord Gen[eral] Fairfax at the siege of Colchester'. The siege began on 14 June, and the town fell on 27 August. The period of composition of the sonnet may be further narrowed if the present tense is meant to be taken literally, because it must have been written after the news reached London of the Scottish invasion on 8 July and before JM heard of the Scottish defeat at Preston on 17 August.

29 Unidentified 'T. C.' mentions *Doctrine and Discipline of Divorce* in *A Glass for the Times* (Thomason's date; his copy is BL E.455 (10)).

August

17 (Thursday) John Sadler sends regards to JM through Samuel Hartlib (Hartlib 45/9/4A-4B). Cromwell engages Scots in battle at Preston.

20 Cromwell defeats Scottish army at Preston.

September

18 (Monday) Parliament opens negotiations with Charles (the 'Treaty of Newport').

29 JM receives rents from Wheatley (£31. 13s. 8d).

October

14/24 (Saturday) Peace of Westphalia ends Thirty Years' War.

25 JM and Mary's daughter Mary born 'on the fast day in the morning about 6 a clock' (BL Add MS 32,310); the date and time are confirmed in Birch's transcription of Mary Milton's Bible (BL Add MS 4244 fol. 52^v). The monthly 'fast day' had been designated a 'day of public humiliation' by Parliament (*Journals of the House of Commons*, VI. 61).

November

7 (Thursday) JM's daughter Mary baptised (Parish Register, St Giles in the Fields, London).

13 JM pays mother-in-law Anne Powell her thirds (£3. 6s. 8d).

24/4 December Carlo Dati writes to JM from Florence; the holograph is BL Add MS 5016* fols. 9–10v.

December

6 (Wednesday) Pride's Purge; Colonel Pride removes many Presbyterians from the House of Commons; those left are known as the 'Rump', which subsequently discontinues negotiations with Charles.

9 JM's fortieth birthday.

23 Parliament votes to bring King Charles to trial.

1649

In an enigmatic undated entry written between January and April 1649 in *Ephemerides* Hartlib seems to mention JM: 'One Sexby or Saxby offers how packets may be opened and sealed again, if he or his associates may be entrusted with Letter-Office. Milton. Sexby.' (Hartlib 28/1/13b); on JM and Edward Sexby see June 1657. JM may have written the 'Digression' in the *History of Britain* in the first few months of 1649. See von Maltzahn (1991 and 1993); for a contrary view see March 1660.

January
JM writes *Tenure of Kings and Magistrates* between 15 and 29 January (see Shawcross, 1966).
19 (Friday) Trial of King Charles opens.
30 King Charles is executed.

February
4 (Sunday) John Warner alludes to the divorce controversy in *The Devilish Conspiracy*, pp. 18–19 (the date is Thomason's, as is the attribution; his copy is BL E.550 (16)).
5 Scots proclaim the Prince of Wales as King Charles II in Edinburgh.
9 *Eikon Basilike* is published (Thomason's date; his copy is BL C.59.a.24.).
13 *The Tenure of Kings and Magistrates* is published (Thomason's date; his copy is BL E.542 (12)). A copy inscribed 'ex dono authoris feb 1648' in Exeter Cathedral Library may have been a presentation copy to John or Henry Bradshaw; the inscription is not in JM's hand. JM's *Tenure* is subsequently attacked by the Presbyterian leader Clement Walker in *Anarchia Anglicana, Second Part*, see 24 October 1649. *LR*, II, 260 is confused about the date.
16 John Canne's· *The Golden Rule, or Justice Advanced* is published (Thomason's date; his copy is BL E.543 (6)); the tract is said to derive in part from *Tenure of Kings and Magistrates*.

March
JM moves from High Holborn to Charing Cross where, according to Edward Phillips, 'he lodged at one Thomson's next door to the Bull-head Tavern at Charing-Cross, opening into the Spring Garden, which seems to have been only a lodging taken till his designed apartment in Scotland Yard was ready for him' (Darbishire, p. 71); see 19 November 1649.
1/11 (Thursday) Treaty of Ruel ends first Fronde.

13 (Noon) Council of State decides to invite JM to be Secretary for Foreign Tongues (PRO SP 25/62, p. 86).

15 JM is appointed Secretary for Foreign Tongues (PRO SP 25/62, p. 89); his annual salary is set at £288.13s.6$\frac{1}{2}$d.

16 *Eikon Basilike* is registered for publication (SR I, 314); it had been published on 9 February.

17 Parliament abolishes the House of Lords.

19 Parliament abolishes the monarchy.

20 JM is inducted into his new post, and takes the oath of secrecy (SP 25/62, p. 94); JM is not named in the order, but it covers 'such as shall be employed as secretaries to attend this Council'.

22 Council of State orders JM to translate into Latin 'letters to be sent to Hamburg in behalf of the Merchant Adventurers' (PRO SP 25/62, p. 104; see 2 April). On the same day Latin and English versions of Bulstrode Whitelocke's *Declaration of the Parlament of England* are published; the tract seems to be influenced by JM's *Tenure of Kings and Magistrates*.

25 JM receives £31.14s.5d in rents from Wheatley (see 22 February 1654).

26 Council of State approves 'the letters brought in by Mr Milton to the Senate of Hamburg'. At the same meeting 'Mr Milton appointed to make some observations on a paper lately printed, called Old and New Chains' (PRO SP 25/62, p. 117). The reference is to two Leveller pamphlets by John Lilburne, *England's New Chains Discovered* (dated 26 February by Thomason; his copy is BL E. 545 (27)) and its sequel *The Second Part of England's New Chains Discovered* (dated 24 March by Thomason; his copy is BL E. 548 (16)). On the next day, 27 March, a one-page *Declaration of the Commons . . . against . . . The Second Part* was published, but there is no indication that JM had a hand in it.

28 JM is ordered by Council of State 'to make some observations' on affairs in Ireland (PRO SP 25/62, p. 125; see 16 May). On the same day Leveller leaders are arrested.

April

2 (Monday) State Paper from Parliament to Hamburg (W151, P1); various additions and revisions on the manuscript of the scribal draft (said erroneously to be in the hand of Henry Marten, Chairman of the Committee for Foreign Affairs) are

in JM's hand (University of Leeds, Brotherton Collection, Marten/Loder-Symonds MSS, 3rd series, 11, fols. 1–2). The official copy of this letter (PRO SP 82/7, fols. 153–4) is endorsed 'the letter not delivered 2 April 1649 sent back by [Isaac] Lee', Deputy of the English Company in Hamburg. The second of the two letters to Hamburg dated 2 April 1649 (P2) was delivered, but perished in a fire in the Hamburg archives in 1849. The draft version of the letter in the Brotherton Library (fol. 2 of the same MS), again said in error to be in the hand of Marten, has revisions in JM's hand. On the letters to Hamburg (2 April, 10 August 1649; 4 January, 2 April, 31 May 1650; 12 March, 13 April (two) 1652; 16 October 1656; 20 August 1657 (two)) see Fallon (1993), 34–43.

5   JM is attacked for views on divorce by Christopher Wase in *Electra of Sophocles* (The Hague, 1649); the date is Thomason's; his copy is BL E. 1216 (2). In an undated letter (in Latin) to Nicholas Grey, Wase again alludes to JM's divorce views (Bodleian MS Add B.5, fol. 17^v).

9   Joseph Hall attacks *Doctrine and Discipline of Divorce* in *Resolution and Decisions* (Thomason's date; his copy is BL E. 1256).

13   Princess Sophie writes from The Hague to her brother Prince Maurice, who is serving in a Royalist squadron off the coast of Ireland. The letter was intercepted and sent to the Secretariat for Foreign Tongues for translation; corrections and additions to the translation from the German are in JM's hand (PRO SP18/1/55, fol. 142; W165, P3); the German original is PRO SP 18/1/54, fol. 140–140v. It is possible that JM had a hand in the translation of the companion letter (in French) to Prince Rupert (PRO SP 18/1/53, fol. 138; the translation is PRO SP 18/1/56, fol. 143).

20   Council of State orders JM or Gualter Frost to examine certain letters to see if they contain anything concerning the export of prohibited goods (PRO SP 25/62, p. 209).

On the same day JM petitions the Goldsmiths' Company for the renewal of a lease; the property, which is not named, is the Red Rose, a large house on the west side of Bread Street; JM offers £150 for a 21-year renewal (Court Book, fol. 46), and subsequently increases his offer to £200. The reason for the renewal is not clear, because the 21-year lease that JM had received (presumably from his father) in March 1632 still had four years to run; the complex rules for renewal are set out in the opening pages of the minutes of the Committee of Contractors of Leases, 1641, 1651–62. See 5 October, 5 November and 21 December 1649; 12 March, 27 March, 5 July 1650; 10 January, 29 July, 20 December 1651; 3 July 1656; 10 June 1659; 30 April 1669.

23 JM pays mother-in-law Anne Powell her thirds (£9. 19s.)

May

11 (Friday) Salmasius' Defence of Charles I (*Defensio regia pro Carolo I*) reaches England (Thomason's date; his copy is BL E.1386 and 1387).

14 John Hall is employed as a writer by the Council of State, possibly to share JM's growing workload (PRO SP 25/62, p. 303). Hall's *Humble Motion to the Parliament* (1649) alludes to *Areopagitica* (pp. 29–30) and seems to draw on *Of Education* (pp. 25–6)

15 A Leveller revolt at Burford is suppressed by Cromwell.

16 *Articles of Peace with the Irish Rebels* is published with JM's *Observations* (Thomason's date; his copy is BL E.555(21)); Fortescue gives 9 March, but 16 May is confirmed in Thomason's catalogue (BL C.38.h.21, Vol. 5, No. 421/21); see 28 March 1649.

18 JM is ordered to translate letters in French given to Parliament by the Dutch Ambassador in time for a meeting at 7.00 the following morning (PRO SP 25/62, p. 325). JM's translations have not survived (W167A, P4).

19 Parliament declares England to be a Commonwealth.

30 JM is ordered to examine the papers of John Lee (PRO SP 25/62, p. 373), who is arrested on 31 May on suspicion of dealing with an enemy of the state. JM's *Tenure of Kings and Magistrates* is cited repeatedly in John Goodwin's *Hubristodkiai: The Obstructors of Justice* (Thomason's date; his copy is BL E.557(2)).

June

1 (Friday) Gilbert Mabbott borrows phrases from *Areopagitica* in his argument about licensing in *The Kingdom's Faithful and Impartial Scout*, No. 18 (25 May–1 June), p. 143.

7 Goldsmiths' Company notes 'a tenement in Bread Street for which Mr Milton is a suitor to renew the lease' (Court Book, fol. 66).

11 JM and Edward Dendy, the Serjeant-at-Arms, are ordered to examine the papers of William Small (PRO SP 25/62, p. 4220, who was ordered to be arrested on 8 June for corresponding

with the enemy.

J[ohn?] H[ackluyt?] comments positively on JM as divorcer in *The Metropolitan Nuncio* No. 3. The same issue reports that an answer to *Eikon Basilike* is being prepared, so JM may already have been at work on *Eikonoklastes*; it is possible that the allusion is to John Selden rather than JM, because Selden had written *Uxor Ebraica* (1646) and had been asked to answer *Eikon Basilike* (but had declined to do so).

16 Court of Chancery dismisses Sir Robert Pye's suit against JM (PRO C33/192, fol. 794).

23 JM is ordered to examine 'the papers of Pragmaticus' and report his findings to the Council (PRO SP 25/62, p. 464b). *Mercurius Pragmaticus* was the royalist newspaper edited by Marchamont Nedham, who was later to become a close friend of JM. A warrant for his arrest had been issued on 18 June; he was imprisoned in Newgate, escaped, rearrested and then released on 14 November and eventually (24 May 1650) employed by the Council of State.

July

13 (Friday) *Tenure of Kings and Magistrates* is cited in *The Discoverer* by John Canne or John Hall (Thomason's date; his copy is BL E. 564(9)).

16 JM is ordered to inspect office of Clerk of State Papers (PRO SP 25/62, p. 533).

20 Latin version of *Eikon Basilike* translated by John Earle is published (Thomason's date; his copy is BL E. 1384). Earle subsequently writes to Charles II enclosing a complimentary copy; his letter is BL MS Egerton 2547, fols. 1–4.

August

JM's translation of an undated Letter of State from the Commissioners of the Great Seal to the Parliament of Paris (W123, P p. 874) may have been written at about this time; the letter intercedes on behalf of the family of one William Sandys, who is said to be 'recently deceased'; this may refer to a William Sandys who died on 19 July 1649.

10 (Friday) Parliament approves JM's translation into Latin of a Letter of State from Parliament to Hamburg (W1, P5).

12 Cromwell embarks for Ireland.

20 JM's *Tenure of Kings and Magistrates* and his views on divorce are attacked by the Presbyterian leader Clement Walker in

Anarchia Anglicana, Second Part (Thomason's date; his copy is BL E.570(1)); see 24 October 1649.

26 *Eikon Alethine,* an anonymous attack on King Charles's author-ship of *Eikon Basilike,* is published on or before this date. A copy now in the NYPL (once owned by Thomas Hollis) is signed 'Jo:s Milton' in a hand that (*pace* the NYPL catalogue) is unlikely to be JM's; see Miller, 1975*b*.

29 John Lilburne publishes *An Outcry of the young men and appren-tices of London,* which is influenced in language and content by *Tenure of Kings and Magistrates* (Thomason's date; his copy is BL E.572(13)).

September

1   (Saturday) Thomas Newcomb is imprisoned for printing Lil-burne's *Outcry;* Parker (1996, p. 977) thinks it likely that JM helped to secure his release on 21 September.

11 Cromwell sacks Drogheda

29 JM receives rents (£32.3s.10d) from Wheatley. Richard Powell's estate is said to be in arrears (PRO E372/493, Oxford)

30 First issue of second edition of *Tenure of Kings and Magistrates* is almost certainly published before this date; the evidence is that the printer changed the formulation of his address on title-pages in October 1649, and the first issue uses the old style.

October

1   (Monday) Richard Powell is reported for unpaid fine of £180 (PRO SP23/39); see 8 December 1646.

5   Goldsmiths' Company votes (by eleven to five) to award JM a lease on the property in Bread Street for 21 years at £400 (Court Book fol. 87).

6   JM publishes *Eikonoklastes* (Thomason's date; his copy is BL E.578(5)); the date is not incontestable, because *A Brief Relation* No. 9 (13–20 November) records that *Eikonoklastes* was 'pub-lished the last week' (p. 96). The manuscript in the British Library (Stowe MS 305/6) is a partial transcription from the printed text, not an original version. At an unknown date after the publication of *Eikonoklastes,* a horoscope of JM, 'Author of Iconoclastes', is cast, perhaps by John Gadbury (Bodleian Ash-mole MS 436, part 1, fol. 119; see Rusche).

11 Cromwell sacks Wexford.

20 JM pays Anne Powell her thirds (£10).

24   JM and Edward Dendy are ordered to seize papers of Clement
      Walker in Kensington and to prepare a report for the Council
      on their findings (PRO SP 25/63, p. 175). Walker is arrested on
      the same day and later imprisoned for high treason; he was to
      die in the Tower in October 1651, before coming to trial.

November
5   (Monday) JM attends a meeting of the Goldsmiths' Company's
      Court of Assistants and accepts their terms for a lease on the
      property in Bread Street and arranges payment in four instal-
      ments of £100 payable at Christmas 1649, Midsummer 1650,
      Christmas 1650 and Midsummer 1651. It was also agreed that
      payment in advance would earn a rebate of six per cent (Court
      Book, fol. 96). This figure may be an error for seven per cent,
      but the agreement of 12 March 1650 may suggest that JM had
      successfully bargained for an extra one per cent; on the other
      hand, the entry is not free of error, because it refers to the
      earlier meeting as having taken place on 12 October rather
      than 5 October.
12   Council of State resolves to confer with Sir John Hippesley
      about 'accommodating Mr Milton with the lodgings he has at
      Whitehall' (PRO SP 25/63, p. 249).
16   Anne Powell's petition for relief is considered by the Commis-
      sioners for Relief (PRO SP 23/194, p. 397).
19   JM is assigned lodgings of Sir John Hippesley in Scotland
      Yard, Whitehall (PRO SP 25/63, p. 274) and moves in with
      his family shortly thereafter.
20   JM's *Eikonoklastes* is praised in *A Brief Relation of Some Affairs*
      No. 9 (13–20 November), p. 96.
21   JM is ordered to present Lady Killigrew's letters to the Council
      of State (PRO SP 25/63, p. 288); the warrant to seize her papers
      had been issued on 12 May; JM passed them to the Council,
      and her passport was issued on 24 November.

December
9   (Sunday) JM's forty-first birthday.
16   JM licenses a book in French on the trial of Charles I (*SR* I,
      333); the *Histoire .. du Procès de Charles Stuart* was published in
      London on 3 March 1650; Thomason's date on the title-page of
      his copy (BL E 1353(1)) is misdated as 20 January 1649, the first
      day of the trial, by Fortescue. On the same day the Committee

for Compounding reports on Anne Powell's petition (PRO SP
23/6, p. 248).

21   JM pays first £100 instalment for lease of the property in Bread
      Street (Court Book, fol. 110).

1650

Samuel Hartlib alludes to *Areopagitica* in *Ephemerides* (Hartlib 28/1/
61B). The first chapter of JM's *Eikonoklastes* is apparently translated
into Latin during this year by Lewis Du Moulin, but no copy is
known to survive (*LR*, II, 284, IV, 326–7). In the same year JM's
English is praised ('few have attained its height') by Durant
Hotham in the preface to his brother Charles Hotham's *Introduction
to Teutonic Philosophy*; the manuscript of the preface is BL Sloane
MS 1325 fol. 13. The Hotham brothers had arrived at Christ's
College just as JM was leaving: Charles migrated from Peterhouse
to Christ's on 7 May 1632 and Durant was admitted to Christ's on
9 November 1632; their brother John and their father Sir John had
been executed by Parliament for treason in January 1645.
    Entries in JM's Commonplace Book in the hands of amanuenses
may be assumed to date from *circa* 1650: Berni, *Orlando Inamorato
Rifatto*; Boiardo, *Orlando Inamorato*, Machiavelli, *Discorsi sopra la
Prima Deca de Tito Livio*; Rivetus, *Commentarii in Exodum*, Augustine,
De Civitate Dei; Dante, *Purgatorio*; Nicetas Acominatus, *Imperii
Graeci Historia*; Buchanan, *Rerum Scoticarum Historia*; Sigonius, *De
Imperio Occidentali*; Angelo di Costanzo, *Historio del Regno de Napoli*.

January

4   (Friday) JM's Latin translation of a Letter of State from Parlia-
     ment to Hamburg is approved by the Council of State (PRO SP
     25/63, p. 467; W2, P6); the letter protests that English Mer-
     chant Adventurers had been prevented from taking the
     Engagement, an oath of allegiance to the Commonwealth.

8   JM is ordered to answer Salmasius and ordered to arrange for
     Thomas Waring's book on Ireland to be printed (PRO SP 25/
     63, p. 486; see Miller, 1987b); the first order is the commission
     for JM's first *Defensio* (see 24 February 1651); Waring's *Brief
     Narration of the Rebellion in Ireland* was published on 19 March
     1650 (Thomason's date; his copy is BL E 596(2)). In the *Defensio
     Secunda* (1654) JM says that when he received the order to

reply to Salmasius he was afflicted with ill health and failing eyesight.

14 JM's books are ordered to be distributed by Luke Robinson, a younger contemporary of JM at Christ's College who was now a member of the Council of State (PRO SP 25/63, p. 519). The books must be *Tenure of Kings and Magistrates* and *Eikonoklastes*, but it is not clear where they are to be distributed, because Robinson's destination is not known.

25 JM is ordered to translate a letter from the Governor of Tetuán (PRO SP 25/63, p. 562). The language of the letter of Mahomet Benisa Necasis is not known, but in a city populated by the descendants of Andalusian Moors, Spanish and Latin are possibilities; alternatively, the phrase 'have the above said letter translated' may imply Arabic or Turkish; the translation is lost.

29 JM is attacked as a divorcer and a regicide in *Mercurius Pragmaticus* (Part 2, No. 39, 22–29 January). JM's *Tenure of Kings and Magistrates* is mentioned in N.W.'s *Discourse Concerning the Engagement*, p. 5 (Thomason's date; his copy is BL E.590(8)). On the same day he is ordered to prepare a reply to the letter from the Governor of Tetuán (PRO SP 25/63, p. 569). The language of the (lost) reply (P9) is not known, but may have been English.

February

2 (Saturday) Civil servants (including a Mr Baker, Mr Willingham, Thomas Challoner and George Weckherlin) are ordered to pass any 'public papers belonging to the Commonwealth to...Mr Milton to be layd up in the Paper Office for public service' (PRO SP 25/63, p. 600); Willingham's copy of the order is dated 4 February (SP 45/20, pp. 230–31, duplicated on pp. 232–3); Weckherlin's copy, also dated 4 February, is now in the BL (MS Trumbull Misc. 22, fol. 15). Papers collected under this Order can no longer be identified, but must include some of the Weckherlin papers now being catalogued in the British Library. On the papers in the library of the Society of Antiquaries sometimes said to have been assembled by JM in response to this order, see the general entry for 1658.

4 JM's translation of Letters of State to King Philip IV of Spain (W3, P12; W4, P11) and to King John IV of Portugal (W5, P10) are signed; the letters are credentials for Anthony Ascham,

Parliament's Ambassador to Spain. On the letters to Portugal see Fallon (1993), 43–55; on those to Spain, pp. 88–100.

15 Second issue of second edition of *Tenure* is published after October 1649 but before this date, which is Thomason's (BL E.593(11)); the third issue is published on or about this date.

16 JM receives interest payment of £5 from Robert Warcupp and signs receipt, now in Ferdinand J. Dreer Collection, 115.2, Historical Society of Pennsylvania, British Poets, II, 102–4.

18 JM is reappointed Secretary for Foreign Languages at the same salary (PRO SP 25/64, p. 3); Council of State orders Salmasius's *Defensio* to be confiscated (PRO SP 25/95, p. 3).

20 William Dugard is imprisoned for planning to print Salmasius' *Defensio Regia* (letter of 7 March 1649/50, pp. 179–80, Scholars' Register, Merchant Taylors' Company; the MS will be moved to the Guildhall Library in 1997).

23 JM takes oath of office (PRO SP 25/64, p. 30); the handwriting is sometimes wrongly said to be JM's.

24 JM's translation of Letter of State from Parliament to King John IV of Portugal (W6, P7) is so dated in the Skinner transcription; this may be the date on which it was despatched, but it may have been signed on 4 February: see Fallon (1993) p. 44 and note. The letter, which protests about the sanctuary given by the Portuguese to the ships of Prince Rupert and Prince Maurice, was passed by Robert Blake to the Portuguese on 10 March.

March

12 (Tuesday) Goldsmiths' Company agrees to JM's request that part payment in advance of his Midsummer instalment would entitle him to a seven per cent rebate (Court Book, fols. 123^v–124).

25 JM receives £31.10s. in rents from Wheatley.

27 JM pays £50 in advance on the second instalment of his purchase of the lease of the Red Rose, and receives a seven per cent rebate (Court Book, fol. 127).

28 JM's translation of a Letter of State to Archduke Leopold of Austria, Regent of Flanders (W9, P13) is signed. Gualter Frost had drafted the English text between 4 and 7 March, and JM translated it in time for signing on 28 March. The letter protests about the retention in Flanders of Jane Puckering, an Englishwoman who had been abducted and forced to sign a marriage contract.

30 JM is ordered to prepare credentials for Richard Bradshaw (PRO SP 25/64, p. 137).

April
2 (Tuesday) JM is ordered to meet Commissioners of the Great Seal (Whitelocke and Lisle) at the door of Parliament at 10.00 a.m. the following morning. The meeting must have concerned the credential letter for Bradshaw, because the *Journals of the House of Commons* entry for 3 April provides for the credential letter to be signed and sealed; JM's translation of the credential letter (W11, P14) is dated 2 April.
10 JM pays Anne Powell her thirds (£10).
11 *Of Education* is praised by Peter Smith in a letter to his uncle, presumably John Beale (Hartlib 67/23/2A-2B).
18 Richard Powell's estate is sequestered (PRO SP 23/251/100).
27 JM's translation of a Letter of State from Parliament to King John IV of Portugal (W10, P15) is signed; the letter, which is cast in JM's most elegant and powerful Latin, requests assistance for Edward Popham, whose ships were being sent to reinforce Blake's blockade of Prince Rupert's fleet in the Tagus. A similar letter to King Philip II of Spain (W137, P8) is probably signed at the same time, but the printed version of the letter is a draft that must have been prepared before 25 January 1650, the day on which Parliament decided to style itself 'Parliament of the Commonwealth of England' (*Parliamentum Republicae Angliae*); the printed draft uses an earlier formulation, 'the Supreme States of the whole nation met in Parliament'. On the same day Montrose is defeated at Carbisdale; he escapes, but is subsequently captured.
30 JM writes memorandum (in his own hand) about the release of Mr Chambers from Gatehouse Prison; the memo is in the draft minute book of the Privy Council, 26 April–17 May (PRO SP 25/6 (unpaged)).

May
In an undated entry in *Ephemerides* written between May and October 1650, Hartlib notes that 'there are no Licences appointed by the last Act so that everybody may enter his book without licence. Provided the printer's or author's name be entered, that they may be forthcoming if required. Mr Milton. Licencing of

books' (Hartlib 28/1/61b); JM is named by Hartlib as the source of this analysis of the implications of Bradshaw's Press Act of 20 September 1649.

6   (Monday) JM is ordered to bring papers of Dr (Francis?) Walsall to Commissioners of Great Seal (PRO SP 25/64, p. 307); the papers concerned the goods of suicides (*felones de se*).

14/24   Gui Patin alludes to *Defensio prima* in a letter to Charles Spon (Patin, II, 17–18).

15   JM is ordered to search the trunks of an unnamed suspect and report to the Council the following afternoon (PRO SP 25/64, p. 350).

21   Montrose is executed and his head is mounted on a spike over Edinburgh prison (see 15 January 1653).

31   JM's translation of a Letter of State from Parliament to Hamburg is signed 31 May (W12, P16); on the date see Fallon (1993), p. 40 and note. The letter requests that Richard Bradshaw, the Commonwealth's envoy, be treated with the honours appropriate to a Resident Agent.

June

1   (Tuesday) A certificate is issued recording that Richard Powell's personal estate has been given to the town of Banbury (PRO SP 33/251/100).

12   An Order of Relief is voted for JM's mother-in-law Anne Powell (PRO SP 23/110); the copy of the order in the BL (Add MS 34,326) is attached to Anne Powell's undated petition to the Council of State.

14   JM is allowed a warrant 'for the furnishing of his lodging in Whitehall with some hangings' (PRO SP 25/64, p. 447; the handwriting of the entry is sometimes wrongly said to be JM's).

18   A warrant for furnishing JM's Whitehall apartment with hangings is issued (PRO SP 25/64, p. 460). It is possible that the warrant was redeemable at the sale of the King's collection of art and furniture at nearby Somerset House.

19   News of the assassination on 27 May/6 June of Anthony Ascham, Parliament's ambassador in Madrid, reaches London. The second edition of *Eikonoklastes*, which alludes to the murder on p. 208, must have been published after this date. Several purchasers or recipients of the second edition

can be identified. One of the BL copies (G.11718) is inscribed (not in JM's hand) 'G. Dury. 1650. Ex dono Authoris', and was probably owned by Giles Dury, an elder of the French church and a friend of JM. A copy now in Trinity College Cambridge (C.9.179) belonged to Richard Vaughan, Earl of Carbery and (from July 1652) husband of Alice Egerton, the Lady of *Comus*; a note in an eighteenth-century hand notes that the inscription is said to be in JM's hand, but it is not. A third copy, now in the Yale University Library, is inscribed (in Latin) to the effect that the book is a gift of JM's nephew John Phillips to John Barker. For a fourth copy see 12 August 1651.

22 JM is ordered to send to the Council the Book of Examinations concerning the risings in Kent and Essex (PRO SP 25/64, p. 473).
24 Charles II lands at Speymouth and takes the Covenant.
25 JM is ordered to summarise information about the rebellion in Essex (PRO SP 25/64, p. 478). On the same day, he is ordered to search William Prynne's rooms at Lincoln's Inn; the search warrant is now in the library of the University of Illinois; the almost identical document in the Order Book has a blank where JM's name is written in the original warrant (PRO SP 25/64, p. 483). Prynne was arrested at his home near Bath on 30 June, and imprisoned without trial until 1 February 1653. On the same day R[obert] B[aron]'s *Pocula Castalia* is published (Thomason's date; his copy is BL E.1221(1)); two of Baron's poems and another by Thomas Moore imitate passages in JM's 1645 *Poems*.
26 JM is ordered to translate *A Declaration of the Parliament of England upon the Marching of the Army into Scotland* into Latin (PRO SP 25/64, p. 483).
28 JM's translation of a Letter of State to Philip IV of Spain (W13, P17), asking that the body of Anthony Ascham be returned to England, is signed.

July
 2 (Tuesday) Responsibility for the Latin translation of *A Declaration* is transferred to Thomas May (PRO SP 25/64, p. 500; see 13 November).
 5 JM completes second payment to Company of Goldsmiths on new lease of property in Bread Street:

At this Court was received of John Milton Esq the sum of
£100 being this second payment in part of £400 fine due and
payable at Midsummer last he having paid £50 at Lady Day
last in part of the said £100 three months before it was due in
the last warden's account for which he was rebated at the
rate of 7% 16s deducting 18d out of 17s.6d being not
received till ten days after Midsummer last (Court Book,
fol. 168v).

The summary of this entry in *LR* II, 319 is entirely wrong.

August

10 (Saturday) JM writes a note about Racovian (i.e. Cracovian)
    Catechism; the context of the note is unknown, though it may
    have been a licence for printing and may have been addressed
    to William Dugard; its existence is recorded in the *Journals of
    the House of Commons* for 2 April 1652.

14 JM, together with a group of five ministers, is ordered to
    inventory the records of the Westminster Assembly (PRO SP
    25/8, p. 79); Gualter Frost is named as an alternate to JM.

15 (?) JM petitions to compound for Wheatley (JM's petition of 25
    February 1651 says that he 'did put in his petition about the
    middle of August last').

23 Anne Powell petitions to compound, mentioning JM's holdings
    (PRO SP 23/110, p. 542). On or about the same day JM's petition
    to compound is approved (PRO SP 23/11, p. 92). On the same
    day John Pye, who is still owed £1,238 by the Powells, petitions
    to compound (PRO SP 23/109, p. 521); his petition is referred to
    John Reading for report (PRO SP 23/11, p. 87).

24 John Pye submits a statement of income from Forest Hill (PRO
    SP 23/109, p. 523).

25 (?) Letter of State from Council of State to the Governor of
    Tetuán (W158, P18), drafted in English by JM, is despatched;
    the letter requests the release of two English hostages.

28 Elizabeth Ashworth petitions to compound for interest from
    Wheatley (PRO SP 23/64, p. 185). On the same day Sir Edward
    Powell petitions to compound for his interest in Forest Hill
    and Wheatley (PRO SP 23/110, p. 587).

September

3   (Tuesday) Cromwell defeats Scots at Battle of Dunbar.

19/29 Second Fronde ends.

29 JM receives rents of £32.2s. from Wheatley.

October

12 (Saturday) JM pays Anne Powell her thirds (£10).
28 *Tenure of Kings and Magistrates* mentioned in G[eorge?] W[ither?]'s *Respublica Anglicana*, p. 41 (Thomason's date; his copy is BL E. 780(25)).

November

7 (Thursday) JM's translations of Letters of State to the governors of Andalusia and Galicia (W14, P19) are signed; the surviving versions of the letters are conflations that address Andalusia in the headings and Galicia in the texts. The letters acknowledge assistance afforded to the English fleet and request that assistance be continued.
13 JM's colleague, the poet and dramatist Thomas May, dies; his death later occasioned 'Tom May's Death', which may have been written by Marvell.
27 Matthew Appleton is ordered to repay a debt of £91.11s.10d to Anne Powell (PRO SP 23/110, p. 551).

December

3 (Tuesday) Sir Robert Pye files an affidavit of Richard Powell's debt of £1,400 to him (PRO SP 23/109, p. 527).
4/14 Sir Edward Nicholas, Joseph Jane's brother-in-law, refers in a letter to 'Mr Smith' (Lord Hatton) to Jane's *Eikon Aklastos* (published 1651, reissued as *Salmasius His Dissection* in 1660), an attack on *Eikonoklastes*, is finished by this date (*LR*, II, 333).
9 JM's forty-second birthday.
19 JM's translation of a Letter of State from the Council of State to the Portuguese envoy (W16, P20) João de Guimarães is submitted to Parliament, which votes not to send the letter, which was neither signed and sealed nor delivered; the letter requests clarification of Guimarães's diplomatic rank.
23 Publication of JM's *Defensio Pro Populo Anglicano* is authorised by Council of State (PRO SP 25/15, p. 39).
24 Edinburgh Castle surrenders to Cromwell.
31 JM's *Defensio* is registered (*SR* I, 357); Anne Powell deposes about Sir Robert Pye's taking of Forest Hill (PRO SP 23/109, p. 524).

1651

Early in the year Joseph Jane's *Eikon Aklastos,* a chapter-by-chapter refutation of JM's *Eikonoklastes,* is published. In his letter to Leonard Philaras of 28 September 1654 JM recalled that for several months before he became completely blind, objects seemed to swim back and forth in front of his eyes, and he became drowsy every afternoon.

January
 1 (Wednesday) John Reading reports on the Pye–Powell case, summarising the history of the dispute (PRO SP 23/109, pp 517–19). On the same day Charles II is crowned as King of Scotland.
 7 JM submits his English translation (from Spanish) of two letters from King Philip IV of Spain to the governor of Cartagena (W156, P22; W157, P23) and of a third letter from Philip IV to Robert Blake (W155, P21).
10 Goldsmiths' Company records that 'At this Court was received of Mr John Milton the sum of £100 in part of the £200 residue of his fine of the £400 for renewing the lease of his house in Bread Street' (Court Book, fol. 66). This is a late payment of the £100 due at Christmas.
23 *Mercurius Politicus* No. 33, which was subsequently to be licensed by JM (see 17 March), reports a request from Leiden dated 7/17 January that Salmasius be answered. The editor replies that a 'victorious reply' (that is, JM's *Defensio*) 'is now in motion at the Press'.
24 Sir Robert Pye pays a fine of £658.15s.3d on Richard Powell's property; the amount and the date are recorded on an endorsement of 25 March 1651 on an affidavit attached to the deed dated 13 December 1650 (PRO SP 23/109, p. 529).
30 JM's *Defensio* said to be in press (*Nouvelles Ordinaires de Londres,* No. 30, 23 January/2 February–30 January/9 February).

February
 2 (Sunday) Sir Henry Wotton's letter to JM (see 13 April 1638) is reprinted in *Reliquae Wottonianae* (Thomason's date; his copy is BL E.1254).
 6 JM's translation of a Letter of State from Parliament to the Senate of Danzig (W15, P25) is signed and sealed. The letter

protests about a tax imposed on English merchants and passed to 'the King of the Scots, our enemy'.

10 JM ordered by Council of State 'to attend the Committee [of Foreign Affairs] at their meetings' (PRO SP 25/17 p. 59). It is not clear whether this is a general order or whether it refers specifically to the meetings with the Portuguese ambassador scheduled for 12 March.

12 3 pm: JM attends meeting with João de Guimãraes in Great Chamber; Charles Vane, the English agent in Portugal, is also present. Joseph Frost, son of Gualter, acts as secretary. JM presumably interprets through Latin.

19 JM is reappointed Secretary for Foreign Languages (PRO SP 25/65, p. 11 and PRO SP 25/18, p. 5).

20 *Mercurius Politicus* No 37 prints a letter from The Hague written on 6/16 February by an unidentified 'gentleman of Leiden' expressing gratitude for the forthcoming reply to Salmasius, 'which we greedily expect'.

24 JM's *Defensio Pro Populo Anglicano* is published. The date is an inference from *Nouvelles Ordinaires de Londres*, No 34, 20 February/2 March–27 February/9 March 1651. JM's *Defensio* is said to have been published the previous Monday (*au jour lundi dernier*). 27 February, the last of the English dates covered by this issue, is said in the journal to be a Thursday; the preceding Monday must therefore have been 24 February. In the text JM excuses his delay in replying to Salmasius on grounds both of a lack of time to write and of insufficient health for the labour of writing. Even now, he explains in the preface, his health is so poor and precarious that he has to take a break virtually every hour, whereas had he been in good health he could have written continuously. There were at least ten further editions by the end of the year, including a Dutch translation which is subsequently mentioned in the February issue of *Hollantse Mercurius* (see Shawcross, 1984). JM presented copies of the first edition to John Morris (now in the British Library (C.114.6.37; see Birrell), Gualter Frost (now in the University of Texas), the Bodleian Library (E.H.2.20.Art; apparently inscribed by Rous) and Charles Vane (now in Harvard University Library 14496.13.4.11F*; apparently inscribed in Vane's hand); cf August 1651. The Earl of Bridgwater, who as a child had acted the part of the Elder Brother in *Comus*, inscribed his copy (now in the Huntington Library) with the

words (in Latin) 'this book is most deserving of burning, its author of the gallows.' There are manuscript copies of the *Defensio* in the Bodleian (MS Rawlinson D.230) and the Royal Library, Copenhagen (GKS 3579, 8vo).

John Rowland's chapter-by-chapter refutation, *Pro Rege et Populo Anglicano contra Johannis Polypragmatici (Alias Miltoni Angli)*, which was initially attributed to Bishop John Bramhall, was subsequently published in two Latin editions in 1651 (and a third in 1652) and in a Dutch translation in 1651. Toland reports that 'on the first appearance of [the *Defensio*, JM] was visited or invited by all the ambassadors at London, not excepting those of Crowned Heads, and particularly esteemed by Adrian Paw' (i.e. Pauw; Darbishire, p. 160); see 7 June 1652.

25   JM again petitions to compound for Wheatley; the main text is in a scribal hand, but JM signs the document and adds a signed attestation in his own hand in the left margin (PRO SP 23/101, pp. 925–8). The endorsements on the document show that on the same day that JM signed the paper, he delivered it to the Committee on Compounding at Haberdashers Hall and swore to it; the Committee immediately acted on the petition, referring it to Peter Brereton for a report 'by Tuesday next'. A schedule of the income from Wheatley (PRO SP 23/101 p. 929) was attached on or about the same day.

27   Anne Powell submits an affidavit confirming that her husband had died at the beginning of January in JM's house in Barbican (PRO SP 23/110, p. 547).

28   Affidavit concerning Richard Powell's debt confirms that JM has received £180 in interest on Powell debt; the signature is in JM's hand (PRO SP 23/101, p. 931). In *LR*, II, 360 the amount is misprinted as £108.

March

4   (Tuesday) A report on JM's petition is issued by Brereton; JM's fine is fixed at £130 (PRO SP 23/14, pp. 26–7). On the same day Brereton reports on Anne Powell's petition to compound (PRO SP 23/110, pp. 539–40); an entry on 6 March seems to imply that her petition was accepted (PRO SP 23/42).

5   The Committee of Examinations is ordered 'to view over Mr Milton's book and to give order for reprinting of it as they think fit' (PRO SP 25/18, p. 31); the book has not been identi-

fied. In the same entry the Council requests that the Committee examine JM's complaint about Peter Cole having printed *A Treatise of the Rickets*, which William Dugard had apparently patented; the reason for the complaint is not clear.

6 *Mercurius Politicus* No. 39 prints a letter from Leiden dated 20 February/2 March reporting that the writer has heard 'in our Academy' and 'at the Hague also' that English ambassadors are bringing copies of 'the answer to Salmasius' to the Netherlands.

11 JM pays half of sequestration fine on Wheatley, i.e. £65 (PRO SP 23/43, p. 73).

12 Sequestration of Wheatley is suspended (PRO SP 23/14, p. 47).

14/24 25 copies of JM's *Defensio* are ordered for members of the Dutch government before this date (Algemeen Rijksarchief, The Hague, MS Leg. Arch. 4582; see Miller, 1986b).

16 JM's son John is born at 9.30 pm in Scotland Yard, i.e. the apartment at the Scotland Yard end of Whitehall (BL Add MS 32,310); the date and time are confirmed in Birch's transcription of JM's wife's (lost) family Bible (BL Add MS 4244, fol. 52^v).

17 Six issues of the weekly journal *Mercurius Politicus* (Nos. 33–38, 23 January–27 February) are licensed in JM's name (*SR* I, 362). JM is usually named as licenser in subsequent registrations until No. 85 (22 January 1652), after which the licenser is normally unnamed but sometimes named as John Thurloe. Under Bradshaw's Press Act of 20 September 1649, licensing of books printed in England was no longer required (though the practice continued), but newsletters and political pamphlets were subject to licensing 'by such person as shall be authorised by the Council of State'.

19/29 Letter from George Richter in Leiden to Christoph Arnold in Nuremburg gives news of publication of JM's *Defensio* (*LR*, III, 9, where writer and recipient are inadvertently reversed, and Lugd[unum] is mistakenly interpreted as Lyons rather than Leiden).

24 JM pays second half of fine on Wheatley, that is, £65 (PRO SP 23/43, p. 73). Before this date, which was the last day of 1650 in the English Calendar, JM translated the *Summarium Damnorum* (W43a, P39) into Latin (Miller, 1992, p. 26). On or about the same day JM is ordered to receive all income from Powell property without deduction of Anne Powell's thirds.

25   JM receives increased (£47.12s.4d) rents from Wheatley. John
     Pye is allowed to compound for Richard Powell's property at
     Forest Hill; the sequestration fine is set at £658.15s.3d, which is
     the amount that Pye had paid on 24 January.

27   JM receives clearance of Powell property in Wheatley through
     payment of fine (PRO SP 14/23, p. 69v). On the same day JM is
     ordered to deliver letters to Cardenas, the Spanish Ambassador
     (SP 25/65, p. 175). By this date JM had already translated the
     first letter, to the Marquis of Lède (W42, P56); he must have
     translated the second letter, to Cardenas (W41, P57), shortly
     thereafter; see Miller 1986a. Both letters are concerned with
     the seizures of an English merchant vessel, the *Ann of Foy*.

28   Sir Henry Vane is ordered to pass the Latin text of the Inter-
     cursus Magna to JM for translation; JM completed the transla-
     tion, but no copy is known to survive (see Miller, 1992, p. 8).

29   Powell's fine is reduced from £658.15s.3d to £576.12s.3d, and
     he pays £329.7s.6d, which is half of the original amount (PRO
     SP 23/43, p. 73).

31/10 April   Letter from Nicholas Heinsius (see *NNBW*) in Leiden
     to Isaac Vossius (see *NNBW*) in Stockholm attests to popular
     ity of JM's *Defensio* in Leiden (Amsterdam Universiteits-
     Bibliotheek, MS III.E.9.40). Leiden and Amsterdam had chan-
     ged to the Gregorian calendar in 1582, so the letters of
     Heinsius are dated N.S.

April

2/12 (Wednesday) Vossius writes to Heinsius saying that he
     received JM's *Defensio* yesterday (1/11 April) and that Queen
     Christina immediately borrowed it (Burmann, III, 595).
     Sweden had adopted the Gregorian calendar in 1582, but
     under King Charles IX (1600–11) had reverted to the Julian
     calendar; the letters of Vossius, however, are dated in the N.S.
     adopted in his native city of Leiden.

3   *Mercurius Politicus* No. 43 reports a letter from the Hague
     dated 20/30 March saying that JM's *Defensio* 'here is very
     much applauded'.

4   Council orders 'that such despatches as come to this Council
     from foreign parts in any foreign tongue are to be translated
     for the use of the council.' (PRO SP 25/65, p. 217) JM doubtless
     translated many of these letters, but no attempt to catalogue
     those translated by him has been made.

6 Thomason secures his copy of JM's *Defensio* (BL E. 1393) and misdates it 'April 6th, 1650'.

8 Pye submits a detailed account of his transactions with Richard Powell (PRO SP 23/109, p. 535).

9/19 Vossius records in a letter to Heinsius that Queen Christina has read JM's *Defensio*, and praised both his genius and his prose style (Burmann, III, 596). On the same day John Pye's fine is further reduced to £554.18s.

10 JM is informed that his forced removal from Whitehall lodgings has been delayed (PRO SP 25/65, p. 253).

16 Anne Powell petitions for the restoration of her thirds from JM (PRO SP 23/110, p. 594)

17 Five issues of *Mercurius Politicus* (Nos. 39–43, 6 March–3 April 1651) are licensed in JM's name (*SR* I, 364). *Mercurius Politicus* No. 45 prints a letter dated 7 April from a correspondent in Amsterdam who approves of JM's *Defensio*; Amsterdam had adopted the Gregorian calendar in 1582, so if the writer is using the local calendar, the date should be 28 March/7 April.

19 Anne Powell's petition for redress from JM is denied (PRO SP 23/14, p. 89ᵛ).

28/8 May Heinsius reports to Vossius that there are five different editions of JM's *Defensio* known in Leiden (Burmann, III, 600).

May

5/15 (Monday) Heinsius writes from Amsterdam to the philologist Johannes Fredericus Gronovius (see *NNBW*) in Deventer to say that Salmasius, who is in Stockholm, is enraged by JM's *Defensio*. (Burmann, III, 257–9)

7 *Mercurius Politicus* No. 48 reports a letter from the Hague dated 23 April/3 May discussing *Eikon Aklastos* (the rebuttal of JM's *Eikonoklastes*), which is attributed to John Bramhall.

8/18 Heinsius writes to Vossius from Leiden discussing presentation copies of JM's *Defensio*, the various editions of the *Defensio*, and the background of JM (Burmann, III, 603).

13 JM buys excise bond from George Foxcroft (see 5 May 1660).

14/24 Heinsius writes to Vossius about JM's *Defensio* (Amsterdam Universiteits-Bibliotheek, MS III.E.9.45).

16 JM is ordered to visit the Portuguese Ambassador with a view to securing names of persons in his retinue (PRO SP 25/19, p. 138).

19/29 Heinsius writes to Vossius about Salmasius and JM (Amsterdam Universiteits-Bibliotheek, MS III.E.9.48).

20 John Dury is ordered by Council of State to translate JM's *Eikonoklastes* into French (PRO SP 25/19, p. 146).

22 Four issues of *Mercurius Politicus* (Nos. 47–50, 1–22 May) are licensed in JM's name (*SR* I, 369). JM's translation of a letter of state to the Grand Duke of Tuscany (W17, P29) is completed but not signed until 20 January 1652; see Miller (1987c).

25/4 June   Vossius enquires about JM and asks Heinsius to send him a copy of *Eikonoklastes* (Burmann, III, 605).

29 *Mercurius Politicus* (No. 51) is licensed in JM's name (*SR* I, 369). On the same day (29 May/8 June) Vossius tells Heinsius that he has learnt from his uncle Junius that JM is a Latin secretary, skilled in many languages, not a nobleman but at least a gentleman, and a disciple of Patrick Young (Burmann, III, 618). 'Patrick' may be a slip for Thomas, JM's tutor, but Francis Junius is not likely to have confused his fellow scholar-librarian Patrick Young with the Smectymnuan Thomas Young, and JM had sent a volume of his writings to Patrick Young (see 4 March 1645). Patrick Young had served as Prebendary and Treasurer of St Paul's Cathedral from 1621 to 1624, so it is at least possible, albeit improbable, that he had taught JM.

30 JM is ordered to translate papers concerning Alderman Dethicke and Cardenas, the Spanish Ambassador (PRO SP 25/19, p. 173). The English draft of the covering letter survives (W167H, P27), dated 27 May 1651, but JM's Latin translation of both Alderman Dethicke's petition and the Council's covering letter are lost.

June

1/11 (Sunday) Vossius tells Heinsius that Salmasius is wholly occupied in preparing an answer to JM's *Defensio* (Burmann, III, 606).

3/13 Heinsius writes to Vossius from Utrecht about JM's slur on Mercera, Salmasius's wife (Amsterdam Universiteits-Bibliotheek MS III.E.9.51); Utrecht remained on the Julian calendar until 1700, but the letter is dated 'Eidibus Junijs Gregorianis' (Ides of June, Gregorian Style). On the same day John Pye's petition arguing that his fine has been miscalculated is referred to the Auditor, Richard Sherwin (PRO SP 23/109, p. 533).

4   John Pye submits another detailed half-yearly account of his income from the Powell property (PRO SP 23/109, p. 537).

5   *Mercurius Politicus*. (No. 52) is licensed in JM's name (*SR* I, 370).

7/17   JM's *Defensio* is ordered to be burnt publicly at Toulouse (Bibliothèque Nationale MS F.L. 602, fols. 21–2).

8/18   Vossius tells Heinsius of progress of replies to JM's *Defensio* by Dirk Graswinkel (see *NNBW*) and Salmasius (Burmann, III, 607); the former seems never to have been printed.

9/19   A letter from Sir George Carteret to Sir Edward Nicholas is signed 'Milton' as a pseudonym (BL MS Egerton 2534, fols. 99–100).

10/20   Heinsius tells Gronovius of the fury of Salmasius about JM's *Defensio*, which Salmasius blames on Heinsius and his father (Burmann, III, 266–7).

11   Council requests Parliament that JM be allowed to remain in Whitehall (PRO SP 25/30, p. 26).

12   *Mercurius Politicus* (No. 53) is licensed in JM's name (*SR* I, 370).

17   Brian Duppa alludes to JM's divorce tracts in a letter to Sir Justinian Isham (Northamptonshire Record Office, MS I(D) 18).

18   Council of State orders JM to be paid a reward of £100 and thanked for the writing of the *Defensio* (PRO SP 25/20, p. 44); this order has been obliterated, and is very difficult to read (the amount payable in Sotheby's facsimile is £200). In another order two pages later (p. 46) the Council declares its 'resentment' (that is, gratitude) but does not offer money, so it seems possible that JM declined the reward, and a revised order was therefore drafted. JM later denied that he had been paid; Salmasius claimed that JM had been paid £4,000. On the same day (18/28 June) Heinsius tells Gronovius that he expects to be attacked by Salmasius along with JM (Burmann, III, 270–71).

19   *Mercurius Politicus* (No. 54) is licensed in JM's name (*SR* I, 371).

23   JM's recommendation that Richard Heath be appointed Vicar of St Alkmund's is recorded (BL Add MS 36, 792, fol. 28; Woolrych (1974)).

25/5 July   JM's *Defensio* is burnt in Paris (the date is given in *Mercurius Politicus* No. 56, 3 July). On the same day Gui Patin writes to M. Belin *fils* reporting that Salmasius's *Defensio Regia* is on sale in Paris, that JM has replied and that Salmasius plans to answer him (Patin, I, 179).

26/6 July   JM's *Defensio* is condemned and burnt in Paris (Bibliothèque Nationale MS F.L.602, fol. 23a). JM is ordered to deliver a letter about Alderman Dethicke to Cardenas, the Spanish Ambassador (PRO SP 25/20, p. 68); this letter must be the Council's covering letter (see 30 May). *Mercurius Politicus* (No. 55) is licensed in JM's name (*SR* I, 372).

July

Hollantse Mercurius reports the burning of JM's *Defensio* in Paris and Toulouse. *Europäische Sambstägige Zeitung* No. 29 (published in Hamburg) reports the burning in Paris, and later in the year *Leipziger Messrelation* and *Wochentliche Donnerstags Zeitung* (Hamburg) carry similar reports (Berghaus, 1983).

1/11   (Tuesday) JM's *Defensio* is again burnt in Paris (Bibliothèque Nationale MS F.L.602, fol. 23).

3/13   Heinsius tells Gronovius that Salmasius's reply to JM is in press in Sweden, but that Graswinkel, who had planned to write a reply for Elzevir's press, had been silenced by the authorities (Burmann, III, 273–4). On the same day *Mercurius Politicus* No. 56, which is licensed in JM's name (*SR* I, 372), reports the burning of JM's *Defensio* in Paris (p. '890', an error for 899).

4   Richard Sherwin submits a detailed report on Robert Pye's appeal against the calculation of his fine (PRO SP 23/109, p. 531).

6   Jacob Matthiesen (see *DBL*) attacks JM's *Defensio* in a letter written from Aarhus (*LR* V, 428); Denmark remained on the Julian calendar till 1700, so the date is probably Julian.

7/17   Heinsius describes JM to Vossius as a wealthy nobleman who is very small and in ill health and has an extraordinary command of foreign languages (Amsterdam Universiteits-Bibliotheek, MS III.E.9.50).

8   Ephraim Elcock mentions *Tenure* and *Eikonoklastes* in *Animadversions on a Book*, pp. 5, 6, 60 (Thomason's date; his copy is BL E.636(2)).

9/19   Heinsius praises JM in a letter to Gronovius (Burmann, III, 276).

10   *Mercurius Politicus* (No. 57) is licensed in JM's name (*SR* I, 373); this issue contains more gossip (dated 21 June/1 July) about

Salmasius and expands on the earlier report of the burning of
the *Defensio* in Toulouse and Paris. A copy of JM's *Doctrine and
Discipline of Divorce* is catalogued in the library of Sion College.
Thomason's copy of the *Catalogus* (BL E.636(7)) is undated, but
he catalogued it with other pamphlets of 10 July (BL C.38.h.21,
Vol. 6, No. 502/7).

11 Anne Powell petitions for increased payments by JM from her
husband's estate, 'to preserve her and her children from star-
ving' (PRO SP 23/110, p. 597).

14 JM's translation of a Letter of State from Parliament to the
King of Spain (W21, P28) is approved. 14 July is the date of
the English text. The date on Skinner's Latin text (10 August
1651) is possible but unlikely, because 10 August fell on a
Sunday when Parliament was not in session.

16 Anne Powell's petition is considered by Commissioners; the
document notes that 'Mr Milton is a harsh and choleric man'
(PRO SP 23/110, p. 595).

17 *Mercurius Politicus* No. 58 is licensed in JM's name (*SR* I, 374);
the burning of JM's *Defensio* in Paris is described in a report
dated 9/19 July.

18 JM's 'Milton against Salmasius' is mentioned in a letter from
William Rand to Hartlib (Hartlib 62/30/1a-4b).

24 *Mercurius Politicus* No. 59 is licensed in JM's name (*SR* I,
374).

26/5 August Vossius praises JM and castigates Salmasius in a
letter to Heinsius (Burmann, III, 621).

29 Goldsmiths' Company describes s.v. 'John Milton' a 'tenement
(called the Red Rose) in the holding of [blank] Hussey' (*Committee of Survey, 1651*, fol. 25).

31 *Mercurius Politicus* No. 60 is licensed in JM's name (*SR* I, 375).

August
Late in the summer John Rowland's *Pro Rege et Populo Anglicano
Apologia*, a chapter-by-chapter refutation of JM's *Defensio*, is pub-
lished; the treatise was popularly but erroneously attributed to
Bishop John Bramhall. A presentation copy of JM's *Defensio* now in
the Pierpont Morgan Library is inscribed in what seems to be JM's
hand, and dated 'August 1651'. John Drew mentions *Tenure* in *The
Northern Subscriber's Plea*, pp. 40–41 (Thomason's date; his copy is BL
E.638 (11)).

2 (Saturday) Perth falls to Cromwell.

6 *Eikonoklastes* is praised in William Lilly's *Monarchy or No Monarchy* (Thomason's date; his copy is BL E.638(17)).
7 *Mercurius Politicus* No. 61 is licensed in JM's name (*SR* I, 375).
14 *Mercurius Politicus* No. 62 is licensed in JM's name (*SR* I, 376).
21 *Mercurius Politicus* No. 63 is licensed in JM's name (*SR* I, 376).
28 *Mercurius Politicus* No. 64 is licensed in JM's name (*SR* I, 377).
30 (?) Hermann Mylius, a diplomat in the service of the principality of Oldenburg, meets Christoph Arnold of Nuremburg at the Old Exchange. Arnold tells Mylius that JM is *vier meilen* away. If these four miles are in German measure, and the point of reference is the Old Exchange, then JM must have been about 18 miles from Westminster (perhaps in Horton?); if in English measure, he may have been in Hammersmith (Miller, 1985, pp. 26, 310).

September
3 (Wednesday) Cromwell defeats Charles II at Battle of Worcester.
4 *Mercurius Politicus* No. 65 is licensed in JM's name (*SR* I, 377).
5 News of Battle of Worcester reaches London. The Committee on Compounding, having considered the Auditor's report, restores Pye's fine to £576.12s.3d and orders him to pay the total amount within six weeks (PRO Sp Dom 23/15, p. 8; see 11 October).
7 London celebrates victory in Worcester with cannon salvoes and services of thanksgiving.
11 *Mercurius Politicus* No. 66 is licensed in JM's name (*SR* I, 378).
17 Charles II flees to France.
18 *Mercurius Politicus* No. 67 is licensed in JM's name (*SR* I, 378).
25 *Mercurius Politicus* No. 68 is licensed in JM's name (*SR* I, 379).
29 JM receives £45.18s.11d in rents from Wheatley.

October
In this month the dissertation of Christian Woldenburg (on Salmasius and JM) and the response of Christoph Turing are printed (in Latin) in *I.N.D.N.J.C. Disputatio politica de potestate regia*.
2 (Thursday) *Mercurius Politicus* No. 69 is licensed in JM's name (*SR* I, 379).
3/13 Graswinkel's reply to JM's *Defensio* is said by Heinsius, in a letter from Leiden to Gronovius, to have been published (Burmann, III, 285). The translation in *LR*, III, 73 translates

Lugdunum as Lyons rather than Leiden. No such publication is known to exist.

6   *A Perfect Diurnal* is licensed in JM's name (*SR* I, 380). Weckherlin writes to Mylius explaining that he has been replaced as Latin Secretary by 'a man of the highest esteem, Mr Milton, who has already often edited state papers, also writing against Salmasius and against the King who suffered capital punishment. He is a sound man, learned in Latin and Greek and especially Italian' (see Miller, 1982 and 1985, pp. 53–5, 316).

7   Christoph Arnold writes to his friend Dr Georg Richter describing English celebrities whom he had met, including JM. The letter is traditionally dated 26 July, but see Miller, 1984. Arnold's meeting with JM must have taken place between 10 July, when Arnold arrived in England, and 7 October, the likely date of this letter. On the same day (7/17 October) Gronovius mentions the revised edition of JM's *Defensio* in a letter to Heinsius (Burmann, III, 286).

9   *Mercurius Politicus* No. 70 is licensed in JM's name (*SR* I, 380).

11 Pye pays £247.4s.9d (PRO SP 23/43, p. 73), which when added to the £329.7s.6d paid on 29 March brings the total paid to £576.12s.3d, the figure specified in the order of 5 September.

16 *Mercurius Politicus* No. 71 is licensed in JM's name (*SR* I, 381). On the same day Mylius writes to JM requesting an interview; Mylius's diary entry introducing his letter to JM notes that JM had returned 'from the country [*vom Land*] the previous day'; the opening phrase of his letter acknowledges that JM has been away from Westminster. Later in the day JM sends word that he must attend the Council of State, but that he might be able to visit Mylius in the evening, or possibly the following morning. Mylius records his suspicion that JM wanted time to establish the facts about Mylius's status and mission (Miller, 1985, 58–9). JM may have been absent since the arrival of Mylius in London on 28 August, and possibly earlier; his protracted absence is a puzzle. Was JM's family living in Whitehall? The local parish records for 1652 do not mention the birth of Deborah on 2 May, the death of Mary on 5 May, or the death of John in June; JM's duties as a licenser did not require his presence.

17 JM had not visited Mylius the previous evening, so Mylius writes again. JM replies through a parliamentary messenger

that he cannot manage a meeting that day, but that a meeting on the following Monday or Tuesday (that is, 20 or 21 October) with the Master of the Ceremonies (Oliver Fleming) was assured (Miller, 1985, p. 60).

19 Fleming sends a parliamentary messenger to Mylius informing him that the official audience will be the next morning at about ten o'clock (*circa decimam*); (Miller, 1985, p. 61).

20 Mylius is received at about 10.00 am. by the Council of State in the Palace of Westminster. He subsequently notes in his diary that the Lords Commissioners (Whitelocke, Vane, Mildmay and Trevor) sat on one side of a long table opposite a chair reserved for Mylius, and that Mr Milton stood to the right of Bulstrode Whitelocke (Miller, 1985, p. 63). Mylius noted that during his speech 'Mr Milton showed himself [to be] very attentive, doubtless for the reason that if I put forth my requests orally, different from the written form, he would correct it, following and taking notice'. Whitelocke responded in English, and JM interpreted into Latin for Mylius's benefit. Mylius also noted the fine tapestries, which must have been those designed by Henry Vroom and executed by Francis Spiring to commemorate the naval victories of 1588. These tapestries, which were destroyed in the fire of 16 October 1834, are among the few works of art that JM is known to have seen (for engravings of the tapestries see Pine). The same afternoon Mylius writes a formal letter to Weckherlin in which he mentions his pleasure in hearing 'the great Milton' reply on behalf of the Council (Miller, 1985, pp. 67–9).

21 Smectymnuus is satirised in *Smectymnuo-Mastix* (Thomason's date; his copy is BL E.1218 (3)).

22 John Pye pays the residue of his fine, and so regains control of the Forest Hill property (PRO SP 23/15 p. 56).

23 *Mercurius Politicus* No. 72 is licensed in JM's name (*SR* I, 381).

24 Day of prayer, thanksgiving and fasting for the victory at Worcester on 3 September.

25 Mylius sends the drafts of the two sections of his *Safeguard* to JM with a covering letter that declares JM to be 'a second Piso'; the reference is not clear, but Mylius may have in mind the Lucius Calpurnius Piso who was declared by Cicero (in *Pro Marco Fonteio Oratio*) to be of such virtue and integrity that he alone was called 'the honest' (Miller, 1985, p. 320). JM reads the letter, examines the drafts, and sends a parliamentary

messenger to Mylius suggesting that JM visit Mylius at 3.00 pm. Mylius happily accepts, but JM cancels at the last moment on the grounds that he had been summoned to the Council of State. Mylius responds to JM's courteous apology with a warm letter requesting an interview at any convenient time. JM replies that he would be able to visit two days later, on Monday. JM reports to the Council, presumably for item 24 on the day's agenda, Whitelocke's report on the progress of the Oldenburg negotiations (Miller, 1985, pp. 72–4).

27 JM cancels the appointment with Mylius, instead attending the Council of State for item 31 on the agenda, as a result of which he is directed to ask 'Mr White' about plans to print a second edition of a book (PRO SP 25/23, p. 66). The book is almost certainly *The Life and Reign of King Charles* (London, 1651, but see 29 January 1652)), which says (with inexplicit reference to JM's *Eikonoklastes*) that the 'whole contexture' of *Eikon Basilike* 'hath already been handled without mittens by a gentleman of such abilities as gives place to none for his integrity, learning and judgement.' Nothing is known of the identity of 'Mr White'. On the same day Limerick surrenders after a long siege.

28 Mylius writes to Dury explaining that it is difficult to be confident about when they might meet, 'since at any moment Mr Fleming, as also the Aesculapius of this Commonwealth and its defender, our Milton, are likely to summon me by their messengers'. Dury responds immediately with an invitation to meet the same day; Mylius visits Dury, and gives an account of his audience with the Council, 'when Mr Milton reported to Council President Bradshaw of my delivery of my proposals' (Miller, 1985, pp. 77–9).

30 *Mercurius Politicus* No. 73 is licensed in JM's name (*SR* I, 382).

31 Mylius tells Fleming that JM has twice had to cancel appointments with him, and wonders whether JM will retain the drafts of the *Safeguard* or return them (Miller, 1985, p. 76). In a partially encoded letter written the same day Mylius reports a meeting of Dury and Bradshaw, with TXNMFY present (in Mylius's code, t=m; x=i; n=l; m=t; f=o; y=n).

November

4 (Tuesday) John Dury visits Mylius, and reports that he has visited Mr Milton to discuss Mylius's mission, and that JM had

been optimistic that the matter would soon be concluded (Miller, 1985, p. 82). This is the first recorded meeting between Dury and JM, but they are likely to have known each other for many years.

5 A day of religious observance in commemoration of the Gunpowder Plot of 1605.

6 *Mercurius Politicus* No. 74 is licensed in JM's name (*SR* I, 382). Mylius writes to JM renewing his request for assistance, asking that JM try to push his case forward and that JM allow him to check the latest drafts of his documents with a view to ensuring that they conform to the needs of Oldenburg as well as those of Parliament. JM replies to the effect that pressure of work had prevented him from concluding Mylius's business, but expressing the wish that they could meet to discuss the matter the same day or the next (Miller, 1985, pp. 83–4).

7 Mylius writes home, recording that he had written to JM the previous day, and that JM had replied that he hoped to visit today (7th). After this letter is completed Mylius receives a letter from JM acknowledging receipt of three letters (Mylius had in fact sent four) and apologising for the delay, which JM attributes partly to pressure of other work and partly to ill-health. The ill-health may have been caused or exacerbated by the horrific treatments that JM was receiving for his failing eyesight. JM encloses the drafts, as Mylius had requested, and explains that he had perused them as carefully as he could in the limited time available and that the matter was now in other hands (Miller, 1985, pp. 84–5). Mylius glances at the drafts, and immediately returns them to JM with a warm covering letter expressing the hope that they would be dealt with promptly. He then returns to his letter home and adds a postscript which expresses frustration that responsibility for the matter has been taken from JM (Miller, 1985, pp. 85–6).

10 Fleming explains to Mylius that the English text of his proposals is in Frost's hands, and that JM probably has the Latin version.

13 *Mercurius Politicus* No. 75 is licensed in JM's name (*SR* I, 383).

15 Dury responds to a letter from Mylius with an assurance that he will try to have a word with JM on Monday (that is, 17th).

18 Dury secretly visits Mylius under cover of a severe storm, and explains that he had visited Mr Secretary Milton, who had confided to him that Whitelocke had assumed personal

responsibility for the Oldenburg negotiations, and that White-locke was angry that Oldenburg's representatives had been negotiating with Stuart agents in The Hague (Miller, 1985, pp. 90–91). This was a sensitive issue, because Scottish support for Charles II had led to discussions in Parliament about the idea of abolishing the name Scotland in favour of North England.

19/29 JM signs Christoph Arnold's autograph album (now BL Egerton MS 1324, fol. 85v). He gives the place as London rather than Westminster, so it seems likely that on that day he was visiting either Samuel Hartlib or Theodore Haak, both of whom signed the album on the same day (see Miller, 1990*b*).

20 *Mercurius Politicus* No. 76 is licensed in JM's name (*SR* I, 383).

21 JM passes the Mylius papers to Whitelocke.

24 JM informs Mylius through a parliamentary messenger that the previous Friday (that is, 21 November) he had passed all the papers to Whitelocke, and expresses his regret that he cannot visit Mylius at present because of 'headache and pain in his eyes' (Miller, 1985, p. 93).

25 Mylius makes a note reminding himself to enquire what sort of farewell gift would be appropriate for Frost and JM (Miller, 1985, p. 325).

26/5 December   Janus Vlitius (see *NNBW*) tells Heinsius that he has arranged to visit JM on his forthcoming visit to England (Burmann, III, 742); the letters of Vlitius are almost certainly dated N.S.

27 *Mercurius Politicus* No. 77 is licensed in JM's name (*SR* I, 385).

December

1 (Monday) Mylius learns from Johan Oste, Secretary of the Dutch legation, that JM is almost blind and that others are assuming his duties (Miller, 1985, p. 97).

4 *Mercurius Politicus* No. 78 is licensed in JM's name (*SR* I, 385).

9 JM's forty-third birthday.

11 *Mercurius Politicus* No. 79 is licensed in JM's name (*SR* I, 385).

12 Mylius records in his diary that negotiations are still stalled, and that JM's hopeful assurance that the matter would be resolved 'shortly' was given 'six long weeks ago' (Miller, 1985, p. 103); Mylius is referring to JM's letter of 7 November, and his German text cites JM's Latin *brevi*. The word becomes a motif in later correspondence.

17 JM moves from Whitehall to 'a pretty garden-house in Petty France in Westminster, next door to the Lord Scudamore's, and opening into St James's Park; here he remained no less than eight years... till within a few weeks of King Charles the 2nd's Restoration' (Edward Phillips, in Darbishire, p. 71). The anonymous biographer (Cyriack Skinner) noted that the house 'had a door into the park' (Darbishire, p. 32). The house was later owned by Jeremy Bentham, whose tenant from 1811 was William Hazlitt; John Stuart Mill was a later resident. The house survived until 1877, when it was demolished by the Metropolitan Railway Company. See *LR* III, 109–10 and Parker (1996), 181. On the same day Mylius writes to JM renewing his request for assistance (Miller, 1985, pp. 109–10).

18 *Mercurius Politicus* No. 80 is licensed in JM's name (*SR* I, 386). Salmasius, who is in Leiden, is said to be angered by JM's *Defensio* (*Mercurius Politicus* No. 82, 25 December 1651–1 January 1652). The report is dated 28 October 1651, but 'October' is presumably an error for December, and Leiden had moved to the Gregorian calendar in 1582, so the most likely date is 18/28 December 1651.

20 JM makes final payment of £100 on the lease of the Red Rose in Bread Street; the lost receipt is recorded in Prideaux I, 288. This payment is late (it was due at Midsummer), which may suggest that JM has been in financial difficulty and so has waited for his quarterly salary of £72.3s.5$\frac{1}{4}$d.

24 John Phillips publishes his *Responsio*, a reply to Rowland's *Apologia*. Scholars misled by Thomason's ambiguous dating of his copy (BL E.1385) as 24 December, with the printed year MDCLII uncorrected, have traditionally dated publication late in 1652 (Parker, 1996, p. 990, n. 139); the tract is occasionally said to have been written by JM (e.g. John Ellis, BL Add MS 28,954, *ca.* 1675).

25 *Mercurius Politicus* No. 81 is licensed in JM's name (*SR* I, 386).

29 JM is reappointed Secretary for Foreign Tongues (PRO SP 25/66, p. 130).

31 JM writes to Mylius, who receives the letter early on 1 January. JM apologises for not having replied sooner to Mylius's letter, explaining that he had moved house on 17 December and that 'ill health, which is now almost my perpetual enemy,' had caused further delay. JM's letter is reproduced in Miller,

1985, p. 122, and discussed on pp. 123–4; on the date of the letter see p. 331. JM later printed the letter in EF (No. 11).

1652

Claude Barthélemy Morisot attacks *Eikonoklastes* in *Carolus I Britanniarum Rex, A Securi et Calamo Miltonii Vindicatus* ('Dublin' [actually Dijon], 1652); John Hacket attacks JM in *Scrinia Reserta*, and Sir Edward Walker attacks JM and his defenders in *A Full Answer to...Lilley* (see 6 August 1651); Marchamont Nedham alludes to JM's *Defensio* in *A Cat May Look Upon A King*. Two further editions of the *Defensio* are printed, Rowland's *Apologia* attacking JM is reprinted. At some point in the year Heinsius writes to Pierre Bourdelot (see *DBF*) saying that he has never met JM (Burmann, V, 713). It is also likely that JM learnt Dutch from Roger Williams in the first half of this year (see 12 July 1654); Williams had arrived in England in December 1651 and left early in 1654, but the last Dutch diplomats left on 30 June 1652, just before the outbreak of war on 7 July. JM's nephew John, son of Christopher and Thomasina, was probably born in this year; he was 15 when admitted to Pembroke College Cambridge on 29 January 1668.

January
1 (Thursday) *Mercurius Politicus* No. 82 is licensed in JM's name (*SR* I, 387).
JM takes Oath of Secrecy (PRO SP 25/26, p. [3]).
Mylius replies fulsomely to JM expressing his distress at the news that JM is suffering from headache and inflamed eyes (Miller, 1985, p. 125).
2 JM is ordered to prepare the Latin text of a letter to Tuscany (PRO SP 25/66, p. 152); the Council is unaware that the Latin text has been ready since 22 May 1651 (see 20 January 1652). Mylius writes home, enclosing a copy of JM's letter; Mylius's amanuensis has dated his copy of JM's letter 2 January 1652. The date on the original has also been adjusted; the 'correction' must have been made by a German, because JM and his amanuensis would not have changed the year to conform to German usage. Presumably Mylius changed the date to give the impression that he was reporting home the moment he received the letter. In another letter written the same day

Mylius describes JM as a friend whom he sees from time to time, but not as often as he might wish because JM does not always drop in and is often absent because of ill health. The surviving documentation only records a meeting at the audience on 20 October; either Mylius is exaggerating the extent of contact, perhaps representing chance encounters as meetings, or some meetings were not recorded by either JM or Mylius. On the same day (2/12) Johannes Rhodius mentions JM in a letter to Heinsius written from Padua (Burmann, V, 456).

3 Mylius visits JM, expressing best wishes for the recovery of his health, 'since he suffers from headaches and suffusion of the eyes'; the fact that the term 'suffusion' recurs in *Paradise Lost* 3.26 raises the possibility that Mylius is citing JM's term. Mylius records that JM undertook to speak to Thomas Challoner about his case and that JM gave Mylius a gift of John Phillips's *Responsio* and asked Mylius for his opinion of it (Miller, 1985, pp. 127–8).

7 Early in the morning Mylius visits Whitehall, and overhears a conversation between Fleming and Colonel William Purefoy, in which Purefoy describes to Fleming what had happened in Council the previous day (Fleming had been in the City on official business), when several members of Council had spoken against the Oldenburg accord on various grounds, especially that Oldenburg had assisted Charles II. Mylius also hears Purefoy say that the Order of the Council would have been passed to JM. Mylius leaves Whitehall and goes straight to JM's house to find out what had happened in Council the previous evening. JM explains that he was working on an urgent document for the Duke of Tuscany (see 20 January), but that he will return to the Oldenburg documents as quickly as possible (Miller, 1985, pp. 129–31).

8 *Mercurius Politicus* No. 83 is licensed in JM's name (*SR* I, 388). Mylius sends his personal secretary to JM with the revised drafts of the Safeguard; JM returns the revised draft to Mylius asking that it be returned by 2.00pm; Mylius in turn quickly sends the document back to JM with a request for further amendments. Mylius then visits JM, still before 2.00pm, to go over the proposed amendments with him with a view to presenting the document to the Council of State that evening (Miller 1985, pp. 131–4)

9   JM visits Mylius, apparently for the first time, and promises
    assistance; JM leaves to ride into the City on unknown busi-
    ness (Miller, 1985, p. 135). Fleming had visited the City earlier
    in the week to sound out merchants about Hamburg, and had
    also enquired about Oldenburg, so JM's visit may have been
    related to Fleming's. In the afternoon JM returns to Westmin-
    ster via Mylius's home, where he collects the draft that he had
    left with him before returning to the Council of State. At some
    point in the day JM collects interest of £16 on the Foxcroft
    bond (see 13 May 1651).

12 Mylius records in his diary that he visited Hugh Peter and
    explained that the Latin draft of the *Safeguard* was still in JM's
    hands (Miller, 1985, pp. 135–6). On the same day Janus Vlitius
    writes to Heinsius from England mentioning his determination
    to visit JM (Burmann, III, 742).

13 Mylius notes receipt of JM's gift of *Pro Rege Apologia*, an attack
    on JM written by John Rowland (though JM thought that John
    Bramhall was the author), and notes JM's request for com-
    ment. Mylius composes several drafts of a letter to JM, the
    final version of which he sends (Miller, 1985, pp. 137–9).

15 *Mercurius Politicus* No. 84 is licensed in JM's name (*SR* I, 388);
    Salmasius is mentioned on p. 1344.

16 JM's brother Christopher is declared delinquent in payments
    (PRO SP 23/12, p. 390).

20 JM's translation of a Letter of State from Parliament to the
    Grand Duke of Tuscany (W17, P29), which he had completed
    by 22 May 1651, is signed. On the same day JM's translation of
    a second letter to the Grand Duke (the one to which he
    referred in conversation with Mylius on 7 January) is signed.
    The original version is lost, but the Bodleian Library contains
    drafts of the Latin text (MS Nalson XVIII, #146, fol. 390) and
    the English original (MS Tanner 54, fol. 68); see Miller (1987c).

    JM writes from Petty France to Mylius, explaining that the
    previous day he had presented the Oldenburg documents to
    the Lord President, who passed the texts (in both English and
    Latin) to the Council. JM predicts that Challoner and Neville
    will support the ratification of the agreement, and that the
    matter will be concluded within two days. The letter is repro-
    duced in Miller, 1985, p. 144. Mylius reads the letter, and
    scribbles in the margin that JM in his innocence is wrong, at
    least as far as Neville was concerned. Mylius then goes

immediately to visit JM for a personal account of what had
happened. Mylius records that as he left JM's home, 'one of the
Dutch' came to him. The Dutch visitor has not been identified,
but may have been Vlitius, who had twice expressed an intention to meet JM (see 26 December 1651 and 2 January 1652).
The only evidence that a visit took place comes from a remote
source: Gerhard Feltmann, Vlitius' colleague at Breda, wrote in
his *Tractatus de Polygamia* (1677) that the private secretary of
the Dutch ambassador debated the subject of polygamy with
JM, and mentions that a 'son of the ambassador' was present.
Mylius visits Theodore Haak the same evening, but does not
disclose anything of what he had heard from JM (Miller, 1985,
pp. 143–8).

21 Mylius writes a formal letter to JM requesting further assis-
    tance (Miller, 1985, pp. 128–50).

22 *Mercurius Politicus* No. 85 is licensed in JM's name (*SR* I, 389);
    this is the last issue licensed in JM's name.

23 JM is ordered to translate (from Latin to English) a paper from
    Holland signed by Vlitius (PRO SP 25/66, p. 252); the transla-
    tion has not been found; the Latin text is printed in Miller
    (1992), p. 95, where it is mistakenly described as JM's Latin
    translation. Mylius notes that his latest memoranda to JM,
    Challoner and Neville had done much good ((Miller, 1985,
    p. 154).

26 JM is ordered to translate reply to Dutch paper of 19 January
    into Latin (PRO SP 25/66, p. 257).

28 JM is ordered to translate into Latin answer to proposals of
    Dutch Ambassadors (PRO SP 25/66, p. 267). Mylius meets JM
    and Fleming, but learns nothing further.

29 JM's translation of a Letter of State from the Council of State to
    the Dutch Ambassadors (W167C, P32) is signed; this is the
    translation ordered on 26 January; see Miller (1992), pp. 14–
    17, 98–102. On the same day JM's translation of another Letter
    of State from the Council of State to the Dutch Ambassadors
    (W167D, P31) is signed; this is the translation ordered on
    28 January; see Miller (1992), pp. 17–21, 103–11. On the
    same day *The Life and Reign of King Charles* is published
    (Thomason's date; his copy is BL E. 1338 (2)), on which see
    27 October 1651.

30 JM's translations of Letters of State from Parliament to the
    King of Spain (W7, P24) and from Council of State to

Cardenas, the Spanish ambassador (W8, P33) are signed. The manuscripts and early printed texts are undated; see Fallon (1993), p. 94, n. 52.

February

2   (Monday) Sir John Birkenhead (?) mocks JM for *Defensio* and divorce tracts in *Paul's Churchyard*; Thomason's copy (BL E.652 (14*)) is undated, but he catalogued it between entries dated 1 and 3 February (BL C.38.h.21, Vol 6, No. 518/14).

5   Council of State orders a Letter to Oldenburg to be translated into Latin (PRO SP 25/66, p. 307); JM is not named in the order. He does not receive the letter until about 11.00pm (*spät circa undecimam* in Mylius' diary entry). Mylius visits JM with a view to establishing whether or not he had received Mylius's papers (he had not); see Miller, 1985, pp. 167–9.

6   Mylius again visits JM, who reports that he has received some of Mylius's papers and has sent his amanuensis for the others (Miller, 1985, p. 170).

8   JM is mentioned favourably by T[homas] M[anley] in his translation of Payne Fisher's *Veni Vidi Vici: The Triumphs of... Cromwell* (Thomason's date; his copy is BL E.1298(1)).

9   Mylius again visits JM, who still has not received all the papers. JM attributes Mylius's difficulties to 'the inexperience and wilfulness of those who enjoyed the plurality of votes... The more prudent men did not even dare to reveal their true opinions' (Miller, 1985, pp. 170–72).

10 JM writes to Mylius explaining that he had lobbied on behalf of Mylius with limited success. On receipt of this letter Mylius immediately goes to JM, but is unable to discuss his draft with him; JM does, however, give him the text of one of the documents as approved by the Council. Later in the day Mylius writes to JM to thank him for his assistance (Miller, 1985, pp. 175–6).

11 Council of State orders *Safeguard* to be translated into Latin (PRO SP 25/66, p. 317); JM is not named in the order.

12 Mylius visits JM to discuss changes to his drafts. JM explains that he had already been criticised for showing the drafts to Mylius, and could not make any more changes without the express order of the Council. After Mylius departs, JM attends to the Council order (number 8 on the previous day's agenda) to check the Latin text of the *Safeguard*. JM then writes to Bulstrode Whitelocke; the letter is in the library of the

Marquess of Bath at Longleat House (Whitelocke Papers xii, fo. 41; see Miller, 1985, p. 180). On the same day Dr Vicqfort (probably the diplomat Abraham de Wicquefort, but possibly his brother Joachim) writes (in French) to Dr Fraser saying that Salmasius is preparing to answer JM's *Defensio* (*LR*, III, 173; the letter may be in the National Library of Ireland, which holds the Ormonde papers).

13   Mylius writes to JM, who replies that he had written to White-locke but had not been present at the previous day's Council meeting because of rain; the letter, now in the Staatsarchiv in Oldenburg, is in the hand of Edward Phillips. Late in the day JM sends another message to Mylius explaining that nothing had been done, because of the law term ending that day. JM did not know that Parliament had decided to consider the Oldenburg accord as the first item of business the following Tuesday morning (Miller, 1985, p. 185).

16   JM meets Mylius in the morning. He does not have business in Chancery that afternoon (*pace* Parker (1996) 1005, n. 234 and *LR* III, 178–9), but is probably occupied with the preparation of the Latin translation of the covering letter to the *Paper of Demands* that was shortly to be presented to the Dutch (Miller, 1992, 22).

17   Parliament accepts JM's translation of Letter of State: the Old-enburg Safeguard (W152, P35). JM signs three versions, two in Latin and one in English (Miller, 1992, 239–55). JM's transla-tion of Letter of State (the *recreditif* for Mylius) from Parliament to the Count of Oldenburg (W39, P34) is signed. On the same day Hartlib presents a copy of JM's *Defensio* (dated 17/27 February 1651/2) to Peter Pels, a Swedish diplomat; the volume is now in the Harvard College Library (14496.13.4.10F).

18   Mylius records in his diary for 20 February that two days earlier he had heard from an unnamed correspondent [John Dury] that Fleming and JM were regarded by some with suspicion because of their friendly attitude to Mylius. Later in the day JM sends his kinsman (presumably Edward or John Phillips) to say that there had been progress in Parliament, despite some opposition (Miller, 1985, p. 191). On the same day JM is attacked in Sir Robert Filmer's *Observations concern-ing the Original of Government*, upon…*Mr Milton Against Salmasius* (Thomason's date; his copy is BL E.655(1)) and

Commissioners investigate property of JM's brother Christopher (PRO SP 23/30, p. 434; cf p. 14).

20 Mylius visits Fleming before 6.00am and is officially notified of his success in Parliament; Fleming explains that Frost and JM would tie up the loose ends, and that the last of the documents had been sent to JM for translation into Latin (Miller, 1985, pp. 191–2).

21 Mylius tries unsuccessfully to visit JM, but JM is out. The reason for JM's absence may be his appearance at the *in camera* hearing (of which this was the last day) concerning the publication of the Racovian Catechism; the Catechism is said to have been licensed by JM, who testifies that he had indeed licensed it, and cites his *Areopagitica* in vindication of his decision to license the book. Mylius writes instead, asking to see the latest version of the documents. JM replies immediately upon his return, offering assurances that the final details will be sorted out by Monday (Miller, 1985, pp. 192–3).

23 Mylius writes farewell letter to JM. JM notifies Mylius, possibly by messenger, that the Safeguard will soon be ready.

24 JM meets Mylius, probably by chance, in St James's Park (Miller, 1985, p. 199). The Dutch-born diplomat Lieuwe van Aitzema (or Leo ab Aitzema; see *NNBW*), who had arrived in London on 20 February as representative of the Hanse cities, records in his Diary (in Dutch) that the printer of the Racovian Catechism had said that JM had licensed it, and that JM had confirmed the allegation and pointed to the principles articulated in his *Areopagitica* (Miller, 1990*d*, 281).

25 The Council orders that the Paper of Demands be translated into Latin (PRO SP 25/66, p. 378); on the division of labour between JM and his colleague Lewis Rosin, neither of whom is named in the order, see Miller, 1992 , pp. 21–30.

March

2 (Tuesday) JM attends farewell audience for Mylius, and interprets into Latin for Mylius's benefit.

3 The Council orders the translation into Latin of a Letter of State to Queen Christina of Sweden (PRO SP 25/66, p. 407); JM is not named, but the translation (see 11 March) is included among his published letters.

5 Mylius meets JM for the last time, and notes that JM 'is wholly deprived of his sight in his forty-second year'; the statement of the age of JM, who had turned 43 in December 1651, may be a

slip, but may reflect the time at which Mylius received his information. Mylius gives JM a cash gift equivalent to £25 (100 Reichstaler); (Miller, 1985, pp. 214–15).

8   JM is ordered to translate papers for the Dutch Ambassadors (PRO SP 25/66, pp. 424–5).

9   Council orders completion of the translation of the answer to the Dutch by the following Thursday afternoon, that is, 11 March (PRO SP 25/66, p. 428); JM is not named in the order.

11 JM's translation of Letter of State from Parliament to the Queen of Sweden (W19, P36) is signed; the letter conveys the condolences of the English government on the death of the Swedish agent Pieter Silfvercrona (Pieter Spiering), on whom see *SMK*. On the same day Council orders that (JM's) Latin translation of Dutch papers be given to the Dutch on 15 March (PRO SP 25/66, p. 428).

12 JM's translation of a Letter of State from Parliament to Hamburg is dated 12 March (W18, P37); *LR* III, 7 dates the letter 12 March 1651, but 1651/52 is intended.

15 JM's translation of Letter of State (the Paper of Demands) from Council of State is presented to the Dutch ambassadors (W43a, P39) together with JM's translation of another State Paper (W167E, P38), a letter listing counterdemands.

25 JM receives rents of £47.2s.7d from Wheatley.

29 A total eclipse of the sun in England (the only one in JM's lifetime), subsequently known as Mirk Monday, is widely discussed and is mentioned in many sermons the following Sunday.

31 The English text of a Letter of State (W23, P40) to Cardenas, the Spanish ambassador, is approved by the Council of State, and JM is ordered to 'translate the said paper out of English into Latin to be sent along as a copy' (PRO SP 25/66, p. 523). The letter asks for clarification of Cardenas's earlier proposals.

April

6   (Tuesday) JM is ordered to translate letters to Hanse towns and Hamburg (PRO SP 25/66, p. 549; see 13 April).

8   JM's translation of Letter of State from the Council of State to the Hanse cities survives in draft form; the English text survives in manuscript (Bodleian, Nalson MS XVIII 159, fols.

423–4) and the Dutch text in Aitzema's *Saken van Staet en Oorlog* (1669), III, 738–9. The letter is not in W or P, but is printed in Miller (1990*d*), 285–6.

12 JM is sometimes said to have translated a paper from the Dutch Ambassadors to the Council of State (W167F, P44), but it is a Dutch paper, not JM's work.

13 JM's translation of Letters of State from Parliament to the King of Denmark (W24, P41), to the Hanse Towns (W25, P43) and to Hamburg (W26, P42) are approved by Parliament (see Miller, 1990*d*).

15 JM is ordered to translate paper to Dutch Ambassadors into Latin (PRO SP 25/66, p. 595); JM translates the letter overnight.

16 JM's translation of the Letter of State to the Dutch Ambassadors is signed; Miller has recovered the English original and JM's translation into Latin (Miller, 1992, 37–9, 180–84).

May

JM composes Sonnet 16 ('To the Lord General Cromwell'). In the Trinity manuscript the poem is dated 'May 1652'. John Lilburne praises JM's *Defensio* in *As You Were* pp. 15–16.

2 (Sunday) JM's daughter Deborah is born; her birth is recorded in JM's family Bible (BL Add MS 32,310) and confirmed in Birch's transcript of JM's wife Mary's (lost) Bible (BL Add MS 4244, fol. 52^v), but the place of birth is not known.

3 Johann Georg, Elector of Saxony, orders the Council of Leipzig to confiscate copies of JM's *Defensio prima*, printed by Hans Bauer and published by Tobias Riese. The letters in this episode (see 22 May, 12 October, 1, 15 and 28 November, 14 and 16 December), all in scribal hands, are in the Leipzig Stadtarchiv (Bücherzensurakten I (1600–1690) Tit. XLVI.152). Leipzig was Protestant, so the dates are Julian; see Berghaus (1983).

5? JM's wife Mary dies, leaving JM, who is by now totally blind, with four young children; her death is recorded in JM's family Bible (BL Add MS 32,310), but the place of death and burial is not known.

8? JM's translation of Letter of State from Parliament to the Duke of Savoy (W138, P45) is signed; the letter is a protest against the seizure of the *Welcome*, an 18-gun warship en route from Lisbon to Genoa; the protest seems to have been efficacious, because the ship was brought ashore in Woolwich in November. The letter must have been written after 16 March 1652 (when the Navy Commissioners were informed of the seizure) and before 22 November, when the Commissioners were informed that the ship was to be brought ashore in Woolwich. The letter is assigned to this date by Max Patrick, the editor of the 'Yale Prose' volume, without any substantiating evidence; I do not know of any document that confirms the date.

17   JM receives interest (£16) on excise bonds.
19   Battle of the Downs: the English fleet under Robert Blake clashes with a Dutch fleet under Marteen van Trump off the coast of Kent.
22   A draft reply from the Council of Leipzig to the Elector denies that Bauer and Riese have printed and published JM's *Defensio* (Leipzig, Stadtarchiv, Bücherzensurakten I (1600–1690), Tit XLVI.152).
24   The Dane Wilhelmus Worm sees the republican inscription on the niche in the Old Exchange from which the statue of Charles I had been taken, and attributes it to JM (Royal Library, Copenhagen MS Rostgaard 39, 4to).

June
Some time during this month JM replies from London to a letter from Leonard Philaras, an Athenian who is living in Paris as an agent of Parma. JM's other private letters in this period are written from Westminster, so the London address may be indicative of the domestic disruption consequent upon the death of his wife; JM may have been living temporarily with a friend or relative in London.

5   (Saturday) John Dury tells Hartlib in a letter from Stockholm that Salmasius 'is making ready an answer to Mr Milton; I pray salute Mr Milton from me and let him know this' (Hartlib 4/2/24a-25b).
7   Adrian Pauw, the final ambassador sent by Holland before the outbreak of war, arrives in England and stays till 30 June. Two years later JM pays tribute to Pauw in *Defensio Secunda*, and recalls that although they were unable to meet, Pauw sent 'many messages' to JM expressing greetings and good will.
16(?)   According to the entry in JM's family Bible, his son John died 'about six weeks after his mother' (BL Add MS 32, 310);

the place of death and burial is not known. Edward Phillips later attributed the child's death to 'the ill usage or bad constitution of an ill-chosen nurse' (Darbishire, p. 71).

July
In the second half of this year Edward Benlowes publishes *Theophilia*, which imitates various of JM's poems, including 'On Time', 'Nativity Ode', 'Il Penseroso', 'Lycidas' and 'Comus'; the date is an inference from Davenant's commendatory poem, which is dated 13 May 1652.

3 (Saturday) JM composes Sonnet 17 ('Vane, young in years') and sends it to Sir Henry Vane (Sikes, pp. 93–4).

8 Letter of State to Danish envoys, the Latin translation of which is probably by JM. See Miller, 1992, pp. 68–9 and 270–72.

9 Parliament publishes the English version of the 'Declaration against the Dutch' (not JM's work), which is in effect a declaration of war; the First Anglo-Dutch War was to continue until 5 April 1654. On the same day (9/19) Vossius mentions JM's blindness in a letter written to Heinsius from Amsterdam (Burmann, III, 639).

11 A copy of the 1650 edition of *Eikonoklastes*, now in Canterbury Cathedral (Elham 732), is inscribed with the words 'the man that wrot this booke is now growne blind and is led up and downe'.

13 Thurloe is ordered to 'appoint fit persons to translate the Parliament's *Declaration* into Latin, French and Dutch' (PRO SP 25/30, p. 29); on JM's role in the translation see Miller (1992), pp. 56–67.

19 Aitzema confirms in his unpublished journal that the *Declaration* justifying the English position on the outbreak of war was translated into Latin by JM (Miller, 1992, p. 45).

20 Dugard is ordered to consult JM about the printing of the French and Latin texts of the *Declaration* (PRO SP 25/30, p. 54). On the same day the Council of State sends an order concerning Walton's Polyglot to JM (PRO SP 25/30, p. 54). Brian Walton, who had known JM since 1624 (he had served as curate of All Hallows from 1624 to 1628), had petitioned the Council of State for assistance in the preparation and publication of the Polyglot Bible (which was eventually printed in six volumes from 1654 to 1657). On 11 July the Council replied to Walton suggesting that he refer the proposal to Parliament. The order of 20 July communicating the decision of 11 July to

JM implies that it was JM who had brought Walton's petition to the Council. See 9 July 1653.

28 The *Scriptum Parlamenti*, JM's Latin translation of the 'Declaration against the Dutch', was probably published on this date, though Thomason's copy (BL E.673 (8)) is dated 'August'. 28 July is the date on the title-pages of the German, Danish and one of the Dutch editions. A copy of the *Declaration* was enclosed with the Letter of State to the Grand Duke of Tuscany on 29 July, and it seems likely that it was the Latin version that was sent; the Italian translation, if the title-page is to be believed, was published in Florence after being officially licensed, and so must have appeared later in the year.

29 JM's translation of Letter of State from the Council of State to Ferdinand II, Grand Duke of Tuscany (W27, P46) is signed and sealed; the letter thanks the Duke for the protection of English ships (against the predations of the Dutch) in his territorial waters.

30 Letter from Dury to an unknown correspondent ('Dear F') copied in Hartlib's hand on the need to acquaint 'Mr Milton and the Lord President himself' (John Bradshaw, who was so styled despite the condemnation of the term by Parliament on 15 February 1649) with matters related to the protection of the plantations (Hartlib 1/2/9a-10b). Proposals for the administration of Virginia had been the subject of earlier letters from Benjamin Worsley to Hartlib on 3/13 August 1649 (Hartlib 33/2/1A) and from Worsley to Dury on 17/27 August 1649 (Hartlib 33/2/3A-4B).

August

Regii Sanguinis Clamor ('A Cry to Heaven of the King's Blood against the English Parricides') is published anonymously, probably late in the month, and certainly after the outbreak of war with the Dutch, to which the printer Adriaan Vlacq (on whom see Miller, 1979*b* and 1989*c*) alludes in his preface, and before it is mentioned in a letter from Leiden dated 17/27 September 1652. The *Clamor* contains a vitriolic personal attack on JM in its opening pages, and concludes with a 245-line poem excoriating JM. It is not known when the book was first read to JM, but Vlacq later said (in his preface to JM's *Defensio Secunda*) that he had sent weekly consignments of proof sheets to Hartlib in London, and suggested that

Hartlib persuade JM to draft a reply, which Vlacq would be pleased to publish. JM later claimed (in *Pro Se Defensio*) that an unbound copy was handed to him during a meeting of the Council of State, that shortly thereafter the Council's Committee of Examinations sent another copy to him, and that he had been told that the government expected him to reply. JM explains that his reply was delayed by poor health, grief over two deaths in his family and total blindness. There is no trace of the order in the fragmentary order books of the period. In the same month Payne Fisher (poet laureate to Cromwell) alludes to JM in the dedication of *Irenodia gratulatoria* (Fortescue's dating of Thomason's copy, BL E.796(30)).

10 (Tuesday) The Council of State orders that a Letter of State to Cardenas, the Spanish ambassador, be translated into Latin (PRO, SP 25/31, p. 42); JM is not named in the order, but the letter appears in the printed texts of his letters; the letter is a reply to Cardenas's paper of 27 May.

12 Parliament passes Act of Settlement for Ireland.

22/1 September Heinsius repudiates JM in a letter to Vossius (Amsterdam Universiteits-Bibliotheek, MS III.E.9.111). On the same day Vossius writes to Heinsius reaffirming that JM is blind and passing on the rumour that he is dead (Burmann, III, 642–3).

23 Edward Hyde ridicules JM's *Defensio*, hoping that it will be burnt in Germany (Bodleian Clarendon MS 43, fol. 259).

September

At about this time Samuel Bochart writes to Salmasius urging him to reply to JM's *Defensio* (*LR*, III, 249–51).

12/22 (Sunday) Heinsius writes to Vossius from Florence to say that in his view JM's blindness is a judgement from God (Amsterdam Universiteits-Bibliotheek, III.E.9.114).

13 JM's translations of two Letters of State from Council of State to the Danish ambassadors (W29, P50; W30, P51) are signed. None of the early texts is dated; see Fallon (1993), p. 104, n. 74). On the same day James Schaller presents a dissertation on JM and the *Defensio prima* in Strasbourg; Strasbourg was Protestant, so the date is Julian. The thesis was published (together with the response of Erhard Kieffer) before the end of the year as *Dissertationis ad quaedam loca Miltoni*, and

subsequently reprinted. The month is mentioned on the title-page, and the day is added in a copy in the Landesbibliothek in Darmstadt. It is possible that the presentation was delayed till 13 November (*LR*, III, 276).

16 JM's translation of a Letter of State from Council of State to the Duke of Tuscany (W31, P49) is signed; the Skinner manuscript misdates the text (2 September).

17/27 A letter of this date addressed to a friend of JM records gossip about Morus's private life; the letter is subsequently read to JM, who cites it in *Pro Se Defensio*.

28 Battle of Kentish Knock begins.

29 JM receives rents of £48.6s. from Wheatley.

October

4 (Monday) Caspar Ziegler attacks JM as a regicide in a dissertation (*Circa Regicidium Anglorum Exercitationes*) presented in the 'Museum' (a university building) in Leipzig. Saxony was Protestant, so the date is Julian. The dissertation was printed before the end of the year and subsequently reprinted.

7 JM is ordered to translate a letter from the King of Portugal into English and bring his translation to the Council of State the next afternoon (PRO SP 25/34, p. 2); the letter is lost.

8 English defeat Dutch at Battle of Kentish Knock.

12/22 Heinsius tells Vossius that he still awaits Salmasius's reply to JM (Amsterdam Universiteits-Bibliotheek, MS III.E.9.120). On the same day Tobias Riese petitions the Elector of Saxony about the publication of JM's *Defensio*; the petition is lost, but see 1 November 1652.

19 Letter of State to Danish Envoys; the Latin translation is probably the work of JM; see Miller (1992), pp. 69–70, 273–7.

20 Commissioners act on Anne Powell's petition for relief (PRO SP 23/110, pp. 524–5).

21/31 Sir Edward Nicholas writes to Sir Edward Hyde about 'that arch-traytor and declared enemy to monarchy Milton' (transcribed by Birch in BL Add MS 4180, fol. 78).

November

1 (Friday) JM's views on divorce, especially the arguments of *Doctrine and Discipline of Divorce*, are attacked by Henry Hammond in *A Letter of Resolution* (Thomason's date, despite

'1653' on the title-page; his copy is BL E.1326). On the same day the Elector of Saxony replies to Tobias Riese's petition of 12 October, reducing his fine for having published JM's *Defensio*.

2/12   Heinsius discusses Salmasius and JM in a letter to Vossius (Amsterdam Universiteits-Bibliotheek, MS III.E.9.123).

4   *Mercurius Politicus* No 126 prints a report (dated 22 October/1 November) of a Dutch translation of the *Clamor* by [Jacobus?] Stermont; an anonymous Dutch translation appeared in 1653. On the same day Sir Edward Nichols reports in a letter to Edward Hyde and 'Mr Smith' (Lord Hatton) that Queen Christina of Sweden is increasingly sympathetic to JM and the Commonwealth government (Birch's transcriptions are BL Add MS 41870, fols. 78–9).

9   JM's translation of Letter of State from Parliament to the King of Denmark (W35, P52) is signed; the letter introduces Richard Bradshaw as a mediator in a dispute over the seizure of ships. On the same day (9/19) Gronovius assures Heinsius that the *Clamor* is mild by comparison to Salmasius's forthcoming reply to JM (Burmann, III, 303–4). On the same day (9/19 November) Gronovius writes to Heinsius, describing the *Clamor* as 'a cold bath for Milton' (Burmann, III, 303–4).

11   JM's translations of Letters of State from Council of State to Cardenas, the Spanish ambassador, are signed (W32, P54; W33, P53).

15   Tobias Riese submits a second petition to the Elector requesting the waiving of his reduced fine on the grounds that others had sold JM's *Defensio* without penalty.

20 (?)   John Dury's French translation of JM's *Eikonoklastes* is published (*Nouvelles Ordinaires de Londres*, No. 125, 18/28 November–25 November/5 December).

23   JM's translation of a Letter of State from the Council of State to the Duke of Tuscany (W34, P55) is approved and sent to the Speaker for signature.

25   JM receives interest (£16) on excise bond. On or about the same day the publication of John Dury's translation of JM's *Eikonoklastes* into French is noted in *Nouvelles Ordinaires de Londres* No 125 (18/28 November–25 November/5 December).

28   The Elector of Saxony writes to the Council of Leipzig denying Riese's petition of 15 November.

30/10 December   The Dutch under Van Tromp defeat the English off Dungeness.

December

1 (Wednesday) JM is reappointed as Secretary (PRO SP 25/36 p. 1 and 25/68 p. 1).

7/17 Heinsius tells Vossius that he is disappointed by Salmasius's failure to answer JM's *Defensio* (Burmann, III, 656).

9 JM's forty-fourth birthday. On the same day William Rowland publishes *Judicial Astrology, Judicially Condemned* (Thomason's date; his copy is BL E.1239(1)), which alludes to 'Mr John Milton's Figure-Caster' on the title-page and prints it on pp. 157–217, apparently in the mistaken belief that this John Milton is the poet.

12 Wilhelmus a Kospoth delivers a Latin oration that refers to JM; the *Oratio* was published in Wittenburg in 1653 (see Miller, 1978).

13 JM writes to his former pupil Richard Heath (*EF* No. 13), on whom see Woolrych (1974).

14 Tobias Riese petitions the Council of Leipzig, paying part of his fine and requesting that the remainder be waived.

16 Council of Leipzig writes to the Elector in response to his letter of 28 November; the letter indicates that Riese had admitted publication of *Defensio prima*.

28/7 January Heinsius tells Gronovius that he awaits Salmasius's reply to JM's *Defensio* (Burmann, III, 307).

29 Anne Powell again petitions for aid (PRO SP 23/110 p. 446).

31/10 January Rhodius writes to Heinsius from Padua reporting a (false) rumour about the death of Salmasius (Burmann, V, 461).

1653

Martin Zeiller discusses JM (and John Phillips) in *Ein hundert dialogi*; see the preface and Dialogues 77, 81, 83–8. Jean Nicholas de Parival deplores the lies (*calomnies*) of JM's *Defensio* in *Abrégé de l'Histoire de ce Siècle de Fer* (Leiden); the book was reprinted at least ten times during JM's lifetime (see Shawcross, 1984). In an exchange of letters between Roger Williams and Anne Sadleir (Cyriack Skinner's aunt), Williams recommends JM's *Eikonoklastes* to Mrs Sadleir. Mrs Sadleir refuses to read the book on the grounds that JM was a divorcer who 'had at that time two or three wives living', that God had struck him blind for writing that 'most accursed libel' (presumably the *Defensio*), which he could not have written without 'the help of one Andrew Marvell' (Trinity College Cambridge MS R.5.5). In this year John Rowland again attacks JM in his *Polemica*, a supplement to his earlier *Apologia* (see 1651). It was probably in this year that JM wrote the satirical epigram *Gaudete scombri* ('Mackerels rejoice'), later included in the *Defensio Secunda*.

January

3 (Monday) JM writes to Andrew Sandelands in Edinburgh; JM's letter is lost but Sandelands' reply (see 15 January) says 'I receaved yors dated the 3d of January'. The exchange of letters was relatively quick: a postal line between Edinburgh and London had been established on 31 July 1635, and the postage of a single letter had been fixed at 8d.

6 Commissioners for Composition report on Anne Powell's petition for relief (PRO SP 23/17, p. 575).

7 Commissioners summarise Anne Powell's case, mentioning JM's action with respect to Richard Powell's estate (PRO SP 23/32 fol. 155).

8 JM's translation of a Letter of State from Parliament to Francisco Molin, Doge of Venice (W36, P58) is signed and sealed; the letter acknowledges the credential letter for Lorenzo Paluzzi, who had been sent from the Venetian embassy in Paris to procure ships and levy soldiers to fight the Turks. On the same day (8/18) Hyde writes to Nicholas about Joseph Jane (see 1651) and JM (Bodleian Clarendon MS 45, fol. 18ᵛ). In the letter, which is partly in a numerical code that has later been deciphered, Hyde professes ignorance of a French translation of 'Miltons booke' (the *Defensio*).

14 JM's translation of a Letter of State from Parliament to Ferdinand II, Grand Duke of Tuscany (W37, P60) is approved by Parliament, but only after some members of the House had withdrawn to ensure that changes in the English text were effected in the Latin version (*Journal of the House of Commons* VII, 246); presumably JM was waiting outside the door of the Chamber to deal with such a contingency (cf 2 April 1650). On the same day the Council of State orders that admonitory letters be sent to ambassadors who had been allowing English citizens to attend mass in their houses (PRO SP 25/68, p. 251). JM was responsible for the Latin translation of the letter to

Cardenas, the Spanish Ambassador (W43, P59), and presumably for others, which must have been virtually identical.

15 Andrew Sandelands writes from Edinburgh to JM 'at his house in Petite-ffrance' (PRO SP 18/23/6); the letter is dated 15 January 1652, and in Scotland the New Year was deemed to begin on 1 January, but internal references make it clear that 1653 is intended. Sandelands's dating is probably a slip, but possibly a polite concession to English usage. Sandelands had overlapped with JM at Cambridge: he had been a Fellow of Christ's from 1624 to 1630, and had been succeeded by Edward King, JM's 'Lycidas'. The letter is principally concerned with a proposal to use Scottish wood for English ships, but also contains a request for the skull of the Marquis of Montrose, which had for the previous three years been mounted on a spike over Edinburgh prison. JM seems not to have acted on this request, or was unable to oblige; the skull remained in place.

17/27 The Swiss minister Jean Baptiste Stouppe writes (in French) from London to a correspondent in Zürich to say that the *Clamor* had been written by Alexander Morus, who is said to 'tear Milton apart' (*Il déchire Milton*). Stouppe had worked for Cromwell, and was later to write about the Piedmont massacre; he apparently knew JM, who was to send money by Stouppe (see JM's letter of 24 March 1657 to Bigot). The letter is in the Zürich Staatsarchiv (Acta Anglicana EII 457g, p. 171).

21/31 Gronovius attributes the *Clamor* to Morus in a letter to Heinsius (Burmann, III, 311). On the same day Vossius writes to Heinsius with news of Salmasius's progress in his reply to JM (Burmann, III, 662); the letter records allegations about JM having sold his buttocks to Italians that did not survive into the published version.

February

2 (Wednesday) The English text of a Letter of State from the Council of State to the Doge of Venice (W22, P61) is approved by the Council of State (SP 25/68, p. 327) and ordered to be translated and sent; JM subsequently undertakes the Latin translation.

4/14 Vossius writes to Heinsius about the Salmasius–Morus feud (Burmann, III, 664–5).

10 'A Masque of the Gentlemen of Gray's Inn and the Inner Temple', said to have been written (apparently in error) by Francis Beaumont, imitates JM's *Comus* (Thomason's date; his copy of the first issue of *Poems, by Francis Beaumont* is BL E. 1236 (3)).

13 Weckherlin dies, leaving a vacancy in the Secretariat.

18/28 Vossius writes to Heinsius reporting that Queen Christina has turned against Salmasius, condemning him as a fool (Burmann, III, 666); on the same day Allatius writes to Heinsius from Rome reporting that Salmasius seems to be losing his mind (Burmann, III, 442). On the same day the English defeat the Dutch off Portland.

19/1 March   Heinsius writes to Vossius from Venice in defence of JM's morals (Burmann, III, 669–70).

21 JM writes letter of recommendation for Andrew Marvell to John Bradshaw (PRO SP 18/33, p. 75; the letter is in the hand of an amanuensis) and admits that he is no longer fit to attend conferences with ambassadors. Marvell was interviewed the following day, but the Council chose to appoint Philip Meadows, who had recently graduated from Cambridge. Meadows may be the subject of an undated entry in *Ephemerides* (written between 1 January and 1 March) in which Hartlib says 'One is adjoined to Mr Milton a Fellow of a college a personable man and versed in all learning especially Civil Law and Histories. His name is [blank].' (Hartlib 28/2/53a).

March
In an undated entry in *Ephemerides* written between 2 March and May Hartlib refers to 'Meddus a universal philologus, historian, civilian and one that translated the army's declaration, a corrival to Mr Milton' (Hartlib 28/2/62a); both Meddus and the army declaration are unidentified, but Meddus could be Philip Meadows, who is also described as historian and 'civilian' (that is, an authority on civil law), or Dr Meddus, the Oxford theologian.

9 (Wednesday) JM's brother Christopher acts as counsel in a sequestration case (PRO SP 23/69, p. 806).

11/21 Heinsius writes to Gronovius from Venice about the Morus–Salmasius lawsuit (Burmann, III, 313).

25 JM receives rents from Wheatley (£47.15s.4d).

29 Andrew Sandelands writes another letter to JM (PRO SP 18/34/105); the letter begs for relief.

April

1 (Friday) Council of State orders waiving of custom fee on export of French translation of *Eikonoklastes* (PRO SP 25/41, p. 48).

20 Cromwell expels the Long Parliament for attempting to pass the Perpetuation Bill.

29 Cromwell establishes a Council of ten members and a nominated Parliament of 140 members, the so-called 'Barebones' Parliament.

May

16 (Monday) *A Letter written to a Gentleman* is wrongly attributed to JM by Thomason (BL E.697 (2)); the author was John Hall, but it seems odd that Thomason, who knew JM well, would write 'by Mr John Milton' on the title-page.

26 Commissioners mention JM in the reconsideration of Anne Powell's petition (PRO SP 23/110, pp. 509–10).

June

3/13 (Friday) Letter in French from an unidentified correspondent in The Hague to John Thurloe mentions the publication in Strasbourg of a 'little book in Latin' against JM and for Salmasius (Bodleian MS Rawlinson A.3.P. p. 160).

7 Commissioners mention JM in their summary of Anne Powell's petition (PRO SP 23/25, p. 89). On the same day Alexander Ross seems to allude to JM as a divorcer in *Pansebia*, pp. 400, 413 (Thomason's date; his copy is BL E.1513).

10/20 Letter in French from an unidentified correspondent in The Hague, probably addressed to Thurloe, mentions JM as a blind man who has a reputation as a good writer (Bodleian MS Rawlinson A.3.P. p. 220).

11 JM receives six months' interest on bond of 13 May 1651 (£16).

July

4 (Monday) 'Barebones' Parliament meets.

6/16 JM's *Defensio prima* is mentioned in the record of discussion and voting of Brunswick-Wolfenbüttel at Diet of Ratisbon/ Regensburg (Munich, Bayerisches Hauptstaatsarchiv, Bestand Kurbayern, Lit. 1636).

9 Council of State records (PRO SP 25/70, p. 32) a letter (now lost) from JM to Sir Gilbert Pickering; the letter seems to have lent support to the request of Brian Walton and Bruno Reeves

(a former chaplain of Charles I) that they be allowed to import paper for the Polyglot Bible free of custom and excise duties. On 15 July Council granted the permit to import 7,000 reams of paper.

13 Letter of State to the Dutch envoys; the Latin translation is probably the work of JM. See Miller (1992), 73, pp. 278–88.

15 Anne Powell's petition is acted on favourably by the Commissioners, who reduce Pye's fine and order a rebate (PRO SP 23/110, pp. 529–31).

21/31 Fronde surrenders in Bordeaux.

26 JM's translation of Letter of State from Council of State to the Duke of Holstein (W38, P62) is signed and sealed. The letter affirms the English desire for good relations in the context of the Anglo-Dutch War.

31 Battle of the Texel; the English under Monck defeat the Dutch under Van Tromp, who is killed in action.

August

1 (Monday) Letter of State to the Dutch envoys; the Latin translation is probably the work of JM. See Miller (1992), pp. 73, 289–93.

8 JM translates Psalm 2 into English; Psalm 1 is simply dated '1653', but is presumably translated in the same week as the others.

9 JM translates Psalm 3 into English.

10 JM translates Psalm 4 into English.

12 JM translates Psalm 5 into English.

13 JM translates Psalm 6 into English.

14 JM translates Psalms 7 and 8 into English.

24/3 September Salmasius dies. On the same day the Synod of Utrecht considers JM's charges against Morus, and clears him on 28 August/6 September (*LR* V, 438–40; for a chronology of Morus's legal battles see Sellin, 1996).

September

1 (Thursday) John Reading submits a report on Anne Powell's petition (PRO SP 23/194, pp. 389–90).

6/16 Heinsius notes death of Salmasius in letter to Gronovius (Burmann, III, 323–4).

9/19 Edward Hyde asks Nicholas to search for Salmasius's reply to JM (Bodleian Clarendon MS 46, fol. 262).

24   Ole Worm mentions the death of Salmasius in a letter to his
     son Wilhelm (*LR* V, 440).
26   Parliament passes 'Act of Satisfaction' for distribution of
     sequestrated property in Ireland.
29   JM receives rents from Wheatley (£47.14s.6d).

October
17   (Monday) Philip Meadows, who is 'now employed by the
     Council in Latin translations' is ordered 'to assist Mr
     Thurloe in the despatch of Foreign Affairs' (SP 25/71
     p. 118); Meadows was formally responsible to Thurloe, but
     it is likely that he was assuming some of JM's responsibil-
     ities.
26   Commissioners release Anne Powell's properties from seques-
     tration, mentioning JM (PRO SP 23/72, pp. 1–2).

November
 3   (Thursday) JM is reappointed Secretary at the same salary
     (PRO SP 25/72 pp. 1–2).
24   Richard Powell (JM's brother-in-law) called to the bar; earlier
     in the month he had paid his £4 subscription to the Inner
     Temple (Inderwick, II, 307–8).
28   JM's translation of Letter of State from Parliament to the Prot-
     estant Swiss Cantons (W40, P63) is signed and sealed, but
     Stockmar, the Swiss Agent, did not receive a passport to
     leave England until 16 January 1654.

December
 1   (Thursday) Mylius writes to Friedrich Matthias Wolzogen,
     who was shortly to travel to England to renew the Oldenburg
     Safeguard, explaining that Frost is dead and JM blind (Miller,
     1985, p. 281). In preparation for the mission a set of briefing
     notes is prepared; JM is mentioned seven times in this *Memor-
     iale* (Miller, 1985, pp. 353–4, n. 258). JM is also listed among
     those who were to receive letters of introduction to the diplo-
     mats (Miller, 1985, p. 282).
 9   JM's forty-fifth birthday.
12   Barebones Parliament is dissolved. MPs resign their powers to
     Cromwell.
13   Whitelocke notes in his Swedish journal that the Consul of
     Köping (a town 60 miles west of Stockholm), 'half drunke for

sorrow', had told him in Latin that he himself 'had Miltons booke [the *Defensio*] att home & loved the Parliam[ent]' (Longleat MS 124a, fol. 41^r). Sweden had reverted to the Julian calendar, so Whitelocke's dates are O.S.

16   Cromwell is installed as Lord Protector. Under the Protectorate responsibility for foreign affairs was to pass from the Council of State to Cromwell and his Secretary of State, John Thurloe. JM ceases to appear in the Council's Order Books (except for his salary and his attendance at Cromwell's funeral). He effectively ceases to work for the Council of State and is instead employed by the Secretary of State (see Fallon, 1993, pp. 123–39).

18   JM's books are ordered to be confiscated in Regensburg (anonymous letter of intelligence, Bodleian Rawlinson MS A.9, p. [73]; see Miller, 1985, pp. 277–80).

28   JM receives interest on bond (£16).

1654

JM's *An Apology* is reissued. Sir Henry Wotton's letter of 13 April 1638 is reprinted in *Reliquiae Wottonianae*; in 1651 the address was 'To Master ————', but JM's name is given in this reprint. In Helmstadt the dissertation of N. Martini is presented; the respondent is Herman Conring. The dissertation and response were printed as *Exercitatio historico politica de republica antiqua* in 1654; in that edition Conring refers in 'Corollarium IV' to 'Parricidium Anglicanum'; in the 1730 edition of Conring's *Opera* this phrase is glossed with reference to JM and Salmasius.

February

3   (Friday) Thurloe nominates JM for reappointment (PRO SP 25/75, p. 93; 25/48, p. 50; 25/73, p. [162]; warrant for six months' salary is issued (15/10½d *per diem*; £144.9s.3d for the half-year from 4 July 1653 to 1 January 1654 (PRO SP 25/105, p. 7). On the same day JM's brother Christopher sells land in London to William Hobson (PRO CP 25/2); the document is dated 'in the morrow of the Purification of the Blessed Mary'.

13   Bulstrode Whitelocke records in his Swedish journal that Queen Christina *'a parlé de tous les autheurs qui ont escrit en*

Italien, en Latin, en françois et autres langages et par dessus tous a loüé Petronius. Je luy ai demandé qu'elle pensait de Milton. Elle dit qu'il a fort bien escrit et en bon langage' ('spoke of all the authors who have written in Italian, Latin, French and other languages, and praised Petronius above all. I asked her what she thought of Milton. She said that he wrote very well and with a good style') (Longleat MS 124a, fol. 110ʳ).

22   JM answers Elizabeth Ashworth's suit, lodged earlier in the month, concerning Richard Powell's property (PRO C10/44/2). On the same day Whitelocke records that various gentlemen *'ont disné avec moy. Nous avons eu beaucoup de discours sur le livres de Mr Selden et du Seigneur de St Alban, Milton et d'autres autheurs Anglais les quels ils ont grandem[ent] loüé'* ('dined with me. We had much conversation about the books of Mr [John] Selden and Viscount St Albans [Francis Bacon], Milton and other English authors whom they greatly praised') (Longleat MS 124a fol. 115r).

April
 5   (Wednesday) Treaty of Westminster concludes First Anglo-Dutch War.
11   Andrew Sandelands explains in a letter to Thurloe that he has employed JM's nephew John Phillips (Bodleian MS Rawlinson A.13 p. 119).
12   Union of Ireland and Scotland with England.
13/23 John Nicholas (son of Sir John) writes from The Hague to pass to William Edgeman (Hyde's secretary) an enquiry from Joseph Jane about French translations of JM's *Eikonoklastes* and his own *Eikon Aklastos* (Bodleian MS Clarendon 48, fols. 135–135ᵛ).
14/24 John Dury informs Hartlib in a letter from The Hague that JM has unjustly accused Alexander Morus (Hartlib 4/3/1A-1B); on the accusations against Morus see Sellin 1994, 1995, 1996.
19/29 Dury again assures Hartlib (in a letter from Amsterdam) that JM is wrong about Morus (Hartlib 4/3/2A-2B).
22/2 May   JM's letter to Philaras is said in a letter to John Thurloe from René Augier's secretary to have been seized (Bodleian MS Rawlinson A.13 p. 301). Augier had been Parliament's Agent in Paris from 1644 to 1650, and since then had been employed as a diplomat by the Council of State. JM had met Philaras through Augier. The letter is misdated 2 May/23 April.

May

4   (Thursday) Commissioners reduce Pye's fine to £384.8s.2s and order a rebate of £192.4s.1d to be paid to Anne Powell PRO SP 23/23, p. 1604ᵛ).

9/19   John Bramhall, in a letter to his son written from Antwerp, attacks JM for attributing authorship of Rowland's *Apologia* to him; he attributes 'that lying abusive book' (presumably the John Phillips *Responsio*) to 'Milton himself, one who was some-time Bishopp Chappell's pupil in Christ Church [sic] in Cambridge, but turned away by him, as he well deserved to have been both out of the University and out of the society of men. If Salmasius his friends knew as much of him as I, they would make him go near to hang himself. But I desire you not to wound the nation through his sides, yet I have written to him long since about it roundly. It seems he desires not to touch upon that subject' (*LR* III, 374–5); the letter survives only in printed form: HMC Vol. 78, *Report on the Hastings Manuscripts*, Vol 4, does not contain an account of the letter in the calendar of Bramhall's correspondence (pp. 55–136), so the letter must have been removed before the Hastings manuscripts were acquired by the Huntington Library. Similarly, Bramhall's letter to JM does not survive. The nature of the sinister undisclosed knowledge of JM is unknown, but the source was presumably Chappell; they must have known each other in Ireland in the 1630s.

21   John Durel writes to William Edgeman saying that he has abandoned his plan to translate Jane's *Eikon Aklastos* and instead proposes to write his own answer to JM's *Eikonoklastes*; the letter is in the Pierpont Morgan Library. Neither translation nor answer was ever published.

30   *Defensio Secunda* is published (Thomason's date; his copy is BL E 1487 (3)). JM sends three copies to Andrew Marvell at Eton College: one for himself, one for John Oxenbridge (a recently-elected Fellow of Eton, and the elder brother of Daniel, who had given a book to JM on 19 June 1643), and one for John Bradshaw; all three copies are now lost, as is JM's covering letter to Bradshaw.

June

2   (Friday) Andrew Marvell writes to JM describing his presentation of the letter from JM and the copy of *Defensio Secunda* to John Bradshaw. The letter survives in an

eighteenth-century transcription by Josiah Owen (BL Add MS 4292, fol. 264).

5   J[ohn?] P[rice?] alludes to *Tenure* in *Tyrants and Protectors*, p. 8 (Thomason's date; his copy is BL E. 738(18)).

6   Queen Christina of Sweden abdicates and subsequently converts to Roman Catholicism.

8   The publication of JM's *Defensio Secunda* is mentioned in *Mercurius Politicus* No. 208.

9   JM receives interest on bond (£16).

11   JM presents a copy of *Defensio Secunda* to the Bodleian. The volume is now missing, but Wood records that it was 'given to the lib. by the author XI June 1654' (Wood MS F.47, fol. 626; von Maltzahn (1994), 59).

16   JM sues Lady Elizabeth Cope and her son Sir Anthony Cope for failure to repay loan (PRO C8/120/72 and C7/452/60).

22   Court of Chancery writ issued to the Copes ordering them to answer JM's suit of 16 June (PRO C8/120/72).

23/3 July   The Dutch ambassador, Willem Nieupoort, writes (in French) from Westminster to Alexander Morus in Amsterdam to describe his attempts to persuade JM not to publish *Defensio Secunda*. Nieupoort had asked Thurloe to intervene with Cromwell, and had arranged for two (unidentified) friends who knew JM to visit him. JM would not be dissuaded from his view that Morus was the author of the *Clamor*, but undertook to say nothing prejudicial to the United Provinces. In Nieupoort's version of events, the English government was so preoccupied with the discovery on 20 May of the Gerard-Vowel plot to assassinate Cromwell that they did not attend to Nieupoort's appeal, and so JM's book had been published (*LR* III, 399–402). JM is later to quote from the letter and respond to it in *Pro Se Defensio*.

29   JM's translations of Letters of State from Cromwell to the Count of Oldenburg (W44, P64, W45, P65) are signed; the first letter acknowledges the Count's congratulations on Cromwell's assumption of the Protectorship, and the second welcomes the Count's son and acknowledges the gift of eight horses. See Miller, 1985, pp. 281–7.

July

1/11   (Saturday) The governors and rectors of Amsterdam affirm that Morus is innocent of all the allegations made about him by JM (*LR* III, 405–7); see Sellin 1994, 1995, 1996.

3/13 An anonymous letter from The Hague, probably addressed to Thurloe, explains that copies of the *Defensio* have reached The Hague, and that Vlacq is reprinting it (Bodleian MS Rawlinson A.15, pp. 462–4). The evidence that letters in this series are dated O.S. (despite the fact that The Hague changed to N.S. in 1582) is contained in the letter of 3 November 1654, in which a split date can be seen on the side of the letter that has virtually disappeared into the binding of the volume.

6 JM writes in Latin to Henry Oldenburg, agent for Bremen to the English Parliament, about the authorship of the *Clamor* (*EF* No. 14). On about this date Vossius sends Heinsius a copy of JM's *Defensio Secunda* (his letter of 20/30 July says that he sent it about a fortnight ago).

12 Roger Williams mentions JM in a letter to John Winthrop, describing how he taught Dutch to JM in exchange for instruction in several other languages (Massachusetts Historical Society, Winthrop Papers 1a, 115).

18 JM's translation of Letters of State from Cromwell to the Archduke of Austria, Governor of the Spanish Netherlands (W122, P66), is signed on or about this date.

20/30 Vossius mentions JM's *Defensio Secunda* in a letter to Heinsius (Burmann, III, 675).

24/3 August An anonymous letter from The Hague, probably addressed to John Thurloe, reports the rumour that Morus has bought the entire consignment of 500 copies of the *Defensio Secunda* shipped to Elzevir to prevent the book from being circulated, but that Vlacq had already printed a large number of copies (Bodleian MS Rawlinson A.16 p. 146).

25 JM's translation of Letter of State from Cromwell to John IV, King of Portugal (W65, P67), is probably signed on this day; the date is an inference from the date on the passport of the Portuguese ambassador, Conde de Penaguião, who was to carry the letter (though he did not sail till 18 August). The letter confirms the ratification of the Anglo-Portuguese treaty.

August

7 (Monday) An unsigned letter, probably from the Netherlands but possibly from England and apparently addressed to Alexander Morus, informs him that JM has been told that Morus was not the author of the *Clamor*, but that JM

was convinced that Morus had at least contributed to it and arranged for it to be printed. JM is also said to have more damaging information about Morus that he will use should he publish a reply (Bodleian MS Rawlinson A.16, fol. 455).

29 JM's translation of Letter of State from Cromwell to Charles X Gustavus, King of Sweden (W46, P68), is signed. The letter congratulates the King on his accession to the throne; it was presented on 21 September 1654.

September

3 (Sunday) First Protectorate Parliament assembles, with representation of Ireland and Scotland.
4 JM's translation of Letter of State from Cromwell to the Spanish Prime Minister (W47, P69) is signed.
12 Cromwell excludes 100 republicans from Parliament.
15 Cromwell readmits excluded MPs.
28 JM writes to Leonard Philaras setting out a detailed account of his blindness to be passed to the French ophthalmologist François Thévenin (*EF* No. 15).

October

In this month JM's *Defensio Secunda* is reprinted at The Hague by Adrian Vlacq, together with Morus's reply, *Fides Publica*.

3 (Tuesday) John Dury writes to Hartlib from Basel about JM and Morus (Hartlib 4/3/38A-38B); JM subsequently cited the letter in *Pro Se Defensio*, which suggests that he was still in contact with Hartlib.
14 Ezekiel Spanheim writes from Geneva to JM attacking Morus; the letter is lost, but JM reprints it, possibly in full, in *Pro Se Defensio*.
16/26 Elizabeth Queen of Bohemia scorns JM (and Dury) in a letter to her son Charles Louis (*LR* V, 444-5).
21 Lady Elizabeth and her son Sir Anthony Cope answer JM's Chancery bill of 16 June (PRO C8/120/72).
27 JM's translation of a Letter of State from Cromwell to the King of Sweden (W48, P70) is signed; the receipt in Stockholm is dated 13/23 November 1654; the letter offers to mediate in the war with Bremen. On the same day JM's translation of a companion letter from Cromwell to Bremen (W49, P71) is signed; the letter acknowledges receipt of a letter from Bremen delivered by Henry Oldenburg and offers to mediate in the dispute with Sweden.

28   John Pell, Cromwell's agent to the Swiss cantons, writes from
     Zurich to Thurloe to report a proposal that Morus, 'against
     whom Mr Hulton writes so sharply', be appointed Professor
     of Divinity at Nîmes' (*LR* III, 442); the original letter is lost,
     but 'Hulton' in the printed text is almost certainly a misprint
     for 'Milton' in the manuscript; Zürich stayed on the Julian
     calendar until 1701, so the date is O.S.
30/9 November   One 'Medonius' writes to Heinsius from Tou-
     louse acknowledging the abilities of JM and anticipating
     receipt of *Defensio Secunda* (Burmann, V, 634).

November
 3/13 (Friday) An unsigned letter, probably addressed to Thurloe,
     says that Morus has left Amsterdam for France (Bodleian MS
     Rawlinson A.19, pp. 713–15; incorrectly paginated).
17   JM receives interest on excise bond (£16).
18   John Dury writes to Hartlib from Zurich expressing hope that
     JM may recover his sight (Hartlib 4/3/61A-61B).

December
 9   (Saturday) JM's forty-sixth birthday. Dury writes to
     Hartlib from Zurich about Morus's controversy with JM.
     The date has been added in a later hand (Hartlib 4/3/65A-
     65B).
22/1 January   Pope Innocent X dies.
29/8 January   Unknown Dutch correspondent writes to
     Hartlib about JM and Morus (BL Add. MS 4,364, fol. 127; the
     copy in BL Sloane MS 649, fol. 30^v is dated 27 December/6
     January).

1655

In approximately this year JM seems to be the object of 'A
Satyr against I.M.', a poem written upside down on the back
flyleaf of the commonplace book of Thomas Stringer (BL Add
MS 33,509).

January
 1   (Monday) The warrant for JM's salary for previous three months
     (£72. 4s. 7$\frac{1}{2}$d) is issued (BL Stowe MS 142/41, fol. 60^v).

17 Andrew Marvell's *The First Anniversary of the Government under His Highness the Lord Protector* is published in celebration of the anniversary on 16 December 1654; the poem imitates JM's 'Nativity Ode' (ll. 151–2) and 'Lycidas' (ll. 218 and 358); the date is Thomason's (his copy is BL E.480 (1)).

22 Cromwell dissolves Parliament.

29 Letter from Aitzema to JM (BL Add MS 5016*, fol. 8) mentions Dutch translation of *Doctrine and Discipline of Divorce*; discovery of two copies of this apparently lost edition was announced in 1994 (see Alblas).

February

At an unknown time between 1/10 February 1655 and 11/21 November 1656, Emery Bigot visits England (Doucette, p. 8) and meets JM (see 3 July 1671).

5 (Monday) JM writes to Aitzema about the proposed Dutch translation of *Doctrine and Discipline of Divorce* (*EF* No. 16).

6 JM files exceptions to the Copes' bill in Chancery; JM's brother Christopher acts as counsel (PRO C33/204, fol. 475).

13 An amanuensis signs the receipt (known as the 'Ashburnham Document') on JM's behalf for his previous quarter's salary (BL Stowe MS 142/41, fol. 61).

28 Court of Chancery sustains JM's exceptions to the Copes' answer to his bill (PRO C38/124).

March

24 (Saturday) JM writes to Ezekiel Spanheim, thanking him for information about Morus (*EF* No. 17); the letter is presumably a reply to Spanheim's letter of 14 October 1654.

27/7 April Fabio Chigi is elected as Pope Alexander VII.

April

At an unknown point in the spring of 1655 Vlacq publishes Morus's *Supplementum* to *Fides Publica*.

4 (Wednesday) JM's translation of a Letter of State from Cromwell to Henri Charles de la Tremoille, Prince of Táranto (W50, P72) may have been signed on this day; the Skinner manuscript is dated 4 April 1654, but the year is almost certainly wrong. The letter is an attempt to stabilise the Prince's wavering Protestant sympathies.

14/24 Duke of Savoy's forces begin a massacre of the Waldenses (Vaudois) in Piedmont.

17 JM's annual salary is reduced from £288.18s.6d to £150 per annum but made payable for life (PRO SP 25/55, p. 28); the salary of Gualter Frost the younger is similarly reduced (but not extended for life) and those of Marchamont Nedham, John Hall, René Augier and others are eliminated altogether. The order was apparently modified at a later date: see 25 October 1659.

28 Blake destroys a pirate fleet from the Bey of Tunis and releases prisoners in Algiers.

May

19/29 (Saturday) J. Frays writes to Ulrich (in French) suggesting erroneously that Dury had translated JM's *Eikonoklastes* into English (Zürich Staatsarchiv E II 457c); he had in fact translated it into French.

25 JM's translation of a Letter of State from Cromwell to the Duke of Savoy (W51, P73) is signed. The letter is a formal protest against the massacre of the Waldenses by the Duke's troops. Companion letters (also translated by JM) to Louis XIV of France (W139, P78) and Cardinal Mazarin (W112, P79) asking them to intercede to stop the persecution, are signed (the signed version of the first letter does not survive). On the same day four letters (translated by JM) deploring the massacre are sent to the Protestant rulers of Sweden (W53, P74), the United Netherlands (W54, P75), the Swiss Protestant Cantons (W55, P76) and Denmark (W58, P77).

26 Samuel Morland leaves London for Paris and Savoy, carrying the letters for Louis XIV and Mazarin, and also carrying the text of a speech which he delivered to the Duke of Savoy in Rivale on 24 June. It is likely that the speech (W153) had been translated by JM (see Fallon, 1995, pp. 145–50).

28 Court orders further examination of the Copes in JM's suit (PRO C7/452/60).

30 Dury writes from Basel to Frays, dissociating himself from JM's antimonarchical tracts (Zürich Staatsarchiv EII 457c); Basel remained on the Julian calendar until 1701, so the date is probably O.S.

31 JM's translation of a Letter of State from Cromwell to George Rakoczy, Prince of Transylvania (W52, P80), is

signed; the letter responds to Rakoczy's letter of 6/16 November 1654 and describes the horrors of the Piedmont massacre; (Transylvania had changed to the Gregorian calendar in 1590, so the date of 16 November is N.S.). Leo Miller has found both letters in the Hungarian State Archives; see Miller 1990c. On the same day JM receives six months' interest on excise bond (£16).

June

7   (Thursday) JM's translation of a Letter of State from Cromwell to the city of Geneva (W59, P81) is signed; the letter is in effect a letter of credit in which Cromwell transfers £2,000 of his personal funds to Geneva for the relief of the Vaudois; the letter also promises more funds from a national gathering of alms (see 14 June).

11 James Howell denounces JM (without naming him) as 'a poor shallow-brain'd puppy' because of his views on divorce (*Epistolae Ho-Elianae*, third edition, 1655; in the index, s.v. the letter 'N', Howell refers the reader to 'a Noddy that writ a book of wifing').

14 A day of humiliation, fasting and collection of money for the victims of the Piedmont Massacre.

18 Lady Elizabeth Cope submits further answer to JM's suit (PRO C7/452/60).

20 JM's sonnet 18 ('On the Late Massacre in Piedmont') is probably written shortly after this date, as it seems to take details from *Mercurius Politicus* 262.

July

The printed order of JM's sonnets seems broadly to conform to the order of composition as reflected in the Trinity manuscript and in various strands of external evidence, so it seems likely that JM's sonnet 19 ('When I consider') was written between July and October 1655; it is possible, however, that the sonnet was written as early as 1651.

14 (Saturday) JM's exceptions to Lady Cope's answer are overruled by Court (PRO C38/127).

31 JM's translations of Letters of State from Cromwell to King Louis XIV of France (W56, P82) and Cardinal Mazarin (W57, P83) are signed; the date is an inference from an unsigned copy of the letter to the King in Paris.

August

Cyriack Skinner records that after the completion of *Defensio Pro Se* (see 8 August), JM 'had now more leisure', because the Council had allowed him a substitute (see 17 October 1653) and sometimes sent messages home excusing him 'from attending in his Office of Secretary' (Darbishire, p. 143); this statement is corroborated by Edward Phillips (Darbishire, p. 72) and Wood (Darbishire, pp. 45–6), both of whom connect this period of leisure with the completion of the *Defensio Pro Se*. It was apparently about this time that JM began to compile a Latin thesaurus, which may have been completed but is now lost. Two octavo volumes said by Wood to have been published by Edward Phillips in 1684 (*Enchiridion Linguae Latinae* and *Speculum Linguae Latinae*) 'were all or mostly taken from the *Latin Thesaurus* writ by Joh. Milton Uncle to Edw. Phillips'; no copy of these books is known to have survived. Toland reported that 'Milton's *Thesaurus Linguae Latinae*...was never publisht, and has been of great use to Dr [Adam] Littleton in compiling his dictionary'; editions of Littleton's *Linguae Latinae Dictionarius* (first published in 1673) do not acknowledge a debt to JM's thesaurus until the eighteenth century. A dictionary published in 1693, the *Linguae Romanae Dictionarium*, acknowledges the debt to JM's manuscript in an advertisement in *A Catalogue of Books...Easter Term 1693*; the title-page acknowledges various debts, including 'a large manuscript in three volumes of Mr John Milton', and in the preface the editors acknowledge that 'we had by us, and made use of, a manuscript collection in three large folios digested into an alphabetical order, which the learned Mr John Milton had made.' Virtually the entire text of this *Dictionarium* is transcribed from Littleton's *Dictionarius*. Cyriack Skinner also records that JM 'had begun a Greek Thesaurus'; this manuscript is lost, but there may be a connection with the Greek thesaurus (also lost) on which Littleton was engaged until his death in 1694.

The early biographers concur in asserting that after the publication of *Pro Se Defensio* JM began to draft a systematic theology entitled *Idea Theologiae*; this may be an early version of the treatise (discovered in 1823) entitled *De Doctrina Christiana*, though the Augustinian title was added to the manuscript after JM's death, and is unlikely to be his.

8 (Wednesday) JM's *Defensio Pro Se* is published (Thomason's date; his copy is BL E. 1661 (2)). JM subsequently presents a copy to the Bodleian; the volume is now lost, but the gift is

noted by Wood (Wood MS F.47, fol. 34; von Maltzahn (1994), 172).

9   Cromwell divides England into 11 districts, each to be administered by a Major-General.

17 JM's nephew John Phillips publishes *A Satyr against Hypocrites*, which is sometimes wrongly attributed to JM (Thomason's date; his copy is BL E.851(19)).

September
10 (Monday) John Bradshaw adds a codicil to his will bequeathing £10 to JM (PRO PROB 11/296/549); on the same day Joseph Jane writes to Sir Edward Nicholas to enquire about the aborted translation of his *Eikon Aklastos* (BL Egerton MS 2,535, fols. 391–2). The letter alludes to Dury's French translation of JM's *Eikonoklastes*.

October
24 (Thursday) Anglo-French treaty against Spain is signed; the French agree to expel Charles II from France.

26 The Latin translation of Cromwell's *Declaration . . . against Spain* (W169, P84) is approved for publication; the translation is unattributed, but could be by JM or Philip Meadows; see Fallon (1995), 98–100.

November
JM may have written Sonnet 20 ('Lawrence of virtuous father') early in the winter of 1655. The sonnet is almost certainly addressed to Edward Lawrence, but possibly to his younger brother Henry. The 'virtuous father' of the two brothers was Henry Lawrence, a prominent member of Cromwell's government and the author of several theological treatises. Edward Phillips records 'young Lawrence' among those who visited JM at his house in Petty France in the 1650s. The other visitor mentioned by Phillips is Cyriack Skinner, the subject of Sonnets 21 and 22, which may have been written before the end of the year.

27 (Tuesday) Writ is issued to examine Lord Say and Sele in JM/ Cope suit (PRO C7/452/60).

28 Thomas Young, recipient of *Elegia Quarta*, dies in Stowmarket; the date is recorded on Young's monument in Stowmarket Church.

29   JM receives interest on bond (£16).

December
 3   (Monday) Writ issued to examine witness in Ashworth–JM
     suit (PRO C22/759/17).
 9   JM's forty-seventh birthday.
15? JM's translation of a Letter of State from Cromwell to
     King Louis XIV of France (W61, P85) is signed on or about
     this day; the letter protests about the French seizure of
     the English merchant vessel *Unicorn* in the Eastern Mediterra-
     nean.
16? JM's translation of a Letter of State from Cromwell to the Doge
     of Venice (W60, P86) is signed on or about this day; the letter
     protests about the Venetian seizure of the merchant vessel
     Great Prince on the grounds that its service with the Turkish
     fleet had been forced.

1656

A bookseller's catalogue published in an anonymous English translation of *The Preacher*, by JM's tutor William Chappell, announces
'The Works of Mr John Milton, concerning Divorce, digested into
one volume'; no such edition is known. JM is mentioned as
the opponent of Salmasius by Antonius Clementius in his biography of Salmasius prefaced to Salmasius's *Epistolarum Liber Primus*
(Leiden, 1656). Parival's *Abrégé de l'Histoire* appears in an English
translation by B. Harris as *The History of this Iron Age*; the slighting
reference to JM is omitted in the translation, in which JM is deemed
to have 'elegantly answered' Salmasius. In an undated entry in
Ephemerides written between January and May 1656 Hartlib refers
to 'Mr Skinner a traveller and a most accomplished gentleman and
universal scholar for mathematics Greek Latin French etcetera not
far dwelling from Mr Milton and mighty studious.' (Hartlib 29/5/
68b); 'Mr Skinner' is Cyriack Skinner, who was living near JM in
Petty France (Marvell's letter of 2 June 1654 says that he is 'exceed-
ingly glad to think that Mr Skyner is got near to you'). 'Peter
Negesch' (the pseudonym of Peter Schultz) discusses JM throughout *Comparatio inter Claudium Tiberium principem & Olivarium
Cromwellium protectorem*, which may have been published in the
Netherlands.

January

In this month JM's translation of a Letter of State from Cromwell to the Evangelical Swiss Cantons (W62, P87) is signed; the letter encourages the Protestant cantons to stand fast against the Catholic cantons.

7   (Monday) JM's dispute with Morus is mentioned in *The Public Intelligencer* No 14.

11 Witnesses are examined in the Ashworth–JM suit (PRO C22/759/17).

13 JM's translation of a Letter of State from Cromwell to King Louis XIV of France (W140, P88) is signed; the letter protests about the protection of a Royalist ship, the *Kinsale*, by the governor of Belle-Ile.

16 Lord Say and Sele answers JM's bill against Cope, himself and others (PRO C7/452/60).

31 Anne Powell's petition is dismissed (PRO SP 25/96, p. 506).

February

7   (Thursday) JM's translation of a Letter of State from Cromwell to the King of Sweden (W63, P89) is signed. The letter congratulates Charles X on his successful conquest of Poland and on the birth of his son.

11 A letter from Paris (dated 29 January/8 February) about Morus, mentioning JM, is printed in *The Public Intelligencer* No. 19.

14/24 A revised version of the letter about Morus (see 11 February) is published in French in *Nouvelles Ordinaires de Londres* No. 298.

19 Philip Meadows, who had been sharing translation assignments with JM, is nominated as a special envoy to Portugal and departs on or about 11 March. In the ensuing months JM had to undertake an increased number of translations; Meadows returned in July, but was recovering from an attempt on his life. He was finally replaced on 8 September 1657.

March

25 (Tuesday) JM receives £65 from John Robinson of Wheatley, bringing the total paid to £345. The dates of the four previous payments (£65 each) are not known, but may be 25 March, 24 June, 29 September and 25 December 1655 (PRO C22/759/17).

29 JM's brother Christopher's daughter Mary is baptised in Ipswich (Parish Register, St Nicholas, Ipswich).

April

The Columbia manuscript contains English texts of two Letters of State from Council to Algiers (for the second see June 1656) and one to 'Lord Hamet Bashaw' (presumably but not certainly Pasha Ahmed VI, Dey of Algiers); JM may have drafted the texts. The first letter to the Council of Algiers (W161, P91), dated April 1656 (with a blank for the day of the month) acknowledges the Pasha's letter 'dated on the third day of the second moon of Rabia in the year 1066 according to your account' (i.e. 30 January 1656); the letter clarifies the use of English flags of convenience. The second letter of April 1656 (W161, P90) also has a blank for the date; the letter assures 'Hamet Bashaw' that English ships visiting Algiers will not have any French or Flemish sailors on board.

1 (Tuesday) JM's translation of a Letter of State from Cromwell to the United Netherlands (W66, P92) is signed; the letter complains about an attack by a Dutch privateer from Flushing (i.e. Vlissingen) on *The Red Lion*, an English merchant vessel.

14 JM's translations of Letters of State from Cromwell to the King of France (W145, P93) and to Cardinal Mazarin (W146, P94) are signed; the original of the letter to Mazarin is dated, and the letter to Louis XIV must have been signed on the same day. The letters are credential papers for Sir William Lockhart, the ambassador to France.

19 JM's translation of a Letter of State from Cromwell to King Charles X of Sweden (W67, P95) is signed; the letter commends the character of Peter Julius Coyet, the departing Swedish ambassador. The Columbia manuscript contains the English text of a Letter of State from Cromwell to Sir Thomas Bendish, the ambassador to Turkey; it is possible that JM drafted the letter, which orders Bendish to support Captain John Casse in his effort to secure compensation for losses inflicted on him by the Algerian Fleet.

21 The Swedish ambassador, Count Christer Bonde, delivers a draft treaty to the commissioners of the Council of State, and asks that it be translated into Latin. JM undertakes the translation (see 6 May and 17 July).

22 *Sportive Wit*, a poetical miscellany edited by JM's nephew John Phillips, is investigated by the Council of State (PRO SP 25/77 p. 69).

25 The Council of State receives a report declaring *Sportive Wit* to be 'scandalous, lascivious, scurrilous and profane', and

orders copies to be seized and burnt, and orders that Phillips be fined and that he appear before the Council 'on Tuesday next' (i.e. 29 April) (PRO SP 25/77, p. 80); there is no record of his appearance before the Council. The Swedish ambassador complains in a letter to King Charles X that the translation of the draft treaty has been assigned to JM (Roberts, p. 282).

26 Cromwell personally approves the burning of *Sportive Wit* (PRO SP 25/77, pp. 82–3).

30 Copies of *Sportive Wit* are burnt in front of the Old Exchange (*Nouvelles Ordinaires de Londres*, No. 309, 1 May 1656).

May

JM's undated letter to his former pupil Richard Jones (later the Earl of Ranelagh) may have been written about this time. The letter (*EF* No. 22) acknowledges a (lost) letter from Jones which had been left for a fortnight in the house of Lady Ranelagh (Jones's mother) in Pall Mall, just across St James's Park from JM's house. Jones had recently gone up to Oxford, and JM's letter is a homily about the need for hard work if the resources of Oxford are to be beneficial.

6 (Tuesday) Bulstrode Whitelocke records in his diary the complaint of the Swedish ambassador that the translation of the Swedish treaty had been assigned to JM. The ambassador was angry that he had had to wait a fortnight for the translation and that an amanuensis had become privy to the treaty because of the necessity of reading it aloud to a blind translator (Whitelocke, p. 439).

10 Court orders action in Ashworth–JM suit (PRO C33/205 fol. 1119^v).

13 JM, represented by his brother Christopher, requests an extension of time to examine witnesses in the Ashworth suit (PRO C33/205, fol. 989).

14 JM's translation of a Letter of State from Cromwell to King Louis XIV of France (W68, P97) is signed. The surviving copies do not specify the day of the month, but a later letter (W86, P120) alludes to this letter 'of 14 May'. The letter requests the return of the merchant ship *Jonas of London*, which had been taken by an English Royalist pirate to Dunkirk.

30 JM's translation of a Letter of State from Cromwell to the United Netherlands (W70, P98) is signed. The letter is a (fourth) request on behalf of two English citizens who were attempting to settle

a disputed estate in the Netherlands. On the same day JM
receives interest payment on bond (£16).

31 JM's translation of a Letter of State from Cromwell to the
United Netherlands (W69, P99) is signed. The letter intercedes
on behalf of the owners of *Good Hope of London*, who had for
six years been seeking an insurance settlement in Dutch courts.
In this month, or possibly earlier, Henry Oldenburg writes to
JM, who replies on 25 June; Oldenburg's copy of his undated
letter to JM is Royal Society MS I, fol 9. The letter was delivered to JM by 'young Ranelagh', that is, Richard Jones.

June

JM may have drafted the English text of a Letter of State from
Cromwell to the Council of Algiers (W163, P100); the letter requests
the release of the merchant ship *Crowned Herring*; see April 1656 for
a related letter to Algiers.

4 (Wednesday) Anne Powell deposes in JM–Ashworth suit as a
witness for JM (PRO C24/796/97).

11 JM presents copies of *Eikonoklastes* and *Tenure of Kings and
Magistrates* to Bodleian Library (MS 4o. Rawl. 408); the inscriptions seem to be in the hand of Thomas Barlow, who had
succeeded Rous as Librarian in 1652. JM probably sent the
books via Edward Phillips, who presented two of his own
books to the Bodleian on the same day.

13 JM's translation of a passport for Dr Peter George Romswinckel, who was returning to his native Germany, is signed;
the date derives from a copy in The Hague archives (W141,
P101). On the same day JM's translation of a Letter of State
from Cromwell to King Charles X of Sweden (W142, P102) is
signed; the letter introduces Romswinckel. The date derives
from a letter in The Hague archives.

25 JM writes (in Latin) to Henry Oldenburg in reply to his recent
letter. Oldenburg is living in Oxford as tutor to Richard Jones
(who was not formally registered at the University). The letter
(*EF* No. 18) grumbles about the 'idle quibblings' of Oxford,
and returns the greetings of Cyriack Skinner.

July

JM's translation of a Letter of State from Cromwell to King John IV
of Portugal (W71, P103) is signed; the letter intercedes on behalf of
English merchants seeking payment from the Brazil Company.

3   (Thursday) Goldsmiths' Company demises the Red Rose in Bread Street to Thomas Hussey from Lady Day 1674. The entry describes the property (which is unnamed) as having been 'in the occupation of John Milton scrivener deceased and are now in the tenure of John Milton Gent[leman]' (minutes of Committee of Contractors and Leases, 1641, 1651–62, fol. 163v).

15 The Anglo-Swedish Treaty (W170, P96) is signed by Cromwell; Bonde signed for Sweden on 17 July and Charles X signed on 14 November. For evidence that JM was the translator see Fallon (1993), pp. 172–5.

30 JM's translation of a Letter of State from Cromwell to King Charles X of Sweden (W72, P104) is signed; the letter praises Christer Bonde, who had earlier complained about JM (see 6 May).

August

Peter Heimbach visits JM before leaving England; JM asks him to look for an atlas abroad, and inscribes a copy of his 1645 *Poems*; the copy is now in private ownership in Chicago; see Shawcross (1991). Andrew Marvell, who is visiting Saumur (a Protestant town on the Loire) with his ward William Dutton, writes to JM to say that JM's book (presumably one of the *Defences*) had been well received in Saumur. Marvell's letter is lost; its existence is an inference from JM's letter of 1 August 1657 to Henry Oldenburg, in which JM mentions that the previous summer a close friend had written to him from Saumur. In this month JM's translations of two letters from Cromwell to King John IV of Portugal (W76, P105; W77, P106) are signed; the first acknowledges ratification of the Anglo-Portuguese peace treaty that had been renegotiated in Lisbon by Philip Meadows, and the second demands that the attempted murderers of Meadows (who had shot him in the hand) be brought to justice. JM's translation of a third letter (W78, P107), from Cromwell to the Conde d'Odemira (John IV's chief minister) is also signed; the letter acknowledges the Conde's letter of 25 June and urges pursuit of those who had wounded Meadows.

21 (Thursday) JM's translation of a Letter of State from Cromwell to the United Netherlands (W75, P109) is signed; the letter urges reconciliation with the Swedes. JM's translation of a similar Letter of State from Cromwell to King

Charles X of Sweden (W79, P108) was presumably signed on the same day.

September

In this month, or possibly earlier, Richard Jones writes to JM; the letter, to which JM replies on 21 September with an apology for his tardiness, is lost.

5/15 (Friday) Treaty of Amity between England and France is agreed.

8 Bishop Joseph Hall, JM's antagonist in the controversy over episcopacy, dies in Norfolk.

9/19 Blake captures Spanish treasure ships off Cadiz.

10 JM's translation of a Letter of State from Cromwell to the States of Holland (W80, P110) is signed; the letter intercedes on behalf of an English claimant to joint ownership of a valuable patent.

17 Second Protectorate Parliament meets.

21 JM writes to Richard Jones (*EF* No. 19); the letter is delivered by his mother, Lady Ranelagh, who visits Oxford on her way to Ireland with her two daughters. In the letter JM says of Lady Ranelagh that she has been a substitute for his family. JM had been widowed for four years, and Lady Ranelagh had long been separated from her husband; JM and Lady Ranelagh had been friends since 1645 and possibly earlier.

25 JM's translations of two Letters of State from Cromwell to King Louis XIV of France (W73, P111; W81, P112) and a third to Cardinal Mazarin (W74, P113) are signed; the date of one of the letters to the King (W73, P111) can be inferred from the dated companion letter to Mazarin; these letters intervene on behalf of the owners of the *Endeavour*, which had been captured by French pirates on 21 November 1655 and taken to the East Indies. The other letter to the King, which may have been signed on the same day, concerns the claim of an English merchant to the ownership of a cargo of 4,000 hides taken from the *Antony of Dieppe*.

26 JM signs the autograph album of the Swiss minister Johannes Zollikofer (Stadtbibliothek Vadiana, St Gallen, Switzerland, MS 92a); see Miller, 1990*b*.

29 JM receives last instalment of rents from Wheatley (£4. 17s. 4d).

October
JM's translation of a Letter of State from Cromwell to King John IV of
Portugal (W82, P114) is signed during this month; the letter introduces Thomas Maynard as Consul for Trade. A second letter from
Cromwell to King John, dated 'October 1656' (W84, P115), renews the
question of payments from the Brazil Company raised in the letter of
July 1656. As this letter refers to the July letter as having been written
'last year' (*superiore anno*), one of the dates would seem to be wrong.
16 (Thursday) JM's translation of a Letter of State from Cromwell
    to the Senate of Hamburg (W85, P116) is signed; the letter
    intercedes on behalf of two Englishmen seeking restoration
    of the estate of their deceased brother.
22 JM's translation of a Letter of State from Cromwell to King
    Charles X of Sweden (W83, P117) is signed. The letter seeks
    payment for Sir William Vavasour, who had fought as a mer-
    cenary for Sweden.
        First publication of banns for marriage of JM to Katherine
    Woodcock (Parish Register, St Mary the Virgin, Alderman-
    bury, London). On Katherine's family and background see
    Parker (1996), pp. 1052–5.
27 Second publication of banns.

November
3 (Monday) Third publication of banns.
4(?) On or about this date JM translates into English (W159,
    P118) a letter (dated 16 February 1656) from King
    Frederick III of Denmark (W159, P118). The date is an infer-
    ence from the order of the Protector's Council (issued that day)
    to prepare a letter on Danish–Swedish relations (see 4 Decem-
    ber 1656).
8 JM writes to Peter Heimbach (*EF* No. 20); the unidentified atlas
    about which JM has enquired is said to cost 130 florins, which
    JM thinks too much for a blind man to pay for maps.
12 JM marries Katherine Woodcock, probably at the Guildhall;
    the civil ceremony was conducted by Sir John Dethicke, whose
    term as Lord Mayor of London had ended on 9 November.
    (Parish Register, St. Mary the Virgin, Aldermanbury)

December
2 (Tuesday) JM receives interest on bond (£16); on the same day
    JM wins a stay in the Ashworth suit on grounds of scandalous

matter in the bill; JM is represented by his brother Christopher (PRO C33/207, fol 221ᵛ).

4   JM's translation of a Letter of State from Cromwell to King Frederick III of Denmark (W87, P119) is signed; the letter acknowledges the King's letter of 16 February (see 4 November) and counsels reconciliation with the Swedes.
9   JM's forty-eighth birthday.
28   Henry Oldenburg writes to JM from Oxford concerning the date of Christmas (Royal Society MS I, fol 11).

1657

JM is visited by the Lutheran theologian Johan Lassenius; see Miller, 1972. JM's 1645 *Poems* are mentioned and quoted in Joshua Poole's *The English Parnassus*. JM's Hobson poems are reprinted in *A Banquet of Jests*. At some time early in this year JM's translation of a Letter of State to King Louis XIV of France (W86, P120) is signed; the letter is dated 'November 1656' in all the sources, but refers to the letter of 14 May of 'last year', i.e. 1656, and mentions that Dethicke was Lord Mayor of London in that year; the letter renews the request for the return of the *Jonas*.

February
28   (Saturday) Two submissions by JM to the Committee for Compounding concerning claims made on him by Anne Powell are signed on his behalf (28 February '1656') by different scriveners (PRO SP 23/101, pp. 929 and 931).

March
JM's translation of a Letter of State from Cromwell to William VI, Landgrave of Hesse (W88, P121), is signed; the letter urges reconciliation between Lutherans and Calvinists. JM's translation of a Letter of State from Cromwell to King Frederick III of Denmark (W64, P122) may have been signed in this month, as it is a response to a petition referred to the Navy Commissioners on 3 February 1657; the letter concerns the seizure of English cargo by the Danish authorities.
13   (Friday) Treaty of Paris between England and France sanctions a joint attack on Gravelines and Dunkirk.
24   JM writes to Emery Bigot (*EF* No. 21; see *DBF* and Doucette), who owns a copy of the late medieval treatise on the relation

between crown and parliament known as the *Modus Tenendi Parliamentum* (see Galbraith), and had asked JM to check certain readings and to see if the original survives in the Tower of London. JM reports that he had confirmed or emended readings from manuscripts in the possession of John Bradshaw and Sir Robert Cotton, and that he had consulted a friend who was responsible for manuscripts in the Tower and established that there was no copy there; the friend was William Ryley, Norroy King-of-Arms. JM asks in return that Bigot try to secure six books from a Parisian publisher, and to have them shipped by Jean-Baptiste Stouppe. Only one of the six was a well-established text: the *Liber Pontificalis* ('Book of Popes'), which was then attributed to the ninth-century anti-pope Anastasius Bibliothecarius, had first been printed in Mainz in 1602. A second, the continuation of the *Alexiad* of Anna Commena by John Cinnamus (which covers the period 1118 to 1176), had been edited in 1662 by Tollius. Three of the books had been published in 1655: Goar's *editio princeps* of the *Chronographia* of Theophanes the Confessor (a chronology of the years 284 to 813), the *Breviarum Historicum* of Constantine Manasses, a 7,000-line metrical chronology from the creation to 1081 AD written in the 'political' metre (which is accentual rather than quantitative) and *Excerpta de Antiquitatibus Constantinopolitanus* of George Codinus, which treats the history, topography and monuments of Constantinople. The sixth book had not yet been published: the *Annales* of Michael Glycas (from the creation to 1118 AD) was not published till 1660.

Bigot had visited England in 1655 or 1656 (see Doucette, p. 8) and had apparently met JM (see 23 June 1671).

25 Parliament votes to offer Cromwell the crown.

27 JM assists William Spenser, grandson of the poet, to recover most of the Kilcolman estate, which had been confiscated in 1654 because of William's Catholicism (Skinner's anonymous biography, in Darbishire, p. 30). William had since reconverted to Protestantism, and JM intervened on his behalf. The nature of JM's intervention is not clear, but he may have facilitated Cromwell's letter of 27 April to the Council in Ireland, and he may have used the good offices of Lady Ranelagh, who was, like the poet's wife, a Boyle.

31 Parliament's Humble Petition and Advice offers the title of King to Cromwell.

April

3   (Friday) Cromwell rejects the title of King.

10 JM's translation of a Letter of State from Cromwell to Danzig (W90, P125) is signed. The letter requests the release of a Swedish general, or, failing that, an alleviation of the harsh conditions in which he is being held. On the same day JM's translation of a Letter of State from Cromwell to Tsar Alexis of Russia (W91, P124) is signed. The paper is a credential letter for Richard Bradshaw, who travelled as far as Mitau in Courland (now Yelgava, Latvia), but was refused entry to Russia. Bradshaw's instructions (W164, P123), which survive (in English) in the Columbia manuscript, were presumably issued on or about the same day.

20/30   The English fleet commanded by Blake defeats the Spanish fleet off Santa Cruz.

May

4   (Monday) Anne Powell and her son Richard are ordered to answer Elizabeth Ashworth's bill (PRO C33/207, fol 809).

8   Cromwell declines the crown.

25 The New Humble Petition and Advice gives Cromwell the right to nominate his successor and create an 'Other House' consisting of 40–70 members.

26 Anne Powell and her son Richard reply to Elizabeth Ashworth's bill of complaint against them and JM (PRO C5/405/2).

June

'William Allen', a pseudonym for Edward Sexby and/or Silas Titus, mischievously cites JM in support of an argument for assassinating Cromwell in *Killing No Murder*; Thomason's copy (BL E.501(4)) is dated 'June 1657' but dated May 1657 by Fortescue.

5   (Friday) JM receives interest payment (£16). On the same day Court of Chancery settles Ashworth–JM suit, and orders JM to return Wheatley to the Powells (PRO C33/207, fols. 1250–1251).

11/21   Emery Bigot writes to Gilles Ménage from The Hague. Bigot explains that *'On m'escrit de Rouën que Mr Milton m'avoit fait response, et m'avoit envoié ce que Mr [Gilles] Nublé m'avoit prié de luy faire venir d'Angleterre'* ('I have been told in a letter from

Rouen that Mr Milton has replied to me, and has sent me what Mr [Gilles] Nublé asked me to obtain for him from England') (Bibliothèque Nationale, Nouvelles acquisitions françaises 1343, fol. 60)

13   JM's *Reason of Church Government and Apology* is advertised in John Rothwell's *Catalogue of the Most Approved Divinity Books*.

17   Henry Stubbe praises JM in *Clamor, Rixa, Joci*; the date is taken from the introductory note to the reader.

26   The Additional Petition and Advice strengthens the powers of Parliament; Cromwell is installed as Protector for the second time.

27/7 July   Henry Oldenburg writes to JM from Saumur, mentioning his meeting with Morus and asking that greetings be passed to [Edward] Lawrence (Royal Society MS I, fols. 22^v–23); an accompanying letter by Richard Jones is lost.

July

Hartlib sends a copy of *Of Education* to the mathematician-astronomer Nicolaus Mercator, who approves of its contents (see Raylor); JM and Christopher are each bequeathed 20 shillings in the will of John Jeffery, a distant relation of their mother (PRO PROB 11/267/349).

15   (Wednesday) JM writes to Henry de Brass about the merits of Sallust as an historian (*EF* No. 23).

August

JM's translation of a Letter of State to the French Ambassador (W93, P126) is signed, probably by Henry Laurence as President of the Council; the letter intervenes on behalf of English ship-owners whose vessel has been seized and sold in France.

1   (Saturday) JM writes to Richard Jones and Henry Oldenburg in Saumur. The letter to Jones (*EF* No. 25) commends the virtues of industry and sobriety; the letter to Oldenburg (*EF* No. 24) deplores the appointment of Morus as minister in Charenton.

20   JM's translations of six credential letters in Cromwell's name for William Jephson, addressed to the King of Sweden (W92, P127), the Elector of Brandenburg (W94, P128), Hamburg (W95, P129), Bremen (W96, P130), Lübeck (W97, P131) and the Duke of Holstein (W99, P132) are signed; the dated originals in Stockholm, Lübeck (a photocopy of the original lost in

the Second World War) , Kiel (Holstein) and Merseburg (Brandenburg) are all dated 20 August, so it seems reasonable to assume that the lost originals in Hamburg and Bremen were so dated. Similarly, a credential letter in Cromwell's name for Philip Meadows, addressed to Hamburg (W98, P133), is likely to have been signed on the same day, especially as Jephson and Meadows sailed together.

September
2 (Wednesday) Andrew Marvell is appointed as a clerical assistant in Thurloe's office. The appointment is not recorded in the order book, but the Thurloe papers in the Bodleian contain an order dated 3 September (MS Rawlinson A.62, p. 49) for Marvell to be paid £50 for one quarter's salary on 2 December 1657.
3 JM's translation of a Letter of State from Cromwell to the Elector of Brandenburg (W101, P135) is signed; this letter is normally dated 23 September, but the original has been discovered in Merseburg and is clearly dated 3 September (see Miller, 1987*a*).
8 'Mr Sterry' (probably Nathaniel, but possibly his brother Peter; there is a blank where the Christian name should be) is appointed as a substitute for Philip Meadows in Thurloe's office (SP 25/78, p. 132).
10 JM's translation of a letter of State from Cromwell to the Grand Duke of Tuscany (W100, P134) is signed; the date is an inference from a companion letter from the Levant Company to the English agent at Livorno; Cromwell requests the arrest of an English captain, William Ellis, who was alleged to have stolen a cargo of rice, tea and coffee.
17 James Schaller's thesis about JM is defended in Strasbourg in a dissertation by Christopher Güntzer, *Dissertationis ad Quaedam Loca Miltoni*, which was published before the end of the year.
25 *Of Reformation, Of Prelatical Episcopacy, Reason of Church Government*, the first *Defensio, Eikonoklastes* and 1645 *Poems* are advertised in William London's *Catalogue of the Most Vendible Books in England*.

October
JM's translation of a Letter of State from Council of State to the French Ambassador (W102, P136) is signed; the letter intervenes in a dispute over a seized ship and cargo.

4 (Sunday) Henry Oldenburg writes to JM from Saumur.

19 JM's daughter Katherine is born 'between 5 and 6 in the morning' (JM's family Bible and the Parish Register of St Margaret, Westminster).

   A receipt for £50 dated 19 October 1657 records that a 'John Driden', almost certainly the future dramatist, is employed in Thurloe's office, presumably working alongside JM (PRO SP 18/180/95; see Hammond).

22 JM's translation of a Letter of State from Cromwell to the Doge and Senate of Venice (W103, P137) is signed. The letter proposes that a Turkish prisoner in Venice be released in exchange for an English sailor who had been captured by the Turks.

23 On an unknown date in Michaelmas term (23 October–28 November) JM appears in court to make an affidavit in the Cope suit. The affidavit seems to be lost, but it is listed in PRO IND/1/1926 fol. 56.

November

4 (Wednesday) Bulstrode Whitelocke notes in his diary an 'application to Wh[itelocke] to buy Mrs Powell's interest in Shottover woods, butt he held it not convenient' (Whitelocke, p. 479); Shotover is close to Forest Hill and Wheatley. Anne Powell's application survives at Longleat (Whitelocke Papers, Vol. 17, fol. 219).

12 JM's translation of a Letter of State from Cromwell to the United Netherlands (W104, P138) is signed. The letter commends Willem Nieupoort, the departing Dutch ambassador.

26 JM receives interest on bond (£16).

December

JM's translation of a Letter of State from Cromwell to the Grand Duke of Tuscany (W107, P139) is probably signed early in the month; the letter thanks the Grand Duke for the arrest of William Ellis (see 10 September); at about the same time JM's translation of a Letter of State from Cromwell to Holland (W106, P140) is signed; the paper is a credential letter for Sir George Downing, Envoy Extraordinary to Holland.

9 (Wednesday) JM's forty-ninth birthday.

16 JM writes to Henry de Brass about the writing of history (*EF* No. 26).

17 The Latin text of a Letter of State from Cromwell to the United Netherlands (W105, P141) is signed; the letter is a *recreditif* for

Sir George Downing. The letter may be the final version of a draft printed with JM's *Letters of State*, but the relationship between the two letters is not clear.

18 JM receives a letter dated 8/18 December (now lost) from Peter Heimbach in The Hague asking for a letter of recommendation, and replies on the same day to the effect that he cannot be of assistance (*EF* No. 27).

1658

A volume of State Papers collected by JM, now in the library of the Society of Antiquaries (MS 138), may have been the subject of an official order issued in this year (see 2 February 1650 for an example of a surviving order) or may have been JM's private initiative. The papers seem to have passed from JM to Thomas Ellwood to his friend Joseph Wyeth, and through his widow to John Nickolls, who published them in 1743.

In this year JM's Hobson poems are reprinted in *Wit Restored*, and *Killing no Murder* (see June 1657) is translated into French. Sir William Sanderson seems to allude to JM's *Eikonoklastes* in *A Complete History of the Life and Reign of King Charles*, p. 324, but the allusion may be to *Eikon Alethine*. In this year JM's *Comus* is copied into a Commonplace Book now in the Yale University Library (James Osborn Collection b. 63).

January
1 (Friday) An unpublished pseudonymous answer to the preface to JM's *Defensio* is dated 1 January 1658; it was written by Henrik Ernst (Royal Library, Copenhagen, GKS 2259, 4to; see Bradley). Denmark remained on the Julian calendar, but had changed the New Year to 1 January.
14 JM lends £500 to Thomas Maundy, taking mortgage on property in Kensington as security; JM's counterpart of the mortgage deed is signed on his behalf by Jeremie Picard and witnessed by Picard and Elizabeth Woodcock, JM's mother-in-law (Rosenbach Museum, Philadelphia, 810/25).
20 Cromwell's third (and last) Protectorate Parliament meets.
23 JM is said to sign an indenture as witness (*LR* IV, 211–12), but the signature on the document, which was sold at Sotheby's (New York) on 14 December 1988, is of another 'John Milton'.

February

2   (Tuesday) Hartlib writes to Robert Boyle about 'that secret which hath been imparted to Mr Milton' (*LR*, IV, 214). The 'secret' is apparently a manuscript copy of Jean Bodin's heretical *Heptaplomeres*; the book, which is a discussion by seven scholars of differing religious opinions, was not published until 1841.

3   (Tuesday) JM's wife Katherine dies, probably of consumption. If, as seems likely, Katherine is the subject of Sonnet 23 ('Methought I saw'), then the sonnet must have been written in 1658. It is possible, however, that the subject of the sonnet is Mary, JM's first wife, in which case the sonnet may have been composed after May 1652 and (if the chronological order of the sonnets is to remain intact) possibly as late as the end of 1656 (see Shawcross, 1956, and Parker, 1996, p. 1045).

4   Parliament is dissolved.

10   JM's wife Katherine is buried in St Margaret's Church, Westminster (Parish Register). The account recording funeral expenses of £5. 3s. 4d survives in the College of Arms (Painters Workbook I.B.7, fol. 46b). A parted shield to the left of the entry contains the Milton arms on the left and the Woodcock arms on the right; the normal practice was for a woman's husband's arms to be on the right and her father's on the left, but exceptions are not unknown. The entry in *LR*, IV, 217 mistranscribes the cost of the buckram escutcheons as £1 instead of £1.10s.

March

JM's translation of a Letter of State from Cromwell to the Duke of Courland (W89, P142) is signed before 25 March, when the new year begins (the letter is dated 'March 1657'). The letter intercedes on behalf of a Scottish captain whose ship had been wrecked by a Courlandian (now Latvian) pilot.

17   (Wednesday) JM's daughter Katherine dies (JM's family Bible).

20   JM's daughter Katherine is buried in St Margaret's Church, Westminster (Parish Register, St Margaret's Church).

April

2   (Friday) JM's translation of a Letter of State from Cromwell to King Charles X of Sweden (W108, P143) is signed; the date is written on the original in Stockholm, but copies of JM's draft

are dated 30 March. The letter expresses pleasure at the signing (on 26 February) of the Treaty of Roskilde, which concluded the war between Denmark and Sweden.

7 JM's translation of a Letter of State from Cromwell to the
Grand Duke of Tuscany (W109, P144) is signed; the letter
intervenes on behalf of several Englishmen who have been
defrauded.

May

4 (Tuesday) JM's edition of *The Cabinet Council*, then attributed
to Sir Walter Raleigh, is registered for publication (*SR* II, 176).
The date of publication is not known, but was presumably in
May or June. In the preface JM claims that the treatise was
given to him many years before by an unidentified 'learned
man' at his death.

14 JM's translation of a Letter of State from Cromwell to the
Grand Duke of Tuscany (W117, P145) is signed; the letter,
which had been commissioned on 12 May, protests against
the treatment accorded to John Stoakes (Commander-in-Chief
of Cromwell's Mediterranean fleet) in Livorno.

15? On or about this day JM's translations of Letters of State to
King Louis XIV of France (W113, P146) and Mazarin (W114,
P147) are signed; the letters introduce Thomas Belasyse, Vis-
count Fauconberg (Cromwell's son-in-law) as Ambassador
Extraordinary to France.

17 Sheriff of Oxford is reprimanded for not expediting
testimonies of witnesses in the JM/Cope suit (PRO C33/210,
fol. 723^v).

18? On or about this day JM translates revised Letters of State to
King Louis XIV of France (W116, P148) and Mazarin (W115,
P149). These revised versions of the letters of ca. 15 May are
occasioned by the news that King Louis had left Paris for
Mardyck, close to besieged Dunkirk.

20 JM's translation of a Letter of State from Cromwell to
Cardinal Mazarin (P150) is signed; the letter is a final
version of the draft that JM had translated a few days earlier.

25 JM's brother Christopher deposes in Chancery; the case concerns one Thomas Agar, probably the brother-in-law of JM and
Christopher (PRO C24/825/89).

26 JM's translations of Letters of State from Cromwell to the King
of France (W110, P151) and the Swiss Protestant Cantons

(W111, P152) are signed. The letters urge intervention to stop the renewed persecution of the Vaudois by the Duke of Savoy.

31 JM receives interest on bond (£16).

June

4 (Friday) JM's translation of a Letter of State from Cromwell to King Charles X of Sweden (W120, P153) is signed; the letter is an explanation and apology for Cromwell's failure to send troops to serve under Charles X. On the same day (4/14) an Anglo-French force defeats the Spanish at the Battle of the Dunes, thus precipitating the fall of Dunkirk.

19 JM's translations of Letters of State from Cromwell to King Louis XIV of France (W118, P154) and Cardinal Mazarin (W119, P155) are signed. The letters rejoice in the surrender of Dunkirk to English and French troops.

July

1 (Thursday) JM's translations of Letters of State from Cromwell to King Louis XIV of France (W143, P156) and to Cardinal Mazarin (W144, P157) are signed; the letters acknowledge the handover of Dunkirk (which had been part of the Spanish Netherlands) to the English.

August

JM's translation of a Letter of State from Cromwell to King Alphonso VI of Portugal (W121, P158) is signed; the letter intercedes on behalf of an English merchant whose stolen cargo had been taken to Portugal. The Lünig version correctly addresses the letter to Alphonso VI; see 23 February 1659.

14/24 (Sunday) Spanish forces are defeated at Gravelines (east of Calais).

September

3 (Friday) Oliver Cromwell dies and is succeeded by his son Richard.

6 JM's translation of Letters of State from Richard Cromwell to King Louis XIV of France (W124, P159) and Cardinal Mazarin (W125, P160) are signed. The letters announce the death of Oliver Cromwell and the accession of Richard Cromwell.

7   JM is authorised to purchase mourning cloth for funeral of Oliver Cromwell (PRO SP 18/182/90 fol. 2); the list of those entitled to buy cloth includes Andrew Marvell, [Nathaniel?] Sterry and Mr 'Draydon' (John Dryden).

21 Court orders examination of witnesses in JM–Cope suit (PRO C21/M44/23).

October

Revised edition of *Pro Populo Anglicano Defensio* published, with a personal postscript by JM; Thomason listed his copy (BL E. 1900(1)) as the third of 17 entries for the month (BL C.38.h.21, Vol. 10, No. 1550/809), so it must have been published early in the month. In this month JM's translation of a Letter of State from Richard Cromwell to King Charles X of Sweden (W126, P161) is signed; the letter assures the king that the alliance established by Oliver will be maintained by Richard.

12 (Tuesday) JM's witnesses Edward Lyde (alias Joyner) and John Robinson depose in JM/Cope suit (PRO C21/44/23).

26? On or about this date JM's translation of a Letter of State from Richard Cromwell to King Charles X of Sweden (W128, P162) is signed. The letter commends Sir George Ayscue, who was travelling to Sweden to take command of the Swedish fleet.

November

11 (Thursday) Sir Anthony Cope petitions for a new set of interrogatories for witnesses in JM/Cope suit (PRO C33/212, fol. 155); the date is inconsistent with the day, which is given as Saturday.

13 JM's translation of a Letter of State from Richard Cromwell to King Charles X of Sweden (W127, P163) is signed. The letter acknowledges Charles X's condolences on the death of Oliver Cromwell. JM seems to have composed his translation on or about 13 October (the date in the Miltonic collections), but signature was delayed until the fleet was ready to depart.

23 JM joins funeral procession of Oliver Cromwell 'from Somerset House in the Strand unto the Abbey Church of Westminster' (BL Lansdowne MS 95, No. 2, fols. 1, 11^v; cf PRO SP 18/182/90).

25 Revised edition of JM's *Pro Populo Anglicano* is advertised in *Mercurius Politicus* No. 443.

30   JM receives interest on bond (£16)

December
9   (Thursday) JM's fiftieth birthday.

1659

Richard Watson praises *Areopagitica* but satirises the *Defensio* in *The Panegyric and the Storm*. John Locke quotes *Of Reformation* in his *Lemmata Ethica Argumenta et Authores* (Bodleian, Locke MS d.10, p. 93).

January
27 (Thursday) JM's translation of a Letter of State from Richard Cromwell to West Friesland (W130, P164) is signed. The letter intercedes on behalf of a widow who has for 18 years been owed money by Thomas Killigrew, a soldier in the service of the States; the poet and dramatist Thomas Killigrew was on the continent at the time, but it seems unlikely that such a prominent Royalist exile would simply be described as 'one of your soldiers', so the debtor is probably another man of the same name. On the same day Parliament meets.
28 JM's translation of a Letter of State from Richard Cromwell to King Charles X of Sweden (W129, P165) is signed. The letter protests against the detention of two ships belonging to Samuel Piggott, a London merchant.

February
10 (Monday) John Draper deposes as witness for Lady Elizabeth Cope in suit against JM (PRO C24/835).
14 JM's *A Treatise of Civil Power* is advertised (*Publick Intelligencer* No. 163, 7–14 February).
16 JM's *A Treatise of Civil Power* is registered for publication (SR II, 214).
17 *Treatise of Civil Power* is again advertised (*Mercurius Politicus* No. 554, 10–17 February). The treatise is published on or about this date; Thomason seems not to have received a copy of the book. In the tract JM mentions that he is planning to write about the corrupting effects of 'hire' (see August 1659).

18 JM's translation of a Letter of State from Richard Cromwell to King Louis XIV of France (W131, P166) is signed. The letter requests toleration of Protestants in Provence.
19 JM's translation of a Letter of State from Richard Cromwell to Cardinal Mazarin (W132, P167) is signed. The letter requests a favourable reception for the Dowager Duchess of Richmond and her son Esmé.
22 JM's translation of a Letter of State from Richard Cromwell to Cardinal Mazarin (W134, P168) is signed. The letter renews an earlier appeal on behalf of Peter Pett, whose ship had been seized at the mouth of the Thames and sold in Boulogne.
23 JM's translation of a Letter of State from Richard Cromwell to King Alphonso VI of Portugal (W133, P169) is signed. The letter congratulates the King on his victory over the Spanish, presumably with reference to the Battle of Elvas on 4/14 January 1659, and requests payment to English merchants. The Lünig collection correctly addresses the letter to Alphonso VI, but all other versions address it to his late father, John IV, who had died in November 1656; see Miller (1970).
24 Thomas Chandler deposes for Lady Elizabeth Cope in suit against JM (PRO C24/835).

March
26(?) (Saturday) Moses Wall writes to JM from Caversham, near Reading (BL Add MS 4292, fols. 264–5). The date of 26 May in the surviving transcript of Wall's letter has been challenged by Austin Woolrych on the grounds that the phrase 'I think a Commonwealth was more friendly to you than a Court' implies that there was still a Court; similarly, the restoration of the Commonwealth on 7 May is not mentioned. It seems likely (but not certain) that '26 May' is a mistranscription of the lost original (*P* 7, 83 n. 2). JM enclosed a copy of his 'last book', presumably *Treatise of Civil Power*, with the letter.

April
19 (Saturday) JM's translations of two Letters of State from Richard Cromwell to Ferdinand II, Grand Duke of Tuscany (W147, P171; W148, P172) are signed. The letters intercede on behalf of English merchants. JM's translation of a similar Letter

of State from Richard Cromwell to King Alphonso VI of Portugal (W149, P170) is likely to have been signed on or about this date, but is simply dated 'April' in the collections, where it is mistakenly addressed to King John IV (cf 23 February 1659).

22   Richard Cromwell dissolves Parliament after an army *coup d'état* designed to prevent Parliamentary control of the army.

25   JM's translation of a Letter of State from Richard Cromwell to King Charles X of Sweden (W150, P173) is signed; the letter intercedes on behalf of an English merchant who had been forbidden to export hemp from Riga, which was part of the Swedish empire.

27 (?)   JM writes to Jean Labadie (see *DBF*), a former Jesuit who had been converted to Protestantism, inviting him to succeed the late Jean d'Espagne (see *DBF*) as minister of the Somerset House Chapel. The letter is dated 21 April 1659 in JM's *EF* (No. 28), but Jean d'Espagne did not die until 25 April, so '21 April' is likely to be a misprint for a later date.

May

2   (Friday) *Treatise of Civil Power* advertised (*Publick Intelligencer* No. 174, 25 April–2 May).

7   Rump Parliament is restored.

12   Derby Petition, drafted by John Lambert, seeks to settle the constitutional relationship of Parliament and the army.

13   William Prynne attacks JM's *Defensio* in *The Re-Publicans* (Thomason's date; his copy is BL E.983(6)).

15   JM's translations of Letters of State from Parliament to King Charles X of Sweden (W135, P174) and King Frederick III of Denmark (W136, P175) are signed by William Lenthall. The letters announce the abdication of Richard Cromwell and introduce Philip Meadows as the English mediator in the war between Denmark and Sweden.

18   William Prynne attacks JM in *A True and Perfect Narrative*. The date is Prynne's, and is more likely to be correct than the alternative of 13 June (the date written on the Gay copy in the Harvard College Library); Fortescue's dating of Thomason's copy (BL E.767(1)) as 7 May cannot be right, because the title-page refers to 7 and 9 May.

21/31   Treaty of The Hague, in which Dutch, English and French governments agree to force Denmark and Sweden to reach a peaceful settlement.

25 Richard Cromwell resigns; the Rump Parliament re-establishes the Commonwealth.

26 Moses Wall may have written to JM on this day; see 26 March 1659.

June

9 (Monday) New edition of *Killing No Murder* repeats citation of JM; see June 1657 (Thomason's date; his copy is BL E.763.1).

10 Lease of the Red Rose in Bread Street is transferred by the Goldsmiths' Company from JM to Thomas Hussey (*Extracts of Leases, 1650–1675*, p. 64). On the same day Hugh Candish testifies for Lady Elizabeth Cope in the suit against JM (PRO C24/835).

11 Court of Chancery gives seven days' notice of its intention to make available to both parties the depositions of all witnesses in the Cope–JM suit (PRO C33/212, fol. 792^v). The suit thereafter disappears from the legal record (except for the return of papers to John Draper on 21 June), and its eventual fate is unknown.

30 Letters of State from Parliament to Denmark (see Kelley (1952)) and Sweden repeat phrases from the letters of 15 May, and may be translations by JM or translations indebted to JM (French and Kelley, 1952).

July

22 (Friday) JM receives interest on bond (£16).

August

JM publishes *Considerations Touching the Likeliest Means to Remove Hirelings out of the Church* (Thomason gives the month but not the date; his copy is BL E.2110(2)). In this month a royalist rising led by Sir George Booth culminates in the capture of Chester and in Booth's subsequent defeat at Nantwich. Charles II had intended to join Booth, but had been unable to obtain a ship in St Malo (Brittany); he instead travelled to Fuenterrabia in a vain attempt to secure French and Spanish support, an incident that JM seems later to have recalled in *Paradise Lost* I 586–7 ('When Charlemagne with all his peerage fell/By Fontarabbia').

31 (Wednesday) James Harrington's *Aphorisms political* seems to echo JM's *Hirelings* in aphorisms 15–38 (Thomason's date; his copy is BL E.995(8)).

September
5   (Friday) William Mewe mentions JM and his divorce tracts in a
     letter to Richard Baxter (Baxter Correspondence IV, fol. 278, in
     Dr Williams's Library).

October
According to Aubrey (and thence Wood), Cyriack Skinner, 'scholar
to John Milton', became chairman of the Rota Club, James Harrington's group, which met at the Turk's Head in the New Palace Yard
in Westminster (*LR* IV, 275).
12   (Wednesday) The army expels the Rump Parliament.
20   JM writes *Letter to a Friend Concerning the Ruptures of the
      Commonwealth*, which was first published in 1698; the identity
      of the friend is not known.
25   The Council of State orders a salary payment (£86.12s) to be
      made to JM (PRO SP 25/107, p. 143). JM's salary is said to be
      £200 per annum, which suggests that the order of 17 April
      1655 had been modified. This is JM's last recorded payment by
      the Council of State.

November
JM's *Proposals of Certain Expedients for the Preventing of a Civil
War* was probably written during this month, and was
certainly written between 27 October and 24 December, when
'the present committee of safety' mentioned in the essay was
in session. The phrase 'this civil war now at point to ensue'
suggests a date of composition between 3 November, when
Lambert departed to take up his command, and 15 November,
when an (abortive) treaty was signed. The tract was first published
in 1938.
8   (Saturday) JM's translation of a tercet from Dante is quoted
     (from *Of Reformation*) and praised by Henry Stubbe (?) in *A
     Light Shining out of Darkness* (Thomason's date; his copy is BL
     E.770.5).
9   JM is attacked as the author of *Eikonoklastes* in an anonymous
     single-sheet broadside, *A Guildhall Elegy* (Thomason's date; his
     copy is BL 669.f.22 (5)).
22   John Bradshaw dies (see 16 December).
29   JM signs in a sprawling hand the discharge of Richard
     Powell's bond of 1627 acknowledging payment of £500 (PRO
     C 152/61).

December

2/12 (Friday) Henry Oldenburg writes to JM from Paris (Royal
Society MS I, fol. 61); Richard Jones probably writes on the
same day, but his letter is lost.

6 JM receives interest on bond (£16). This is the last
recorded payment during the period when JM possessed the
bond, which he was to sell to Cyriack Skinner on 5 May 1660.

9 JM's fifty-first birthday.

16 The will of John Bradshaw is proved, bequeathing £10 to JM
(see 10 September 1655).

20 JM writes letters to Henry Oldenburg (*EF* No. 29) and Richard
Jones (*EF* No. 30).

26 Long Parliament meets again, excluding those expelled in
Pride's Purge of December 1648.

1660

In this year Francis Siefert publishes a poem (in German) that
alludes to JM and Salmasius (*Applausus gratulatorius* Carolo II,
Gdansk). Heinsius explains in an undated letter to Gronovius
(printed between letters dated December 1659 and April 1660) that
[Francis] Junius says that JM might be contributing to a supplement
to Jan Gruyter's *Lampas*, a collection of annotations on classical texts
(Burmann, III, 407). Johannes Andreas Gerhard publishes a *Discursus Publicus* (Jena) that discusses the Salmasius–JM controversy at
length, especially in sections 3, 5, 6, 8 ('Contra Miltonum Disputatur') and 9. Robert Creighton attacks JM's anti-royalist views (without naming him) in the preface to his translation into Latin of a
Greek treatise (Sylvester Sguropulus, *Vera Historia Unionis*).

January

1 (Sunday) General Monck leads his army across the Tweed into
England.

16 JM's *Defensio* is praised for its style and condemned for its
substance by Pierre du Moulin (*LR* IV, 298); on the same day
JM's blindness is mocked in *The Outcry of the London Prentices*
(Thomason's date; his copy is BL E.1013(12)).

February

3 (Friday) General Monck's army enters London.

11 An anonymous *Exact Account of the Receipts and Disbursements Expended by the Committee of Safety* seems to satirise JM's sonnet 20, to Lawrence (Thomason's date; his copy is BL E.1079(3*)).

16 General Monck calls for a free Parliament.

18–21 JM writes the first edition of *Ready and Easy Way*, which is published early in the last week of February.

21 The Rump Parliament recalls the Presbyterian members excluded in Pride's Purge.

March

In the first week of March JM drafts 'The Present Means... of a Free Commonwealth', a letter to General Monck; it is not clear from the surviving draft (published in 1698 from a manuscript that was subsequently lost) whether it was intended as a private letter or a public tract. JM may write the 'Digression' in the *History of Britain* in the first half of this month (so Woolrych, 1986 and 1993, but cf von Maltzahn, 1991 and 1993).

3 (Saturday) Thomason dates his copy of *Ready and Easy Way* (BL E.1016(11)).

8 *Ready and Easy Way* is advertised in *Mercurius Politicus* No. 610, 1–8 March; the advertisement includes errata.

13 JM is mocked by Sir Roger L'Estrange in *Be Merry and Wise*; Fortescue dates Thomason's copy (BL E.765(6)) 13 March, the date printed on the title-page.

16 The Long Parliament dissolves itself.

16–27 JM prepares second edition of *Ready and Easy Way*, which is published no later than the first week in April 1660.

17 *Ready and Easy Way* attacked in *The Character of the Rump* (Thomason's date; his copy is BL E.1017(20)); on Butler's authorship see von Maltzahn (1995a). On the same day JM's *Doctrine and Discipline of Divorce* seems to be mocked in a broadsheet called *A Free Parliament Litany* (Thomason's date; his copy is BL 669.f.24(19)).

24 William Colline mocks JM's *Ready and Easy Way* in *The Spirit of the Phanatiques Dissected* (Thomason's date; his copy is BL E.1017(39)); on the same day Sir Roger L'Estrange mocks JM (without naming him) in a broadside, *The Fanatique Powder-Plot* (Thomason's date; his copy is BL 669.f.24(38)).

30 JM said by the anonymous author of *The Censure of the Rota* to have 'achieved the honour to be styled the founder of a sect'

(Thomason's date; his copy is BL E.1019 (5*)); on Butler's authorship see von Maltzahn (1995*a*). At about the same time Dr William Fairebrother ridicules JM as a member of Harrington's *Rota* in *An Essay of a Loyal Breast*.

31 G[eorge?] S[tarkey]'s *Dignity of Kingship*, an attack on *Ready and Easy Way* by 'G.S.', is registered for publication (*SR* II, 255); the preface is dated 29 March; the tract was presumably published early in April.

April

The second edition of *Ready and Easy Way* is published no later than the first week of April. In the first half of the month JM publishes *Brief Notes upon a late Sermon*, an answer to a sermon preached by Matthew Griffith on 25 March and registered for publication on 31 March (*SR* II, 255). JM's tract must have been published after the publication of the sermon in the first few days of April but in time for Sir Roger L'Estrange to attack it in *No Blind Guides*, which is dated 20 April.

3 (Tuesday) Sir Roger L'Estrange mocks JM as the author of *Plain English* in *Treason Arraigned* (Thomason's date; his copy is BL E.1019(14)).

4 Charles II issues Declaration of Breda, promising a general amnesty and religious toleration.

5 Sir Roger L'Estrange mocks JM as the author of *An Alarum to the Armies* and *Plain English* in *Double Your Guards* (Thomason's date; his copy is BL E.1019(19)).

20 Sir Roger L'Estrange attacks *Brief Notes* in *No Blind Guides*. The date is taken from the title-page, but Thomason's copy (BL E.187(2)) is dated 25 April and that date is confirmed in Thomason's catalogue (BL C.38.h.21, Vol. 8, No. 826/13).

25 Monck calls a Convention Parliament to consider the Declaration of Breda. .

27 Sir Roger L'Estrange attacks JM as the author of *An Alarum* and *Plain English* in *Physician Cure thy Self*. Thomason catalogued his copy (BL E.1021(15)) s.v. 27 April (BL C.38.h.21, Vol. 8, No. 826/17); Fortescue gives 23 April in error.

28 JM's brother-in law Richard Powell is listed among the gentry of Oxfordshire who remained faithful to Charles I (*A Declaration of the Nobility ... of Oxon which have adhered to the late king*; Thomason's date; his copy is BL 669.f.25(2)).

May

JM goes into hiding at the house of an unidentified friend in Bartholomew Close (West Smithfield), where he is to stay 'till the Act of Oblivion came forth' (that is, 29 August); Phillips, in Darbishire, p. 74.

1   (Tuesday) Convention Parliament invites Charles II to return to England as a monarch with limited powers.

5   JM transfers excise bond to Cyriack Skinner; the document, signed on JM's behalf by Jeremie Picard, is now in the Richard Moncktori Milnes Collection. The document was offered for sale on 29 June 1995, and is reproduced in the Christie's catalogue of that date, but was subsequently withdrawn.

8   The restoration of Charles II is proclaimed. In the subsequent collapse of the Excise Office JM loses savings of £2,000 (Cyriack Skinner, Edward Phillips and Wood, in Darbishire, pp. 32, 78, 48).

14   G[eorge] S[tarkey?] mocks JM's political and divorce tracts in *Britain's Triumph*, and suggests that he commit suicide (Thomason's date; his copy is BL E.1023(13)).

17   JM's anti-monarchical tracts are mocked in the anonymous *Third Conference* (Thomason's date; his copy is BL E.1025(3)).

23   Bate's *Elenchus Motuum* is registered for publication (*SR* II, 265); see January 1661.

25   Charles II returns to England.

29   Charles II enters London in triumph.

31   William London publishes a *Catalogue of new books*, including *Treatise of Civil Power* and *Considerations* (Thomason's date; his copy is BL E.1025(17)).

June

JM is said by John Heydon in *The Idea of the Law Charactered* to have been struck blind by God as he wrote the second word of *Eikonoklastes* (Thomason gives the month but not the date; his copy is BL E.1916(2)).

1   (Friday) Joseph Hall alludes (posthumously) to JM's views on divorce in *The Shaking of the Olive Tree* (Thomason's date; his copy is BL E.185(1)).

6   Sir Roger L'Estrange attacks JM in *L'Estrange his Apology* (Thomason's date; his copy is BL E.187(1)); Peace of Copenhagen ends war between Sweden and Denmark.

16 JM is ordered to be arrested, and *Eikonoklastes* and *Defensio Prima* ordered to be burnt (Whitelocke's *Diary*, p. 606). JM is subsequently attacked in a reissue of Jane's *Eikon Aklastos* as *Salmasius his Dissection*, the title-page of which refers to the banning of *Eikonoklastes* (*Journal of the House of Commons* VIII 65–6; *Parliamentary Intelligencer* No '26' [that is 25]). On the same day Anthony Wood notes the removal of JM's books from the 'public library', i.e. the Bodleian (Bodleian MS Tanner 102, fol. 71^v; see Miller (1988) and von Maltzahn (1994), 172).

21 Parliamentary order against JM is summarised in *Mercurius Publicus* No. 25, 14–21 June.

25 The Parliamentary Intelligencer No. 26 corrects the statement in the previous issue (see 16 June), insisting that Parliament did not order JM's books to be burnt but rather 'resolved that his Majesty should be desired to order it'.

27 Council orders the Attorney-General to prepare a proclamation 'in consequence of an Order of the House of Commons [see 16 June] relating to books written & published by John Milton' (PRO PC 2/54, part 2, p. 46).

July

5/15 (Thursday) Gui Patin writes to André Falcourt reporting the rumour that JM's books have been burned and that JM has been taken prisoner and may have been hanged (Patin, III, 238). JM was still in hiding, and had not yet been arrested when the proclamation of 13 August was issued.

13 George Starkey attacks JM in *Royal...Blood crying aloud to Heaven* (Thomason's date; his copy is BL E.1032(7); on the last page of the book the date of composition is given as 18 June 1660).

14 JM is said in a broadside (*The Picture of the Good Old Cause*) to have been struck blind by God for his anti-monarchical tracts (Thomason's date; his copy is BL 669.f.25(57)).

26 David Lloyd attacks JM as a 'blind beetle' and a mercenary in *Eikon Basilike* (Thomason's date; his copy is BL E.1922(2)); another edition published by the same bookseller on the same day attributes the tract to 'R. F. Esq: an Eye-witness'.

31/10 August A letter from QNB (?) in Amsterdam to an unknown recipient enquires (in Latin) about 'Milton and the prisoners' (BL MS Sloane 649, fol. 42).

August

13   (Monday) Publication of a proclamation to call in books by JM
      (and John Goodwin) that are to be burnt; the official copy is PRO
      SP 45/11, p. 14. The printed date is confirmed on Thomason's
      copy (BL 669.f.25(70)) and in Whitelocke's *Diary* (p. 612). JM and
      Goodwin are said to have fled and obscured themselves.

16   The proclamation is reprinted in *Mercurius Publicus*. No. 33 (9–
      16 August).

17   Colonel Baker mocks JM in *The Blazing Star* (Thomason's date;
      his copy is BL E.1040(3)).

20   The proclamation is reprinted in *Parliamentary Intelligencer* No.
      34 (13–20 August).

22   The proclamation is reprinted in the Edinburgh edition of
      Mercurius Publicus No. 29 (15–22 August).

27   JM's books are burnt by the hangman at the Old Bailey (*LR*, IV,
      334).

29   Act of Free and General Pardon, Indemnity and Oblivion
      given Royal Assent; JM is not named, and therefore escapes
      the death penalty.

September
'Soon after [the Act of Oblivion]...he took a house in Holborn near
Red Lion Fields; where he stayed not long before his pardon hav-
ing passed the seal, he removed to Jewin Street.' (Phillips, in
Darbishire pp. 74–5); JM was to live in the house in Holborn, in
St Giles in the Fields, until December.

 3   (Monday) JM is mocked in *The London Printer His Lamentation*
      (Thomason's date; his copy is BL E.765(16)).

 5   The burning of JM's books in London is recorded in *Mercurius
      Publicus* No. 37 (6–13 September), p. 578 and *Parliamentary
      Intelligencer* No. 37 (3–10 September), p. 589 (see Miller, 1988);
      the date is confirmed in Whitelocke's *Diary* (p. 613). On the
      same day (5/15 September) the French edition of Salmasius's
      posthumous reply to JM is published in Dijon. The dedication
      by Salmasius's son Claude to Charles II is dated 22 August/1
      September.

10   JM's views on divorce are attacked in the anonymous *Brief
      Description or Character of the Fanatics* (Thomason's date; his
      copy is BL E.1765(1)).

19   English edition of *Salmasius Posthumus* is registered for pub-
      lication (*SR* II, 278).

28/8 October   Gui Patin alludes to JM in a letter to André Falcourt (Patin, III, 280).

October
In this month, or possibly later, JM is arrested. The dates of his incarceration are uncertain, and the evidence is conflicting (see Parker, 1996, p. 1087), but Cyriack Skinner's statement that JM 'was quickly set at liberty' suggests a short imprisonment.
2/12   (Tuesday) Gui Patin alludes to JM in a letter to M. Belin (Patin, I, 255).
4/14   Jean Chapelain (see *DBF*) writes to Claude Salmasius *fils* attacking JM and praising Claude's father (*LR* IV, 340–41).
18   Thomas Forde's *Faenestra in Pectore* is published shortly before this date, when it is advertised in *Mercurius Publicus* 42 (11–18 October); Forde mocks JM's views on divorce, and alludes to JM's coat of arms in his reference to those 'who are thus joined in you know whose phrase, like a Spread Eagle, with one body but two heads' (pp. 103–6).
25/4 November   Jean Chapelain writes to Heinsius attacking JM as impudent and sophistical and praising *Salmasius Posthumus* (*LR*, IV, 343–4).

November
22/2 December (Thursday): Heinsius writes to Spanheim about the posthumous publication of Salmasius's *Ad Ioannem Miltonum Responsio* (see Miller, 1974a).
25   JM's brother Christopher is called to the Bench of the Inner Temple (Inderwick, III, 1). Masters of the Bench were the senior members of the Inns of Court.

December
English edition of Salmasius's posthumous reply (in Latin) to JM is published; Thomason's copy of *Ad Ioannem Miltonum Responsio* (BL E.1926(2)) only gives the month, but he listed it 13th of the 14 books received during December (BL C.38.h.21, Vol. 10, No. 1913/835), so probably received his copy at the end of the month.
3/13   (Monday) Johann Christian, Baron Boineburg mentions the publication of Salmasius's attack on JM in a letter from Mainz to Hermann Conring (Wolfenbüttel, Herzog-

August-Bibliothek, 'Commercium literarium Joh. Christiani de Boineburg et Hermanni Conringii a. 1660–1664' fol. 649.84.12. Extrav., fol. 3). Mainz had adopted the Gregorian calendar in 1582, so Baron Boineburg's date of 13 December is probably N.S; on Boineburg and Conring see *NDB*.

6   Salmasius's posthumous reply to JM is advertised (*Mercurius Publicus* No. 49, 29 November–6 December).

8   Ezekiel Spanheim writes (to Baron Boineburg?) from Heidelberg, alluding to Salmasius's *Defensio* and *Responsio* (Wolfenbüttel, Herzog-August-Bibliothek, 'Commercium', fol. 5^v). Heidelberg was on the Julian calendar, so the date ('the Ides of December') is probably O.S.; on Spanheim see *ADB*.

9   JM's fifty-second birthday.

13 Spanheim writes to Heinsius from Heidelberg deploring Salmasius's posthumous attack on JM and Heinsius (Burmann, III, 812).

15 JM is ordered to be released from custody in the Tower and to pay his fees (*Journals of the House of Commons*, VIII, 208); his pardon does not survive, but it is listed in the PRO's Index to Warrant Books, 1660–1722, A-P, (IND/1/8911, p. 201) and the Index to the Signet Office Docket Books, 1660–1737 (PRO SO 4/5 fol. 164), both s.v. December 1660. According to *Hollandsche Mercurius* No. 249 (1661), p. 163, JM 'was freed through good promises' (*nu uytging door goe belaften*). His pardon is deplored in anonymous verses in a lost copy of *Eikonoklastes* (*LR* IV, 352–3).

17 JM protests at excessive fees (£150) for his imprisonment; the matter is raised by Andrew Marvell in Parliament and referred to the Committee of Privileges (*Journal of the House of Commons*, VIII, 209); the eventual outcome is not known.

1661

Andrew Marvell recalls in *The Rehearsal Transprosed* (1672) that 'after the royal clemency' Samuel Parker (the future Bishop of Oxford who was to attack JM in 1673) 'frequented JM incessantly and haunted his house day by day'. The house must have been JM's new home in Jewin Street (see general entry for September 1660), to which JM moved after his release from prison. He lived in this house until his third marriage (on 24 February 1663), but according to Phillips 'stayed not long after his new marriage' (Darbishire, p. 75).

In this year Philip von Zesen reviles JM in *Die Verschmähete doch wieder erhöhete Majestäht* (Amsterdam), pp. 185–6; the book is dated 1662, but the title-page is dated 1661. Johannes Böckelmann alludes to JM's divorce tracts in the preface to his inaugural lecture; the lecture was printed in Heidelberg in 1659, but the preface was separately printed in Duisburg in 1661. John Fell attacks JM's views on divorce (without naming him) in *The Life of H. Hammond*, pp. 67–8.

January
George Bate attacks *Eikonoklastes* and *Defensio* in *Elenchi Motuum Naperorum in Anglia* (revised edition, 1661, pp 237–8; there is no allusion in the first edition of 1650).

7 (Monday) A German-speaking owner of JM's *Defensio* notes JM's release from prison in a manuscript note inside the back cover; the volume is now in the Rutgers University Library (X DA/396/A.3S32/1652).

18/28 Heinsius writes to Spanheim about Salmasius's *Ad Ioannem Miltonum Responsio* (see Miller, 1974a).

30 On the anniversary of the death of Charles I the bodies of Bradshaw, Cromwell and Ireton are disinterred, taken to Tyburn, hanged until sunset, and then decapitated and buried under the gallows; their skulls are impaled in Westminster Hall, where they remain until 1684. The public degradation of the bodies seems to be recalled in *Samson Agonistes* 693–4 ('their carcases/To dogs and fowls a prey').

31 Robert Baillie condemns JM in a letter to William Spang (*LR* IV, 360).

April
20 (Saturday) Sir Edward Hyde is created Earl of Clarendon.

23 Charles II is crowned.

May

8 (Wednesday) Charles II's second Parliament (the 'Cavalier Parliament') meets.

June
5/15 June (Wednesday) Conring replies to Baron Boineburg condemning both Salmasius and JM (Wolfenbüttel, Herzog-

August-Bibliothek, 'Commercium', fol. 82ᵛ). The letter is dated
(in Latin) 'the Fast of the Four Seasons, June 1661', a reference
to the Ember Days (Latin *jejunia quatuor temporum*) that follow
Whit Sunday. In 1661 the Ember Days were 5, 7 and 8 June.
Helmstedt was a Protestant city, so the dating is O.S.

6   Baron Boineburg writes from Mainz to Hermann Conring in
Helmstedt asking for his opinion on Salmasius's attack on JM
(*LR*, IV, 362). Mainz was on the Julian calendar, so Boineburg's
letters are probably dated O.S.

21/1 July   Baron Boineburg agrees with Conring's views of Salmasius and JM (Wolfenbüttel, Herzog-August-Bibliothek,
'Commercium', fol. 96).

30   JM's brother Christopher's son, Christopher, enters Inner Temple 'at the request of his father' (Inderwick, III, 3).

November
9   (Saturday) Thomas Flatman dates the first of the entries in his
'Miscellanies', poems that often imitate JM's poems (University of Pennsylvania Library, Thomas Flatman MS ENG 28); the
collection was completed in 1670 and published in 1674.

December
9   (Monday) JM's fifty-third birthday.

1662

In this year Aitzema mentions the reaction of an unnamed learned
man (*geleert man*), presumably Heinsius, to JM's *Defensio* (*Historie of
Verhael van Saken van Staet en Oorlogh*, 1662, VII, 205); the comment,
to the effect that Salmasius had defended a good cause badly
whereas JM had defended a bad cause well, echoes Heinsius's
letter of 8/18 June 1651. Henry Foulis lists JM among 'Billingsgate
[i.e. foul-mouthed] authors' in *The History of the Wicked Plots* (1662),
p. 4, 24. Richard Perrinchief describes JM as a 'base scribe' and a
'needy pedagogue' in the introduction to his edition of *Basilika: The
Works of King Charles the Martyr* (1662), pp. 94–5. 'I.T.' attributes
JM's blindness to divine retribution in *The Traitor's perspective Glass,
or, Sundry Examples of God's Just Judgements executed upon many
Eminent Regicides* (1662), p. 21; a copy in the British Library (BL
1326.c.10) contains a handwritten note filling out 'I.T.' as 'John
Taylor, the Water Poet'; the attribution is uncertain.

It is likely that in this year the Quaker Thomas Ellwood is introduced to JM by Isaac Pennington (Quaker son of the regicide of the same name) and Dr Nathan Paget. Ellwood records that he took lodgings near JM's house in Jewin Street, 'and from thenceforth went every day in the afternoon (except on the first-days of the week) and sitting by him in his dining room, read to him in such books in the Latin tongue, as he pleased to hear me read' (*The History of the Life of Thomas Ellwood*, 1714); 'first-day' is the Quaker term for Sunday.

March
13 (Thursday) Clarendon mentions JM in a letter to John Gauden in connection with the authorship of *Eikon Basilike* (*LR* IV, 369).

May
19 (Monday) Act of Uniformity, according to which all clergymen, academics, teachers and private tutors are required to renounce the Solemn League and Covenant and accept the liturgy of the Church of England before 24 August.
21 Charles II marries Catherine of Braganza, daughter of King John IV of Portugal; her dowry includes the ceding of Tangier and Bombay to Charles.

June
14 (Saturday) Sir Henry Vane is executed (on the anniversary of the Battle of Naseby).

July
 3 (Thursday) JM sends his sonnet on Sir Henry Vane to George Sikes (Sikes, p. 93).

August
 6 (Wednesday) Baron Boineburg tells Conring in a letter from Mainz that JM has sent a copy of Jean Bodin's *Arcana* (presumably the *Colloquium Heptaplomeres* of 1593) to a friend in Germany (*LR* IV, 371); the friend is probably Aitzema.
24 (?) JM's blindness is scorned in an anonymous poem entitled 'Democracy Rampant'. The manuscript was calendared by HMC in 1891 (Eleventh Report, Part 9, p. 140), but sold at Sotheby's on 30 March 1936; its present location is unknown. The date

is highly uncertain, but the poem refers to St Bartholomew Sunday, and in 1662 many non-conforming ministers were ejected.

September
5   (Friday) JM's sonnet to Sir Henry Vane is published on or before this date in *The life and Death of Sir Henry Vane*. The date is inscribed on a copy presented by Lady Vane to Sarah Calvert; the volume is now in the Lilly Library at Indiana University.

October
14/24   (Tuesday) Conring tells Boineburg that he still wants Bodin's book, that he has not seen JM's book on divorce, and that JM's writings against Salmasius may be unsound but are shrewd and inventive (Wolfenbüttel, Herzog-August-Bibliothek, 'Commercium', fol. 282^v).
16   Boineburg tells Conring that he is still looking for the Bodin *Arcana*, that horrible book, which had been sent from London by JM (though Boineburg has still not seen a copy), and that JM had also sent some of his other books in English, including his influential divorce tract (*LR* IV, 373).
27   Charles II sells Dunkirk to France for 2,500,000 livres (£400,000).

November
3/13   (Monday) Boineburg tells Conring that the man who owns the Bodin volume [Aitzema?] also has JM's divorce tract (Wolfenbüttel, Herzog-August-Bibliothek, 'Commercium', fol. 284).

December
9   (Tuesday) JM's fifty-fourth birthday.
29   JM's niece Ann Agar is licensed to marry David Moore of Richmond; see Parker (1996), 1094 n. 70.

1663

The anonymous *Treatise of the Execution of Justice* often echoes JM's *Tenure*; the printer (and author?) John Twyn was to be executed for printing the book on 20 February 1664. Johann Heinrich Boecler (on whom see *NDB*) includes an account of JM in his *Museum ad*

Amicum (Strasbourg, 1663), pp. 27–41. Hans Wandal discusses *Defensio prima* in *Juris regii* (Hünfeld).

January
30 (Friday) Robert South attacks JM in sermon preached before Charles II at Court; the manuscript is in the Bodleian (MS Rawlinson E.69).

February
8 (Sunday) JM's brother-in-law Richard Powell is called to the Bench (Inderwick, III, 13).
11 JM signs declaration of intention to marry Elizabeth Minshull (Lambeth Palace MS FMI/3B fol. 149), giving his age as 'about 50' (he was 54) and hers as 'about 25' (she had recently turned 24); JM's red-haired bride was the granddaughter of Nathan Paget's aunt, so it is possible that the match was arranged by Dr Paget. On the Minshull family see *LR*, IV, 381–3.
16 Sir Roger L'Estrange attacks JM's *Tenure* in *Toleration Discussed*; the date is taken from the imprimatur.
17 JM's brother Christopher appears as a witness in a Chancery case (PRO C24/877/45).
24 JM marries Elizabeth Minshull in St Mary Aldermary (Parish Register); 'after his new marriage . . . he removed to a house in the Artillery Walk leading to Bunhill Fields' (Phillips in Darbishire, p. 75). After JM's death his servant Elizabeth Fisher deposed to the effect that 'a little before he was married to Elizabeth Milton' [see 24 February 1663] JM's daughter Mary was informed of the impending wedding and replied 'that it was no news to hear of his wedding but if she could hear of his death that was something'; Elizabeth Fisher adds that JM's children 'had made away some of his books and would have sold the rest to the dunghill women' (PRO PROB 24/13/313).

March
21 (Saturday) James Heath condemns JM's regicide tracts in *A Brief Chronicle of the Late Intestine War*. The date is taken from the imprimatur; the volume was subsequently registered on 30 March (*SR*, II, 322)
23/2 April Gaston de Comminges (see *DBF*) writes from London to King Louis XIV explaining (in French) that the arts and sciences have migrated from England to France, leaving only

the memory of Bacon, More, Buchanan and, more recently, 'one named Milton, who has made himself more infamous through his dangerous writings than are the executioners and assassins of their king' (Bibliothèque Nationale, MS fr.10712).

May
28 (Thursday) British and Portuguese forces defeat the Spanish at Amegial.

June
3 (Wednesday) Sir Roger L'Estrange condemns *Tenure* as treasonous in *Considerations and Proposals*; the date is taken from the title-page.

August
1 (Sunday) Before this date JM talks to the Danish Resident, probably Simon de Petkum (see *DBL*), about a disagreement with John Dury about divorce, and about Salmasius. The conversation is recorded in the 'Itinerarium' of Oluf Borch (Copenhagen, Kongelige Bibliotek, MS NKS 373c, 4to, pp. 27–8), on whom see *DBL*.

October
17 (Saturday) John Beale mentions JM in a letter to Robert Boyle (Boyle, V, 438)
24 John Evelyn records in his diary that 'Mr Edward Phillips came to be my son's preceptor; this gentleman was nephew to Milton, who wrote against Salmasius' *Defensio*, but was not at all infected with his principles, though brought up by him'.

December
9 (Wednesday) JM's fifty-fifth birthday.
25 JM's writings are ridiculed in *Cabala, or an Impartial Account of the Non-Conformists' Private Designs*; the date is the last date mentioned in the title.

1664

JM's poem on Shakespeare is reprinted in Third Folio. JM is satirised as 'blind Milton' in the almanac *Poor Robin*, s.v. 5 November. The allusion is repeated in the annual editions of 1665–70 and 1674–77. Johannes Andreas Gerhard discusses JM and *Defensio prima* in sections 5–10 of *Discursus exoterici* (Jena).

April
28 (Thursday) JM is mentioned in a manuscript history by Roger Ley entitled 'Gesta Britannica' as an opponent of James Ussher (BL Stowe MS 76, fol. 301^v); the date is written on the final page of the manuscript.

May
The Conventicle Act, directed against Nonconformists, forbids meetings of more than five people except in private households.
1 (Sunday) JM's brother Christopher is named as attendant to Thomas Foster, Reader in the Inner Temple (Inderwick, III, 23).

June
Anglo-Dutch War.

August
27 (Saturday) Peter Stuyvesant surrenders New Amsterdam to the British.
29 The British rename New Amsterdam as New York.

November
3 (Thursday) JM's brother Christopher is named as attendant to Sir Richard Foster, Reader in the Inner Temple (Inderwick, III, 24).

December
9 (Friday) JM's fifty-sixth birthday.

1665

In this year JM's *Defensio prima* is mentioned by Johann Joachim Zentgraf in a dissertation on the Quakers (*Colluvies Quackerorum*, Strasbourg). *Eikonoklastes* is discussed in Thomas Sprat's *Observations on Monsieur de Sorbier's voyage into England*, pp. 58–9. Georg Horn discusses JM's views on divorce (and refers to Cromwell's letters concerning the Piedmont massacre) in *Historia ecclesiastica et politica* (Leiden and Rotterdam).

January
30 (Tuesday) Henry King alludes to *Eikonoklastes* in a sermon preached at Whitehall and subsequently published.

February
22 (Wednesday) Outbreak of the second Anglo-Dutch naval war.

April
23 (Sunday) JM's brother Christopher is appointed Reader in the Inner Temple for the Summer Vacation (Inderwick, III, 36).

June
7 (Wednesday) JM assigns Maundy's statute staple of 14 January 1658 to Baldwin and Jeremy Hamey; the document is signed on JM's behalf (Rosenbach Museum, Philadelphia, 810/25). At the same time JM authorises an acquittance (that is, receipt) for £500 to Jeremy Hamey; the document is signed on JM's behalf (Folger Library, MS X.d.161).

July
JM moves to a cottage in Chalfont St Giles rented on his behalf (from Anne Fleetwood, daughter of the regicide George Fleetwood) by Thomas Ellwood; the cottage is the only residence of JM still standing, and is now a museum. JM moves from London at an unspecified time when the plague was 'growing hot in London'; Ellwood records that he made the arrangements 'some little time before I went to Aylesbury Prison', which was on 1 July 1665.
2 (Sunday) The Dutch are defeated off Lowestoft.

August
Thomas Ellwood is released from Aylesbury prison, and returns to Chalfont, where he 'soon made a visit to [Milton] to welcome him into the country. After some common discourse had passed between us, he called for a manuscript of his, which being brought he delivered it to me, bidding me take it home with me, and read it at my leisure, and when I had done, return it to him, with my judgement thereupon. When I came home, and had set myself to read it, I found it was that excellent poem which he entituled *Paradise Lost*. After I had, with best attention, read it through, I made him another visit, and returned him the book, with due

acknowledgement of the favour he had done me, in communicating it to me. He asked me how I liked it, and what I thought of it, which I modestly but freely told him; and after some further discourse about it, I pleasantly said to him, "Thou hast said much here of *Paradise Lost*, but what hast thou to say of *Paradise Found*?" He made me no answer, but sat some time in a muse, then brake off that discourse and fell upon another subject' (*History of the Life of Thomas Ellwood*, 1714, p. 233).

September
7/17   (Thursday) Philip IV dies and is succeeded as King of Spain by his son Charles II.
25   'Jn°. Melton' of Cripplegate is reported in arrears of 1s. 4d for taxes on eight hearths (PRO E179/147/630). The tax, which had been instituted in 1662, was levied at the rate of two shillings per hearth until it was abolished in 1689.

October
9   (Monday) Fifth session of Cavalier Parliament is held in Oxford (until 31 October) because of the plague in Westminster.

December
9   (Saturday) JM's fifty-seventh birthday.

1666

Pierre Nichole (?) denounces JM as an advocate of regicide in the preface of *The Pernicious Consequence of the New Heresy of the Jesuits against the King*. The 'John Phillips, schoolmaster' living in Aldersgate Street in 1666, when he is taxed on six hearths, is probably JM's nephew (PRO E179/252, p. 32).

January
16/26   (Tuesday) France and Holland declare war on England.

February
JM returns from Chalfont to London 'after the sickness was over', which suggests a date in February. Some time after JM returned to London he was visited by Thomas Ellwood, to whom, according to Ellwood, he showed 'his second poem, called

Paradise Regained, and in a pleasant tone said to me, "This is owing to you, for you put it into my head by the question you put to me at Chalfont, which before I had not thought of..." (*History of the Life of Thomas Ellwood*, 1714, p. 234).

May

6   (Sunday) JM's brother Christopher is reappointed as Reader in the Inner Temple (Inderwick, III, 39), again for the Summer Vacation.

27/6 June Heimbach writes to JM from Cleves (BL Add. MS 5016*, ff. 6–7); the letter is dated 6 June 'by the common Christian era' (*Vulgaris aerae Christianae*) which presumably means Old Style; if the phrase means New Style, the date should be 6/16 June.

June

1   (Friday) Naval engagement with the Dutch off the Dunes of Dunkirk lasts for four days but ends inconclusively.

27 John Pell mentions JM in a letter to Theodore Haak, explaining that he has advised 'my Lord' (William Brereton) 'to be a little wary in speaking to Mr Milton [about the "business of Mr Gr."] because he is one of those who have lent M. Gr. mony upon his land' (Bodleian MS Aubrey 13, fol. 92). 'Mr Gr.' has not been identified.

July

25/4 August (Wednesday) The English fleet under George Monck, Duke of Albemarle, defeats the Dutch at the Battle of St James' Fight.

August

15 (Wednesday) JM writes to Peter Heimbach (*EF* No. 31).

September

2   (Sunday) Outbreak of Fire of London; JM's house in Bread Street is destroyed, 'which was all the real estate he had' (Wood, in Darbishire, p. 48); by 6 September the city was virtually destroyed, including St Paul's Cathedral.

November

5   (Monday) JM's brother Christopher is appointed Reader in the Inner Temple for the Lent Vacation of 1667. The Lent

Readerships were reserved for 'double readers', i.e. benchers who had previously read in the August vacation (Inderwick, III, 40).

30 JM's brother-in-law Richard Powell is described as a 'Master of the Bench' (Inderwick, III, 42).

December
9 (Sunday) JM's fifty-eighth birthday.

1667

Samuel Woodford seems to allude to JM's shorter poems in the preface to *A Paraphrase upon the Psalms*. A book list in the hand of John Locke, drawn up in approximately this year, includes *Of Reformation*, *Doctrine and Discipline of Divorce* and *Of Education* (PRO 30/24).

April
27 (Saturday) JM signs a contract with Samuel Simmons for publication of *Paradise Lost* (BL Add MS 18861; see Lindenbaum, 1992); the poem had already been licensed by Thomas Tomkins (see von Maltzahn, 1996).
28 JM's brother Christopher is chosen Reader in the Inner Temple for the last time; on the same day JM's brother-in-law Richard Powell's son is granted special admission to the Inner Temple 'at the request of his father' (Inderwick, III, 45).

May
12/22 (Sunday) Pope Alexander VII dies.
22 JM's brother Christopher is sued by John Gray of Ipswich in a dispute over the conveyance of land (PRO C5/49/18).

June
JM's brother Christopher answers the suit of John Gray (PRO C5/49/18).
10/20 (Monday) Giulio Rospigliosi is elected Pope Clement IX.
12 The Dutch fleet razes Sheerness and sails up the River Medway, raiding Chatham dockyard and escaping the next day with the royal barge.

July

21/31   (Sunday) Peace of Breda between Holland and France with
England.

August

20   (Tuesday) *Paradise Lost: A Poem in Ten Books* is registered for
publication (*SR* II, 381).

30   Fall of Clarendon, who resigns as Lord Chancellor.

31   John Beale mentions JM in a letter to John Evelyn (BL Evelyn
MSS Letters 63; see von Maltzahn (1992)).

September

4   (Wednesday) Marvell's 'Last Instructions to a Painter' echoes
Paradise Lost in several passages; if the date (taken from Bod-
leian MS Eng. poet.d.49) is correct, Marvell must have read
Paradise Lost before publication.

11   John Beale again mentions JM in a letter to John Evelyn (BL
Evelyn MSS Letters 64; see von Maltzahn (1992)).

October

10   (Thursday) Parliament reconvenes. Some time after this date
Paradise Lost is published; the first indication of its publication
seems to be Beale's letter of 11 November. Sir John Denham is
said to have come 'into the House [of Commons] one morning
with a sheet [of *Paradise Lost*], wet from the press, in his hand'
and proclaimed it 'part of the noblest poem that ever was
wrote in any language or any age' (Richardson, in
Darbishire, p. 295). On the publication date see von Maltzahn
(1996).

16   John Beale again mentions JM in a letter to John Evelyn
(BL Evelyn MSS Letters 67; see von Maltzahn (1992)).

November

3   (Sunday) JM's brother-in-law Richard Powell is elected as
Auditor of the Inner Temple (Inderwick, III, 47).

11   John Beale discusses rhyme with likely reference to *Paradise
Lost* in a letter to John Evelyn (BL Evelyn MSS Letters 69; see
von Maltzahn (1992)).

18   John Beale discusses *Paradise Lost* in a letter to John Evelyn (BL
Evelyn MSS Letters 68; bound out of sequence; see von
Maltzahn (1992)).

24 JM's brother Christopher's son Richard is admitted to the Inner Temple (Inderwick, III, 49).
29 Clarendon goes into exile on the advice of the king.

December
9 (Monday) JM's fifty-ninth birthday.

1668

Two more issues of *Paradise Lost* are published. Hobbes mentions JM slightingly (*Behemoth*, 1679, p. 172). David Lloyd attacks *Eikonoklastes* in *Memoires of the Lives, Actions, Sufferings and Death*. Roger Palmer, Earl of Castlemaine, mentions JM in *A Reply to the Answer of the Catholic Apology*, p. 143. Johann Friedrich Pöpping discusses *Defensio prima* in *Orbis Illustratus* (Hamburg), pp. 300–1.

January
13/23 (Monday) England and the United Provinces sign Treaty of The Hague, which pledges both countries to mutual defence and to an undertaking to mediate between France and Spain; Sweden subsequently signs the treaty, thus creating a Triple Alliance.
22 Sir John Hobart mentions *Paradise Lost* appreciatively in a letter to John Hobart (Bodleian MS Tanner 45, fol. 258; see Rosenheim).
27 John Hobart mentions JM in a letter to Sir John Hobart (Bodleian MS Tanner 45, fol. 264).
29 JM's brother Christopher's son John is admitted to Pembroke College Cambridge.
30 Sir John Hobart again mentions *Paradise Lost* favourably (Bodleian MS Tanner 45*, fol. 271; see Rosenheim).

February
3/13 (Monday) Spain recognises the independence of Portugal in the Treaty of Lisbon.
9 JM's brother Christopher's son Christopher is called to the Bar (Inderwick, III, 49).

March
12 (Thursday) JM's brother Christopher's son, Christopher, is buried (Parish Register, St Nicholas, Ipswich).

28 John Hay, Earl of Tweeddale, alludes to JM and Morus in a letter to an unknown recipient. The location of the letter is not known (see *Atheneum*, 18 May 1878, p. 633).

April
2 (Thursday) John Beale mentions *Paradise Lost* in a letter to John Evelyn (BL Evelyn MSS Letters 71); see von Maltzahn (1992).

September
9/19 (Sunday) John II, King of Poland, abdicates.

November
8 (Sunday) JM's brother Christopher is chosen as attendant to the Reader in the Inner Temple; on the same day JM's brother-in-law Richard Powell is chosen as auditor (Inderwick, III, 52).

December
9 (Wednesday) JM's sixtieth birthday.

1669

Two more issues of *Paradise Lost* are published; Simon Patrick appropriates some passages from the second edition of *Eikonoklastes* (pp. 206–7) in his *A Continuation of a Friendly Debate*, pp. 127–9. Francis Vavassor attacks JM's grammar in *De Epigrammate Liber*, on which see Miller (1975c).

January
9 (Saturday) JM's brother Christopher sits as Justice of the Peace in Ipswich (PRO SP 29/254)

April
26 (Monday) JM receives £5 more for *Paradise Lost*; the receipt, now in Christ's College, Cambridge (MS 8), is signed on his behalf, possibly by Thomas Ellwood (Shawcross, 1959), but arguably by another scribe (Beal, 76).
30 A record in the Company of Goldsmiths' *Extracts of Leases* notes three garrets 'abutting east upon Bread Street north part on Milton then Hussey and part on Goare'.

This entry could refer to JM's occupancy of a rebuilt house, but is more likely to refer to his earlier status as a lease-holder.

June
9/19 (Wednesday) The Lithuanian Michael Wisniowiecki is elected King of Poland.
28 *Accedence Commenced Grammar* announced, and probably published (*Mercurius Librarius* No. 4, licensed 28 June).

November
30/9 December (Tuesday) Pope Clement IX dies.

December
9 (Thursday) JM's sixty-first birthday.
18 John Beale mentions *Paradise Lost* in a letter to John Evelyn (BL Evelyn MSS Letters 93; see von Maltzahn (1992)).
29 JM's brother Christopher's son John is buried at Ipswich (Parish Register, St Nicholas).

1670

According to Richardson (who tells the story twice), in this year JM lodged for a period at the house of the bookseller Edward Millington (Richardson, in Darbishire pp. 203, 275). The circumstances of this temporary residence are not known, but the move may be connected with JM's decision to sell a large part of his library on the grounds that the collection would be of no use to his heirs and that 'he thought he might sell it more to their advantage than they could be able to do themselves' (Toland in Darbishire, pp. 192–3). John Eachard refers slightingly to *Of Education* and *Doctrine and Discipline of Divorce* in *The Grounds and Occasions*. A heavily-revised second edition of Sir Roger L'Estrange's *Toleration Discussed* (see 16 February 1663) reformulates the attack on JM's *Tenure*.

March
5 'And when the subject of divorce was under consideration with the Lords, upon the account of Lord Roos, [JM] was consulted by an eminent member of that House' (Cyriack

Skinner, in Darbishire, p. 33); the debate extended from 5 March to 11 April. On the divorce of John Manners (son of the Earl of Rutland) and his wife Anne see *LR* V, 11–15.

April
19/29   (Tuesday) Emilio Altieri is elected as Pope Clement X.

May
Edward Phillips praises *Paradise Lost* in Johann Buchler's *Phrasium Poeticarum Thesaurus* (17th edition, 1669), p. 399; the title-page is dated 1669, but the Term Catalogues list the book s.v. Easter Term 1670.
22/1 June   (Sunday) Treaty of Dover is signed in secret; according to its terms Charles agrees to declare his conversion to Catholicism and subsequently to restore Catholicism to Britain; he also agrees to give Louis XIV a free hand in Holland and Spain. In return England is to receive subsidies of £150,000 and an additional £225,000 as long as the war lasts.

July
2   (Saturday) *Paradise Regained* is licensed by Thomas Tompkins.

September
10   (Saturday) *Paradise Regained* and *Samson Agonistes* are registered for publication (*SR*, II, 415)

November
1   (Tuesday) JM's *History of Britain* is published on or before this date, when its publication is noted in a letter from Thomas Blount to Wood (Bodleian MS Wood F40, fol. 80); the price is six shillings. The first issue was printed 'for James Allestry', who died on 3 November; a second title-page (dated 1671 and naming a new publisher) was quickly printed, and subsequently advertised in the Term Catalogue licensed on 22 November. The engraved portrait of JM by William Faithorne that was printed in the *History* is labelled 'Ætat: 62.1670', which in this case means in his sixty-second year, at the age of 61. On the historiographical context of JM's *History* see von Maltzahn (1991).
10   Thomas Blount notes reputation of JM's *History of Britain* in a letter to Wood (Bodleian MS Wood F40, fol. 82).

22 Term Catalogue advertising *History of Britain, Paradise Regained* and *Samson Agonistes* is licensed for publication. The same catalogue announces Pierre du Moulin's *Parerga*, which attacks JM in an account of the *Clamor* controversy.

27 JM's brother Christopher's son Thomas is admitted to Inner Temple (Inderwick, III, 74).

December
9 (Friday) JM's sixty-second birthday.

12 Henry Oldenburg drafts memorandum to send copy of JM's *History of Britain* to Francis Vernon in Paris (Royal Society MS 5, No. 15).

21/31 A bogus Treaty of Dover makes public the secret Treaty of Dover, but omits reference to Charles's conversion to Catholicism.

24 John Beale, who has seen the Michaelmas Term Catalogue (22 November) asserts in a letter to John Evelyn that JM 'is now abroad again, in prose and in verse, epic and dramatic' (BL Evelyn MSS Letters 108; see von Maltzahn (1992)).

1671

JM's brother Christopher is named among gentry of Suffolk (BL Add MS 19,142, fol. 79^v).

January
9 (Monday) John Beale praises JM's *History of Britain* in a letter to John Evelyn (BL Evelyn MSS Letters 109; see von Maltzahn (1992)).

25/4 February Bigot tells Heinsius in a letter from Rouen that *'Milton a fait imprimer en Angleterre l'Histoire d'Angleterre jusques à Guillaume le conquérant'* ('Milton has had *The History of England up to William the Conqueror* printed in England') (Rijksuniversiteitsbibliotheek, Leiden, BPL 1923/II, letter 101).

February
4 (Saturday) John Beale mentions JM in a letter to Henry Oldenburg (Royal Society MS 5, No. 28).

April
22 (Saturday) Charles II prorogues Parliament (till February 1673).

May
24 (Wednesday) JM's brother-in-law Richard Powell is appointed as Reader in the Inner Temple (Inderwick, III, 75).
29 *Paradise Regained* and *Samson Agonistes* are advertised in John Starkey's *Catalogue* (along with *Tetrachordon* and *Accedence*) and must therefore have been published before this date. The date of composition of *Samson Agonistes* is not known (but see Introduction, p. 4).

June
23/3 July (Friday) Emery Bigot writes from Rouen to Lorenzo Panciatichi (then in Amsterdam) to report that *'ces Antiquités d'Angleterre recueillis de plusieurs autheurs pourroient bien estre de Mr. Milton, luy mesme m'ayant dit qu'il travailloit à semblable ouvrage'* ('those English Antiquities collected by several authors could well be by Mr Milton, as he told me himself that he was working on a similar project') (Biblioteca Nazionale, Florence, MS Panciatichi 194, letter 43); Bigot's biographer comments that 'Bigot never uses *"on m'a dit"* as a synonym for *"on m'a écrit"*, so the reference must be to a personal acquaintance with Milton' (Doucette, p. 36).

December
9 (Saturday) JM's sixty-third birthday.

1672

Thomas Blount quotes JM's *History of Britain* in *Animadversions upon Sir Richard Baker's Chronicle*. JM's nephew John Phillips appropriates a passage from *Paradise Lost* in *Montelion's Predictions*. Samuel von Pufendorf (see *SMK*) cites *Doctrine and Discipline of Divorce* in *De Jure Naturae* (Lund).

February
15 (Thursday) JM's brother Christopher is said to be one of the leaders of the Inner Temple Parliament. (Inderwick, III, 84).

March
15 (Friday) Charles II issues Declaration of Indulgence towards Roman Catholics and Nonconformists.
17 England declares war on Holland.
22 Frances Jones, daughter of JM's friend Lady Ranelagh, dies and is subsequently buried in St Martin in the Fields; Marvell's 'An Epitaph Upon ——' commemorates her.

May
1 (Wednesday) JM's brother Christopher is again said to be one of the leaders of the Inner Temple Parliament (Inderwick, III, 84).
13 *Term Catalogue* advertising JM's *Artis Logicae* is licensed, which implies that the *Art of Logic* had already been published. On the same day JM's brother Christopher deposes in Court about his work as a solicitor in advising on the preparation of a will (PRO C24/974/13).

June
10 (Monday) JM's brother-in-law Richard Powell is elected to the Parliament of the Inner Temple (Inderwick, III, 85).

November
12/22 (Tuesday) The Marquis Turon de Beyrie praises JM's *Defensio Secunda* in a letter to Elie Bouhéreau, on whom see *DBF* (MS Z2.2.16(9) in Archbishop Marsh's Library, Dublin).

December
9 (Monday) JM's sixty-fourth birthday.
29 JM's *History of Britain* registered for publication (*SR* II, 451–2).

1673

Samuel Butler (?) refers to JM's episcopal tracts, *Areopagitica*, *Accedence* and *Paradise Lost* in *The Transproser Rehearsed* (on Butler's authorship see von Maltzahn 1995a) as does Samuel Parker in *A Reproof to the Rehearsal Transprosed*. Sir Roger L'Estrange (?) cites *Accedence* in *A Commonplace Book out of The Rehearsal Transprosed*. Christian Funck discusses JM and *Defensio prima* in *Quadripartitum historico-politicum orbis*. Anthony Hodges (?) alludes to JM and the Salmasian controversy in *S'too him Bayes*.

March

8   (Saturday) Charles II withdraws Declaration of Indulgence.
29   Charles II signs Test Act excluding Catholics from office in England.

May

6   (Tuesday) Andrew Marvell defends JM against Parker's attacks in *The Rehearsal Transprosed: The Second Part*. The book contains a (spoof?) licence dated 1 May, but the *Term Catalogues* specify a licence of 6 May. The catalogue also lists JM's *Of True Religion* as licensed, so JM's tract must already have been published; on the tract's political significance see Dzelzainis (1992).

June

12   (Thursday) James, Duke of York, is forced under the terms of the Test Act to resign as Lord High Admiral.

August

11/21   (Monday) Prince Rupert (who succeeded the Duke of York) is defeated by the Dutch off the coast of Texel.
12/22   The Marquis Turon de Beyrie again praises JM in a letter to Elie Bouhéreau in La Rochelle (MS Z2.2.16(9) in Archbishop Marsh's Library, Dublin).

October

31/9 November   (Friday) Michael, King of Poland, dies.

November

JM engages Elizabeth Fisher as maid; the date is an inference from her deposition of 15 December 1674, in which she is said to have worked for JM 'for about a yeare before his death'.

1   (Saturday) JM's brother-in-law Thomas Agar dies, and is succeeded in the office of Deputy Clerk of the Crown Office in Chancery by JM's nephew Thomas, son of his brother Christopher (Phillips, in Darbishire, p. 53); Agar's bequests include £200 to his 'son-in-law' (that is, stepson) Edward Phillips (PRO PROB 11/343/142).
24   Second edition of JM's *Poems* is published before this date, on which it is entered in the Term Catalogues. The only wholly undatable poem in the collection is JM's translation of

Horace's Pyrrha Ode (I.5). Its prosodic experiments resemble those of *Samson Agonistes* (Shawcross, 1963a), but that too is undatable.

December
9 (Tuesday) JM's sixty-fifth birthday.
23 Sir Peter Wentworth bequeaths £100 to JM in his will (PRO PROB 11/341/26); JM predeceased Wentworth, and it is not known if the money was paid to JM's family.

1674

In this year the Dutch printer Elzevir advertises JM's *Poems* and his three *Defences* in his *Catalogus Librorum*. Vincent Placcius refers to JM's response to Salmasius in *De scriptis et scriptoribus* (Hamburg). John Fell alludes to JM in the preface to Book Two of Antony à Wood's *Historia et antiquitates universitatis Oxoniensis* (Oxford). Thomas Flatman's *Poems and Songs*, many of which echo JM's poems (see 9 November 1661) is published.

January
30 (Friday) Richard Meggott seems to allude to JM's antimonarchical works in a sermon preached in the Guildhall Chapel and subsequently published.

February
1 (Sunday) JM's brother Christopher is recorded as one of the leaders of the Inner Temple Parliament (Inderwick, III, 94).
9/19 Treaty of Westminster, according to which the British withdraw from the Dutch war.
11 JM's brother Christopher is again recorded as one of the leaders of the Inner Temple Parliament (Inderwick, III, 95).

March
25 (Wednesday) JM is rated for four hearths for tax (PRO E179/143/370, m.57); it is not clear, except in terms of tax payable, why the eight hearths of the 1665 assessment should have shrunk to four.

April

17   (Friday) Dryden's *State of Innocence*, a dramatisation of *Paradise Lost* is registered (*SR* II, 479).

May

10   (Sunday) JM's brother Christopher is reappointed a leader of the Inner Temple Parliament (Inderwick, III, 95). On the same day Christopher and his son Richard sign an indenture (now in the Pierpont Morgan Library).

11/21   John Sobieski is elected King of Poland as John III (see July 1674).

13   JM's brother Christopher and his son Richard witness an indenture (BL Add. Chart. 10260).

26   Catalogue advertising JM's *Epistolarum Familiarium* is licensed; it seems likely that JM's *Familiar Letters* were published on or before this date.

31   JM's brother Christopher and his brother-in-law Richard Powell are listed as leaders of the Inner Temple Parliament (Inderwick, III, 96). This is the last time that Christopher was to hold this office during JM's lifetime, though he continued to hold it regularly until 1685; see *LR* V, 232–4.

June

1   (Monday) JM's daughter Deborah marries Abraham Clarke, a weaver, in Dublin (Parish Register, St Peter and St Kevin); the wedding must have taken place in St Kevin's Church, because St Peter's, which had been merged with St Kevin's in 1673, was in ruins, and was not rebuilt till 1685. Deborah's sisters had not heard of the marriage by the time their father had died, so it seems likely that JM never learned of the marriage.

July

JM's translation of the Latin version of *A Declaration, or Letters Patent* was probably published in this month; the Latin version had been issued early in July. JM's translation of a Polish document advocating an elective monarchy is a contribution to the Exclusion debate, in that it contests the Catholic succession.

1   (Wednesday) JM's *Epistolarum Familiarium* is registered for publication (*SR* II, 481)

6 Catalogue advertising the second edition of *Paradise Lost* is licensed, so it seems likely that the poem was published on or before this date; the price is three shillings. In this edition the poem is expanded from 10 books to 12, and commendatory poems by Marvell and S. B. are added; on the identification of S. B. with Samuel Barrow see von Maltzahn (1995*c*).

20? JM is ill, and prepares a nuncupative (i.e. orally declared) will with the help of his brother Christopher; on 5 December 1674 Christopher is to state in a deposition that the will was prepared 'on or about the twentieth day of July 1674 the day certaine he now remembreth not'.

27 JM receives bond of £40 from Richard Hayley (NYPL).

November

2 (Monday) Eight of JM's books are advertised in Robert Clavell's *General Catalogue*. JM's *History of Britain* is priced at 6s, *Of True Religion* at 3d, *Poems* and *Paradise Regained* and *Samson Agonistes* at 2s 6d, *Accedence Commenced Grammar* at 8d, *Artis Logicae* at 2s, *Epistolarum Familiarium* at 1s.

9? JM dies, probably of renal failure associated with his gout, aged sixty-five, in his house in Jewin Street 'in the 9th or 10th of Novemb 1674' (Aubrey, in Darbishire, p. 5).

AFTER MILTON'S DEATH

Dates within this section are restricted to information about JM's immediate family and about the first publication of books by him or closely associated with him. A full bibliographical listing is presented in John Shawcross's *Bibliography*; on JM's posthumous reputation see von Maltzahn 1994 and 1995*a* and his forthcoming book entitled *The Making of a National Poet: Milton and his Readers, 1650–1750*. The Chancery actions of Christopher Milton and his family are summarised in *LR* V, 469–72.

1674

November

12 (Thursday) JM is buried near the altar in St Giles Cripplegate (Parish Register).

23   JM's brother Christopher writes and files JM's nuncupative
     will.

December

 1? Elizabeth Milton's solicitor initiates legal action to have JM's
     will probated (*LR*, V, 207–9); the document should be among
     the Allegations for 1674 in PRO PROB 18/6, but is not there,
     nor is it listed in the indices; it seems not to have been seen
     since the mid-nineteenth century.
 2   JM's brother Christopher and his son Richard buy property in
     Oxfordshire (PRO C54/4405/13)
 5   Depositions on JM's will begin; brother Christopher testifies
     (PRO PROB 24/13/238ᵛ).
15   Elizabeth Fisher and her sister Mary are examined about JM's
     will (PRO PROB 24/13/311–313).

1675

February

22   JM's daughter Mary signs release to stepmother Elizabeth
     Milton in exchange for a payment of £100; on the same day
     JM's daughter Anne makes her mark on a virtually
     identical document. Both releases are now in the NYPL. On
     the same day JM's brother Christopher gives a bond of £200
     to Richard Powell. The purpose of the bond is not known,
     but it is likely to be related to the payments to JM's daugh-
     ters; it is mentioned in the release signed by Deborah on 27
     March 1675.
25   Elizabeth Milton receives letters of administration for settling
     estate (PRO PROB 6/50/14).

March

27   JM's daughter Deborah and her husband Abraham Clarke
     sign release to Elizabeth Milton in exchange for a payment
     of £100. The release, which is now in the NYPL, is written in
     a different hand from the releases signed by Deborah's
     sisters; the difference in handwriting, together with the later
     date, suggest that the document was prepared and signed in
     Dublin.

July
6 JM's brother Christopher's daughter Thomasine is buried in Ipswich (Parish Register, St Nicholas, Ipswich).

1676

October
18 JM's *Literae Pseudo-Senatus Anglicani* (Letters of State) is published before this date, when Daniel Skinner mentions the publication (PRO SP 29/386/65).

November
26 JM's brother Christopher's son Richard is called to the bar (Inderwick, III, 109).

1678

October
24 JM's mother-in-law Anne Powell makes will leaving bequests to JM's daughters Mary and Deborah (PRO PROB 11/358/138); the failure of the will to mention Anne, JM's eldest daughter, suggests that she was already dead. Between 22 February 1675, when she was alive and unmarried, and 24 October 1678, she had married a master builder and subsequently died in childbirth along with her child (BL Add MS 4320, fol. 232).

1679

January
7 Dr Nathan Paget bequeaths £20 to Elizabeth Milton (PRO PROB 11/359/9); see 11 February 1663.

1680

June
4 Elizabeth Milton receives a bond from her brother Richard Minshull (now in NYPL).

December
21   Elizabeth Milton receives £8 from Samuel Simmons and relinquishes her rights to *Paradise Lost* to him (Christ's College MS 8).

1681

JM's widow Elizabeth moves to Nantwich in or about this year.

April
JM's *Character of the Long Parliament* is probably published this month.
29   Elizabeth Milton signs another release to Simmons (Christ's College MS 8); the document is partly in her hand.

1682

February
JM's *History of Moscovia* is probably published this month.

1683

February
9   JM's brother Christopher's daughter Anne receives a licence to marry John Pendlebury (*Allegations for Marriage Licences issued from the Faculty Office of the Archbishop of Canterbury*, London, 1543–1869, in *Publications of the Harleian Society* 24 (1886), p. 165). Anne declared in her application that her parents were dead, but her father was to live for another ten years; her fiancé was a Protestant clergyman, so if her father was a Roman Catholic she may have chosen to suppress the fact. She also gave her age as 22, so she may or may not be the same Anne who had been baptised on 27 August 1641, who would by now have been 41 years old. John Pendlebury, her fiancé, gave his age as 42; he was actually about 30.

July
21   JM's books are burnt at Oxford on the same day that William, Lord Russell is executed in London for complicity

in the Rye House plot to assassinate the king (see Miller (1988), 431–3).

24   Brabazon Aylmer registers *Paradise Lost* (*SR* III, 76).

August

17   Aylmer sells half-right in *Paradise Lost* to Jacob Tonson (*LR* V, 264).

21   JM's *History Of Britain* is registered as part of the estate of John Martin (SR III, 184).

1685

July

8   JM's brother Christopher is named as Deputy Recorder of Ipswich (PRO C66/3241/6)

1686

April

21   JM's brother Christopher is made Serjeant-at-Law (*London Gazette*, 22–26 April); the oath is taken in the presence of Judge Jeffreys, who had recently been appointed Lord Chancellor in recognition of his 'faithful services' in the 'Bloody Assizes' of September 1685.

24   JM's brother Christopher is appointed as a Baron of the Exchequer (PRO T52/10, p. 424); his wife Thomasine 'dyed before her husband was made a Baron, bur^d. in St Nich^s. Parish Ipswich' (BL Add MS 19,142, fol. 78). John Evelyn noted in his diary (2 June 1686) that Christopher was a 'Papist' and was therefore excused from the requirements of the Test Act. Christopher's alleged Roman Catholicism is a persistent rumour, but proof is lacking.

25   JM's brother Christopher is knighted.

1687

April

14   JM's brother Sir Christopher is appointed Justice of Common Pleas (*LR* V, 280).

May

10 JM's brother Sir Christopher's salary is fixed at £1,000 per annum (PRO T 53/8, p. 141).

1688

July

6 JM's brother Sir Christopher retires as Justice (*London Gazette*, 5–9 July); the retirement may have been forced.

November

JM's granddaughter Elizabeth Foster, daughter of Deborah, is born in Ireland (BL Add MS 4472, fol. 3).

1691

March

24 Aylmer sells second half of his rights to *Paradise Lost* to Tonson (*LR* V, 290).

1693

March

22 JM's brother Sir Christopher is buried in Ipswich (Parish Register, St Nicholas).

1694

October

17 JM's brother Sir Christopher's son Thomas is buried (Parish Register, St Dunstan in the West).

1695

June

24 Elizabeth Milton signs a document 'at Mainwarings Coffee house in ffleet Street' assigning copyright of JM's prose works (which are listed in full) to Joseph Watts for a payment

of 10 guineas (Bedfordshire Record Office P 11/28/2, fols. 309, 313–15; see Lindenbaum, 1995).

1703

June
2 Abraham Clarke, son of Caleb and Mary Clarke and grandson through his father of JM's daughter Deborah, is baptised in Madras (Parish Register, St Mary's).

1707

March
17 JM's daughter Deborah's son Caleb's daughter Mary is baptised in Madras (Parish Register, St Mary's).

1711

February
13 JM's daughter Deborah's son Caleb's son Isaac is baptised in Madras (Parish Register, St Mary's).

1713

April
11 JM's widow Elizabeth gives bond to Randle Timmis (now in NYPL).

1716

January
26 JM's daughter Deborah's son Caleb's wife Mary is buried in Madras (Parish Register, St Mary's).

December
15 JM's daughter Deborah's son Caleb's daughter Mary is buried in Madras (Parish Register, St Mary's).

1719

Joseph Addison visits and befriends JM's daughter Deborah. The visit takes place shortly before his death on 17 June. In the same year JM's granddaughter Elizabeth Clarke marries Thomas Foster.

October
26   JM's daughter Deborah's son Caleb Clarke is buried in Madras (Parish Register, St Mary's).

1720

October
22   JM's widow Elizabeth signs an agreement with John Darlington about the rental of a farm at Brindley, in Cheshire; the document is now in the NYPL.

1721

February
20   JM's brother Sir Christopher's daughter Ann Pendlebury dies and is buried alongside her husband at Farningham, Kent.

August
10   George Vertue visits JM's daughter Deborah.
12   George Vertue describes his visit to Deborah in a letter to Charles Christian (BL Harleian MS 7003, fol. 176).

1725

June
16   JM's widow Elizabeth renews agreement with John Darlington (NYPL).

September
22   JM's daughter Deborah's son Caleb's son Abraham marries Anne Clark in Madras (Parish Register, St Mary's).

1727

April
5 JM's daughter Deborah's son Caleb's son Abraham's daughter Mary is baptised in Madras (Parish Register, St Mary's).
29 Public appeal for JM's daughter Deborah.

August
22 JM's widow Elizabeth signs her will (Cheshire Record Office, WS 1727).
24 JM's daughter Deborah dies; the date was recorded by John Ward in conversation with Deborah's daughter Elizabeth Fisher (*LR*, V, 328). Elizabeth Milton is referred to as 'late' in the inventory of her goods, so she must have died between 22 and 26 August.
26 JM's widow Elizabeth's estate is inventoried (Cheshire Record Office). The 108 items include '2 Books of Parradice'.

October
10 Probate of Elizabeth Milton's will (NYPL).

1729

October
4 JM's daughter Deborah's son Caleb's son Abraham's daughter Mary is buried in Madras (Parish Register, St Mary's); her parents are not named, so it is not certain that she is the child that was baptised on 5 April 1727.

1737

Monument to JM by John Rysbrack is erected in Westminster Abbey at a cost of £21 (Westminster Abbey Muniment 33,880).

1738

February
10 John Ward visits JM's granddaughter Elizabeth Foster in Pelham Street, Spitalfields.

11 Thomas Birch visits JM's granddaughter Elizabeth Foster.

March
24 Thomas Birch visits JM's granddaughter Elizabeth Foster and her brother Urban Clarke.

1742

Elizabeth Foster moves to Lower Holloway, London.

1743

September
 5 Abraham Clarke, the last known direct descendant of Deborah, is buried in Madras (Parish Register, St Mary's); the entry lists Clarke as one of a number of soldiers, so it is not certain that he is Caleb's son.

1749

Elizabeth Foster moves to Cock Lane, near Shoreditch Church, where she runs a chandler's shop.

1750

January
 6 Thomas Birch records a visit to Elizabeth Foster (BL Add MS 4,244, fol. 52^v).

April
 5 Benefit performance of *Comus* at Drury Lane for Elizabeth Foster.

November
13 Birch again visits Elizabeth Foster (BL Add MS 35,397, fol. 321^v).

1754

May
9 JM's granddaughter Elizabeth Foster, his last known direct descendant, dies in Islington 'of an Asthma & Dropsy' (BL Add. MS 4472, fol. 3).
14 Thomas Birch attends the funeral of Elizabeth Foster (BL Add. MS 4472, fol. 3).

1823

The manuscript of *De Doctrina Christiana* is discovered in the State Papers Office by Robert Lemon (PRO SP 9/61); it is subsequently translated by Charles Sumner and published (in English and Latin) in 1825.

1874

Alfred Horwood discovers JM's Commonplace Book at Netherby Hall, Cumberland; in 1876 Horwood publishes facsimile and printed versions.

Glossary of Legal Terms

Administration The process of settling the affairs of one who has died, including the ingathering of assets, the paying of debts and the distribution of the balance under either the will of the deceased or the laws on intestacy. Letters of Administration are the judicial authority required to administer the estate of a person who has died without leaving a will.

Allegation In ecclesiastical courts, a pleading after the libel (i.e. a response to the first pleading).

Answer In judicial proceedings, an affidavit in reply to interrogatories; in ecclesiastical courts the equivalent term is Allegation.

Baron of Exchequer The title of senior judges in the Court of Exchequer. Barons were appointed from the ranks of Serjeants and were required to serve as circuit judges.

Chancery The office of the Chancellor, originally the office in which writs for all common law actions were initiated. Chancery's common law jurisdiction was discharged through its offices, chiefly the Petty Bag Office, the Hanaper Office and the Enrolment Office. Its equitable jurisdiction was discharged through the Court of Chancery.

Chancery Country Depositions Depositions taken by Commission and recorded on parchment, retained initially by the court clerk and eventually passed to his superior, the Six Clerk.

Chancery, Court of In Tudor and Stuart England the Court of Chancery functioned chiefly as an equity court concerned with contracts, fraud, forgery, corruption and, in general, in cases where the common law could not act effectively. Chancery Courts routinely granted injunctions against proceedings under common law judgements, a practice which brought common law and equitable jurisdictions into dispute. In 1616 James I ruled in favour of the Chancery view that principles of equity could overturn common law, thus silencing the debate until after the Restoration.

Chancery Town Depositions Depositions recorded on paper and stored in the Examiners' Office in which they had been taken.

Close Rolls Chancery records containing royal commands to individuals from 1205 to the present. The commands are closed and sealed, in contrast to the open letters recorded in the Patent Rolls.

Concord of fine (Latin: *Finalis concordia*) A legal mechanism for the conveyancing of land. The legal record of the transaction was a summary of the proceedings drawn up by the chirographer of the Court of Common Pleas at the foot of the deed; these feet of fines were preserved in the Treasury. The system was abolished in 1833. See 'Feet of fines'.

Common Pleas, Court of The court that travelled with the King, the King's Bench, was distinguished by Magna Carta Article XVII from an inferior royal court to be held in a certain place, in practice Westminster Hall. The Court of Common Pleas was a common law court that exercised jurisdiction over personal actions such as debt and covenant and also supervised local and manorial courts. In the early seventeenth century it acquired jurisdiction to issue writs of prohibition and habeas corpus.

Court of Equity A court that judged claims and pleas and principles of equity, justice and fairness rather than strict principles of law. The major Court of Equity was the Court of Chancery, and important minor Courts of Equity included the Court of Requests and the Star Chamber.

Court of High Commission A prerogative court that used civil (rather than common law) procedures to deal with ecclesistical offences and suppress movements deemed to endanger the Church. It was strenuously opposed by the common lawyers and abolished in 1641.

Court of Requests A minor Court of Equity, widely used in the early Stuart period as a popular alternative to the Courts of Star Chamber and Chancery. Courts of Common Law denied that it was a legal court, and it was abolished in 1641, though the term survived until 1864 to describe various small claims courts.

Decree An order of an Equity Court.

Dedimus potestatem (Latin: 'We have given the power') A writ, of which this is the opening phrase, empowering someone who is not a judge to act in place of a judge.

Deposition A declaration or statement taken under oath and recorded for subsequent use in legal proceedings.

Docket books Collection of short summaries of bills and legal judgements.

Exchequer, Court of The Exchequer, the department of state responsible for the King's revenue, had financial and judicial branches. The financial branch, the Lower Exchequer, developed into the Treasury, which became a Department of State in 1688. The jurisdiction of the Court of Exchequer, the judicial branch that originated in the Upper Exchequer, was for centuries limited to revenue cases, but in the late sixteenth century developed supplementary equitable and common law jurisdictions.

Feet of fines A foot of fine is the botton third of a document summarising a conveyance, executed in triplicate and divided into three by a cut down the middle and another parallel to the bottom. The two top parts were given to the parties to the transaction, and the foot was returned by the keeper of the writs. Collections of feet of fines are filed in the PRO by county. See 'Concord of fine'.

Lord Chamberlain's Department The Department of State responsible for the administration of the royal household.

Patent Rolls Chancery rolls (from 1202 to the present), now in the PRO, recording documents related to the Crown, such as revenue, grants and appointments to offices.

Petty Bag Office The principal office responsible for the discharging of the common law obligations of the Court of Chancery; it was chiefly concerned with the issuing of writs and with the seizure of escheated and forfeited land. Its royal proceedings were preserved in a small bag rather than entered on rolls.

Pipe Rolls The record of accounts of the English Exchequer from 1156 to 1833. The origin of the name is disputed.

Pleas Rolls The records of the Royal Courts at Westminster (the *de banco* rolls of the Court of Common Pleas) and of the justices travelling with the King (the *coram rege* rolls). The Pleas Rolls contain pleas entered by Council for the parties and a record of decisions on the points raised.

Prerogative Court of Canterbury An ecclesiastical court that sat in Doctors' Commons, in Paternoster Row. The court exercised the testamentary jurisdiction of the Archbishop of Canterbury. A similar court was held for the Province of York.

Privy Council The executive and administrative branch of the Royal Council, as distinct from the judicial branch, the Court of Star Chamber.

Privy Seal (i.e. private seal) A seal ranking below the Great Seal and above the signet. The Privy Seal was used in financial transactions as a warrant for payments from the Exchequer.

Probate A certificate granted by the Prerogative Court of Canterbury or York certifying that the will of a deceased person has been proved and registered and that a right to administration has been granted to the executor. 'Proving a will' is another term for obtaining probate.

Reader In the Inns of Court, a judge who gave a series of lectures to student members of the Inns in the Lent and August vacations.

Recognizance An acknowledged obligation or bond enrolled in a Court of Record. The person bound acknowledges obligations such as discharging debts, keeping the peace and appearing to stand trial.

Recusant Rolls Records of fines levied on persons who refused to conform to the rites and ceremonies of the Church of England and to attend church on Sundays and holy days.

Rolls Pieces of parchment on which most legal records were written; the pieces were stitched together and rolled up for storage. Common law courts maintained Plea Rolls, Issue Rolls and Judgement Rolls. Other rolls, all of which are now in the PRO, include Patent Rolls, Subsidy Rolls, Close Rolls, Charter Rolls and Exchequer Rolls.

Serjeants-at-Law The highest order of counsel at the English bar. Masters of the Bench had to be elevated to Serjeants before they could be appointed to the King's Bench or the Court of Common Pleas.

Signet Office The office responsible for the administration of the royal signet and the drawing up of the King's Bills.

Star Chamber, Court of A court of criminal equity that met in the Star Chamber, a room in the Palace of Westminster in which, formerly, starra (deeds and bonds of Jews) had been deposited. The late medieval Royal Council had sometimes met in the Star Chamber, but after 1526 a distinction was drawn between council meetings at Court, which became the Privy Council, and council meetings in the Star Chamber. Both courts dealt with offences imperilling the safety of the state. Under the Stuarts the criminal jurisdiction of the Court of Star Chamber dealt with misdemeanours of a public character such as riot, forgery, libel and conspiracy; as an equity court free from the constraints of common law, it used fines, imprisonment, whipping, branding and mutilation as instruments for the repression of Puritans. The court's tyrannical and illegal exercise of its powers led to its abolition in 1641.

Staple A designation given to certain towns designated for specified areas of trade and commerce. Courts of the Staple had jurisdiction in pleas concerning debt covenant and trespass. The law applied was the Law Merchant rather than the common law.

Statute Staple A bond of record acknowledged in the presence of the Mayor of the Staple.

Subsidy Subsidies were originally import and export duties, but in the seventeenth century the term was extended to other taxes.

Writ Any written order can be described as a writ. Writs ordered in the name of the King were necessary to initiate action in the courts.

Bibliography

MANUSCRIPTS (INCLUDING BOOKS WITH MANUSCRIPT ANNOTATIONS)

Amsterdam, Universiteits-Bibliotheek
MS III.E.9 (letters from Nicolas Heinsius to Isaac Vossius)
Austin, Harry Ranson Humanities Research Center
Pre-1700 Manuscript 127 (see 1615)
Austin, University of Texas Library
Milton, John, *Defensio Pro Populo Anglicano* (1651) (see 24 February 1651)
Aylesbury, Buckinghamshire County Record Office
DAT 107 Horton, Bishop's Transcript, 1637
PR 107/1/1 (Horton Parish Register)
Bedford, Bedfordshire Record Office
MS P11/28/2 (see 24 June 1695)
Bloomington, Lilly Library, Indiana University
George Sikes, *The Life and Death of Sir Henry Vane* (see 5 September 1662)
Boston, Massachusetts Historical Society
Winthrop Papers
Boulder, Colorado University Library
Leo Miller Collection Box XXII, File 17 (Leo Miller, 'Milton in Geneva and the significance of the Cardoini Album')
Brussels, Bibliothèque Royale
MS II 4109 Mus. Fétis 3095 (a collection of 100 songs in the hand of Thomas Myriell)
Cambridge, Christ's College
Admissions Book
MS 8 ('Milton Autographs')
Cambridge, Trinity College
MS R.3.4 (JM's workbook)
MS R.5.5 (Anne Sadleir's letterbook)
MS 0.ii.68 (MS copy of John Lane's *Triton's Trumpet*)
JM, *Eikonoklastes* (C.9.179; see 19 June 1650)
Cambridge University Library
Justa Edouardo King 1638 (Add MS 154); annotated by JM
University Archives

Matriculation Book
Subscription Book
Supplicats 1627, 1628, 1629
Supplicats 1630, 1631, 1632
Canterbury, Cathedral Library
JM, *Eikonoklastes* (Elham 732); See 11 July 1652
Chester, Cheshire Record Office
Parish Register, Wistaston
WS 1727 (Elizabeth Milton's will and inventory)
Copenhagen, Kongelige Bibliotek
GKS 3579, 8vo (MS copy of JM's *Defensio*)
GKS 2259, 4to (see 1 January 1659)
NKS 373c, 4to (Oluf Borck 'Itinerarium')
Rostgaard 39, 4to (see 24 May 1652)
Dublin, Archbishop Marsh's Library
Z2.2.16(9) (contains letters from the Marquis Turon de Beyrie to Elie Bouhéreau)
Dublin, The Representative Church Body Library (Church of Ireland)
MS P.45.1.1 (Parish Register, St Peter's Church); printed in *Parish Register Society of Dublin* 9 (1911)
Dublin, Trinity College
R.dd.39 (volume of ten of JM's tracts with his autograph inscription to Patrick Young, the King's Librarian)
Ely Cathedral Library
Chrysostom, *Orationes LXXX* (Paris, 1604) (see 1636)
Polycarp and Ignatius, *Epistolae* (Oxford, 1644) (see 1644)
Eton College Library
MS Records 16 (survey of the Spread Eagle in Bread Street)
Exeter Cathedral
Milton, John, *Tenure of Kings and Magistrates* (see 13 February 1649)
Florence, Biblioteca Nazionale
MS Magliabecchiana Cl. IX cod. 60 (Svogliati Academy, Minute Book)
MS Palatina E.E. 15,2 (*Descrizione del numero delle case e delle persone della città di Firenze fatta l'anno MDCXXXII*)
MS Panciatichi 194 (letters from Emery Bigot to Antonio Magliabecchi and Lorenzo Panciatichi)
Geneva, Bibliothèque Publique et Universitaire
MS fr. 141C/Inv. 345 (Matricula Studiosorum)

The Hague, Algemeen Rijkskarchief
  MS Leg. Arch. 4582 (Gerald Schaep's accounts)
Harvard College Library
  MS 14496.34 (MS of Digression in JM's *History of Britain*)
  Farnaby, Thomas, *Systema Grammaticum* (1641) (see 1641)
  Gildas, *De Excidio Britanniae* (Heidelberg, 1587) (see 1638)
  Milton, John, *Defensio Pro Populo Anglicano* (1651) (see 17 February 1652)
  Pindar, *Olympia, Pythia, Nemea, Isthmia* (Saumur, 1620) (see 15 November 1629)
  Terence, *Comediae* (Leiden, 1635); see 1635
Harvard, Houghton Library
  MS Sumner 84, Lobby XI.3.43 (Cardoini Album, signed by JM)
Hereford, Hereford and Worcester County Record Office
  MS K11/3232/3/23 (indenture signed by JM's father)
Ipswich, Suffolk Record Office
  Parish Register, St Nicholas (ed E. Cookson, Parish Register Society, 1897)
Leeds, Brotherton Library
  Marten/Loder-Symonds MSS, 3rd series
Leiden, Rijksuniversiteitsbibliotheek
  BPL 1923/II (Letters from Emery Bigot to Nicolas Heinsius)
Leipzig, Stadtarchiv
  Bücherzensurakten I (1600–1690), Tit XLVI.152 (see 22 May 1652)
Lewes, East Sussex Record Office
  FRE 690 (poem by Alexander Gill)
London, British Library
  Add Chart 10,260 (deeds related to the hundreds of Carlford and Colneis, Suffolk)
  Add MS 4,180 (Thomas Birch's transcriptions of papers of Sir Edward Nicholas)
  Add MS 4,244 (miscellaneous biographical and literary memoranda by Thomas Birch)
  Add MS 4,292 (transcriptions by Thomas Birch)
  Add MSS 4300–4323 (letters addressed to Thomas Birch)
  Add MS 4,364 (State Papers relating to the Swiss Evangelical Cantons and Piedmont)
  Add MS 4,472 (Literary diary of Thomas Birch, 1754–64))
  Add MS 4,478 (Catalogue of Birch's MSS)
  Add MS 5,016* (Letters including several related to JM)
  Add MS 11,044 (Letters and Papers of John Scudamore)

Add MS 11,518 (Henry Lawes's five songs for JM's *Comus*)
Add MS 18,861 (contract for *Paradise Lost*)
Add MS 19,142 (Vol. 28 of Pedigrees of Suffolk, 43 vols)
Add MSS 24,487–92 (Joseph Hunter's 'Chorus Vatum Anglicanorum')
Add MS 24,501 (collections of Joseph Hunter relating to JM and his family)
Add MS 28,637 (Francis Peck's transcriptions of JM's poems, etc.)
Add MS 28,954 (Notebook of John Ellis)
Add MSS 29,372–29,377 (part-books of Thomas Myriell's 'Tristitiae Remedium')
Add MS 29,427 (anonymous collection of anthems and madrigals)
Add MS 32,310 (JM's family Bible)
Add MS 33,509 (Notebook of Thomas Stringer)
Add MS 34,326 (Petitions to Parliament and Council of State, 1648–54)
Add MSS 35,396–35,400 (Hardwicke Papers, correspondence of Philip Yorke and Thomas Birch)
Add MS 36,354 (JM's Commonplace Book)
Add MS 36,792 (Register of Presentations to Benefices, 1649–54)
Add MS 38,100 (Dispatches from agents and ambassadors to King Charles X of Sweden)
Add MS 52,723 (songs from JM's *Comus* in hand of Henry Lawes)
Aratus, *Phenomena*, 1635 (C.60.1.7); annotated by JM
Justa Edouardo King 1638 (C.21.c.42); annotated by JM
Milton, John, *Defensio Pro Populo Anglicano*, 1651 (C.114.6.37); presentation copy to John Morris
MS Cart Harl 112
MS Cottonian Charters 1/5/4
MS Egerton 1324 (Christoph Arnold's *album amicorum*)
MSS Egerton 2533–62 (papers of Sir Edward Nicholas, 30 vols.)
MSS Evelyn (605 volumes and unnumbered papers recently moved from Christ Church Oxford and not yet recatalogued)
MS Harleian 1557 (Visitation of Oxfordshire, 1634)
MS Harleian 5243 (John Lane, 'Historie of Sir Gwy, Earl of Warwick')
MS Harleian 6802 (7 November 1644)
MS Harleian 7003
MS Lansdowne 95 (see 23 November 1658)

MS Reg. 17 B xv (Lane)

MS Roy. App. 63 (MS version of Leighton's *Teares*, with music by JM's father)

MS Sloane 649 (29 November 1654, 10 August 1660)

MS Sloane 1325 (see 1650)

MS Sloane 1446 (copy of JM's 'Epitaph on the Marchioness of Winchester')

MS Stowe 76 (Roger Ley, 'Gesta Britannica')

MS Stowe 142/41 (the 'Ashburnham Document'; see 1 January 1655, 14 February 1655)

MS Stowe 305/6 (transcription of JM's *Eikonoklastes*)

MS Tanner 466 (William Sandcroft's MS anthology)

MS Trumbull Misc 22

Thomason Tract Collection (22,255 pieces in 2,008 volumes; for printed catalogue see Fortescue)

[Thomason, George?], Catalogue of the Thomason Collection of Civil War Tracts, 12 vols (1665?), catalogued as C.38.h.21; transcription, 12 vols (1669?) catalogued as C.37.h.13.

London, City of Westminster Archive Centre

Parish Register, St Martin in the Fields, printed in *PHSR* 66 (1936)

Parish Register, St Clement Danes (unpublished)

London, College of Arms

Painters Workbook I.B.7

London, Corporation of London Records Office

Historical Papers 1/11 (bond witnessed by JM's father)

London, Dr Williams's Library

Baxter Correspondence, 6 vols

London, Dulwich College

Muniment 503 (muniment witnessed by JM's father)

London, Goldsmiths' Hall

Committee of Contractors and Leases, 1641, 1651–62 (No. 1915.B393)

Committee of Survey, 1651

Court Book, 1648–1651

Extracts of Leases, 1650–1675

London, Guildhall Library

MS 1503 (Miscellaneous Rate and Subsidy Assessments, St Botolph's Parish, Aldersgate)

MS 3572 (Parish Register, St Mary the Virgin, Aldermanbury; printed in *PHSR* 61, 62, 65, 1931–5)

MS 4508 (Parish Register, St Anne Blackfriars; unpublished)

MS 5031 (Parish Register, All Hallows, Bread Street; printed in *PHSR* 43, 1913)

MS 5370 (Common Paper of the Company of Scriveners; printed in Steer)

MS 6419 (Parish Register, St Giles without Cripplegate; *Records* ed. W. Denton, 1883)

MS 7857 (Parish Register, St Dunstan in the East; printed in *PHSR* 69–70, 84–7 (1939–58)

MS 8319 (Parish Register, St Stephen Walbrook; printed in *PHSR* 69, 1919)

MS 8716 (Charters, Company of Scriveners)

MS 8820 (Parish Register, St Peter's upon Cornhill, printed in *PHSR* 1,4, 1877–9)

MS 8990 (Parish Register, St Mary, Aldermary; printed in *PHSR* 5, 1880)

MSS 10343–10348 (Parish Register, St Dunstan in the West; ed. T. C. Ferguson, 1898–1901)

London, Hammersmith and Fulham Record Office

DD/818/56 (Copies of Papers Relating to Hammersmith Chapel)

PAF/1/21 (Rate Books of the Vestry of Fulham)

London, Inner Temple Archive

Admissions Book, 1571–1640

London, Lambeth Palace Library

MS FM1/3B (Allegations for Marriage Licences)

London, Merchant Taylors' Company

Nomina descipulorum qui admissi sunt in scholam mercatorum scissorum Gulielmo Dugard Archididascalo 1644–62 (Scholars' Register); the MS will be moved to the Guildhall Library in 1997.

London, Public Record Office

30/24 (Shaftesbury Papers, 50 bundles)

C2 (Chancery Proceedings, Series I, 2,240 bundles)

C5 (Chancery Proceedings, Bridges, 640 bundles)

C7 (Chancery Proceedings, Hamilton, 671 bundles)

C8 (Chancery Proceedings, Mitford, 658 bundles)

C10 (Chancery Proceedings, Whittington, 546 bundles)

C21 (Chancery County Depositions, 767 bundles)

C22 (Chancery County Depositions, 1,052 bundles)

C24 (Chancery Town Depositions, 2,509 bundles)

C33 (Chancery Entry Books of Decrees and Orders, 1,262 vols)

C38 (Chancery Reports and Certificates, 3,330 vols)

C54 (Chancery Close Rolls, 20,899 rolls)

C66 (Chancery Patent Rolls, 5,573 rolls and volumes)

C152 (Chancery Certificates and Recogizances of Statute Staple, Rolls Chapel Office, 12 bundles, numbered 55–66)

C228 (Chancery Proceedings on the Statute Staple, Petty Bag Office, 35 bundles)

CP24/3 (Court of Common Pleas, Concords of Fines, Charles I, 33 files)

CP25/2 (Court of Common Pleas, Feet of Fines Files, 1,574 files)

CP40 (Court of Common Pleas, Plea Rolls, 4,135 rolls)

E112 (Exchequer Bills, Answers etc., 2,387 bundles)

E125 (Exchequer Entry Books of Decrees and Orders, Series III, 39 volumes)

E179 (Exchequer Subsidy Rolls, 401 boxes)

E372 (Exchequer Pipe Rolls, Pipe Office, 676 rolls)

E377 (Exchequer Recusant Rolls, Pipe Office Series, 82 rolls)

IND/1/1926 (Index to Chancery Reports & Certificates, 1657)

IND/1/8911 (Index to Warrant Books, 1660–1722, A–P)

LC4 (Lord Chamberlain's Department, Recognizance Rolls, 219 rolls and vols)

PC2 (Privy Council Office, Registers, 872 vols)

PROB 6 (PCC Administration Act Books, 206 vols)

PROB 10 (Registered Copy Wills, PCC and other probate jurisdictions, 7,457 vols)

PROB 11 (PCC Registered Copy Wills, 2,263 vols)

PROB 18 (PCC Allegations, 149 vols)

PROB 24 (PCC Deposition Books, 114 vols)

Req 1 (Court of Requests, Miscellaneous Books, 210 vols)

Req 2 (Court of Requests, Proceedings, 829 bundles)

SO4 (Indexes to Signet Office Docket Books, 15 vols)

SP9 (State Papers Domestic, Miscellaneous, 273 vols, built around the collection of Joseph Williamson, Keeper of the State Papers, 1661–1702)

SP14 (State Papers Domestic, James I, 218 vols)

SP18 (State Papers Domestic, Interregnum, 228 vols)

SP23 (State Papers Domestic, Interregnum, Committee for Compounding with Delinquents: Books and Papers, 269 vols)

SP25 (State Papers Domestic, Interregnum: Council of State, 138 vols)

SP29 (State Papers Domestic, Charles II, 450 vols)

SP45 (State Papers Domestic, Various, 89 vols)
SP82 (State Papers Foreign, Hamburg and Hanse Towns, 103 vols)
T52 (Treasury, King's Warrants, 122 vols)
T53 (Treasury, Warrants Relating to Money, 68 vols)
London, Royal College of Music
  MS 1940 (contains songs by JM's father)
London, Royal Society
  MS 1 (Notebook of Henry Oldenburg)
  MS 5 (Correspondence of Henry Oldenburg)
London, St Giles in the Fields
  Parish Register (unpublished, kept in the church)
London, Society of Antiquaries
  MS 138 (see 1658)
London, Westminster Abbey
  Muniment 28,515 (see 22 October 1628)
  Muniment 33,770 (see 1737)
  Parish Register, St Margaret, Westminster (Printed in *PHSR*, 64 (1935) and 88 (1968))
Longleat, The Marquess of Bath's Collection
  MS 124a Sir Bulstrode Whitelocke, Journal of the Swedish Embassy
  Sir Bulstrode Whitelocke, Collected Papers, 30 vols and 9 parcels
Madras, Fort St George Museum
  Parish Register, St Mary's Church (transcription made in 1739 by Alexander Wynch)
Munich, Bayerisches Hauptstaatsarchiv
  Bestand Kurbayern, Lit. 2636 (see 6/16 July 1653)
New Brunswick, NJ, Rutgers University Library
  Milton, John, *Defensio Pro Populo Anglicano* (1652) (X DA396. A3S32.1652) (see 7 January 1661)
  Lease signed by JM's father (14 December 1638)
New Haven, Yale University Library
  James Osborn Collection b63 (MS copy of *Comus* dated 1658)
New York, Carl H. Pforzheimer Library
  A Masque Presented at Ludlow (see 1638)
New York, Columbia University Library
  MS X823 M64/S52 (Milton's Letters of State)
New York, Pierpont Morgan Library
  Indenture signed by Christopher and Richard Milton (10 May 1674)

Milton, John, *Defensio Pro Populo Anglicano* (1651) (see August 1651)

MS MA 953 (see 17 November 1623)

MS of Book I of *Paradise Lost*

MS of Tonson letter

Letter (see 21 May 1654)

New York Public Library

anon, *Eikon Alethine* (see 26 August 1649)

Milton family MSS (27 July 1674, 22 Feb 1675, 27 March 1675, 4 June 1680, 4 June 1689, 11 April 1713, 22 October 1720, 16 June 1725 (*LR* V. 226–32, 253–5, 303–5, 312–14, 317–18)

Della Casa, Dante, Varchi (*KB 1529) (see December 1638)

Letter from Carlo Dati to JM (see 22 October 1647)

Letter from JM to Carlo Dati (see 20 July 1647)

Northampton, Northamptonshire Record Office

MS 1(0)18 (see 17 June 1651)

Oldenburg, Niedersächsische Staatsarchiv

Best. 20, Tit. 38 No. 73, fasc 13 (Hermann Mylius's diary and correspondence with JM, including seven letters by JM in the hand of an amanuensis)

Oxford, Bodleian Library

Best, Paul, *Mysteries Discovered*, 1647 (Pamph.84 (39))

Euripides, *Tragoedia*, 2 vols, Geneva, 1602 (Don.d.27,28)

Library Records, Bills to 1763 (b.36)

Matriculation Register (University Archives)

Milton, John, *Defensio Pro Populo Anglicano*, 1651 (E.H.2.20.Art)

Milton, John, *Eikonoklastes*, second edition 1656 (MS 4°.Rawl 408)

Milton, John, *Poems* (1645) (4°.F.56.Th, kept at Arch.G.e.44)

MS Add B.5 (Notebook of Christopher Wase, apparently in the hand of Henry Some)

MS Ashmole 36, 37 (English poetry, including verses by Alexander Gill)

MS Ashmole 436, part I (Nativities, including JM's horoscope)

MS Aubrey 6–9 (John Aubrey's 'Brief Lives')

MS Aubrey 13 (Letters to Aubrey)

MSS Clarendon (Papers of Edward Hyde, Earl of Clarendon, 152 vols)

MS Douce 170 (John Lane's continuation of Chaucer's 'Squire's Tale')

MS Lat. misc. d.77 (JM's *Ad Joannem Rousiam*, kept at Arch.-G.f.17)

MS Locke d.10 (John Locke's 'Lemmata Ethica Argumenta et Authores 1659')

MSS Nalson (State and Parliamentary Papers, 20 vols)

MS OAP Oxon.e.11 (Oxford Archdeaconry Papers: Visitation Books)

MSS Rawlinson A (English history, including papers of Thurloe and Pepys, 499 vols)

MS Rawlinson D.51 (fols. 23–41 are the Annual Catalogue of the Company of Scriveners printed in Steer, pp. 76–127).

MS Rawlinson D.230 (MS copy of JM's *Defensio*)

MS Rawlinson E.69 (Sermon by Robert South)

MSS Tanner (papers of Thomas Tanner, 473 vols, including papers of Archbishop Sandcroft, 144 vols)

MS Top. Oxon.c.289 (30 Dec 1646)

MS Wood D4 (anonymous life of Milton by Cyriack Skinner; printed in Darbishire, who attributes it to John Phillips)

MS Wood F39 – F45 (letters to Anthony Wood)

MS Wood F51

Wood 515 (Wood printed book collection)

Oxford, Christ Church College Library

    MS 44 (collection of music in the hand of Thomas Myriell, including a setting by JM's father; see 1632)

Oxford, Oxfordshire Archives

    Wills 183/236 (Henry Milton's will)

    Wills 184/2 (Agnes Milton's will)

Paris, Bibliothèque Nationale

    MS F.L. 602 (see 7/17 June and 26 June/6 July 1651)

    MS FR 10712 (letters from Gaston de Comminges)

    Nouvelles acquisitions françaises 1343 (letters from Emery Bigot to Gilles Ménage)

Philadelphia, Historical Society of Pennsylvania

    Ferdinand Dreer Collection 115.2 (see 16 February 1650)

Philadelphia, Rosenbach Museum

    MS 810/25 (see 7 June 1665)

Philadelphia, University of Pennsylvania Library

    Thomas Flatman MS ENG 28 (formerly 821/F61.1)

Princeton University Library

    Ames, William, *Conscientia* (Amsterdam, 1635) (see 1635)

Reading, Berkshire Record Office

    Parish Register, St Laurence, Reading

MS R/HMC XXXIX (Corporation of Reading, Muster Roll, 1642)
Rome, English College
  Pilgrim Book
Rome, Vatican Library
  MS Barb. Lat. 2181 fols. 57–8 (JM's letter to Holstenius)
St Gallen, Stadtbibliothek Vadiana
  MS 92a (*album amicorum* of Johannes Zollikofer; see 26 September 1656)
San Marino, California, Henry E. Huntington Library
  Bonds signed by JM's father (see 4 July 1633)
  Milton, John, *Defensio Pro Populo Anglicano* (see 24 February 1651)
  Creccellius, Johannes, *Collectanea* (Frankfurt, 1614) (see 21 October 1633)
Sheffield University Library
  Hartlib Collection, published on CD-ROM by UMI (1995)
Urbana, Illinois University Library
  Boiardo, *Orlando Innamorato* (Venice, 1608) (see 19 June 1643)
  Heraclidus of Pontus, *Allegoriae* (Basel, 1544) (see 1637)
  Lycophron, *Alexandra* (Geneva, 1601) (see 1634)
  Search Warrant (25 June 1650)
Vienna, Österreichische Nationalbibliothek
  MS 19287 (see 1614)
Washington DC, Folger Shakespeare Library
  MS X.d.161 (see 7 June 1665)
Wolfenbüttel, Herzog-August-Bibliothek
  MS Fol 649.84.12. Extrav. ('Commercium literarium Joh. Christiani de Boineburg et Hermanni Conringii a. 1660–1664')
Zürich, Staatsarchiv
  MS EII 457C (see 20/30 May 1655)
  MS EII 457g (see 17/27 January 1653)

PRINTED BOOKS AND ARTICLES

Alblas, Jacques (1994), 'Milton's *The Doctrine and Discipline of Divorce*: The Unknown Dutch Translation Discovered', *MQ* 28, 35–9.
Beal, Peter (1993), 'Milton', in *Index of English Literary Manuscripts* II Part 2 (Poole, Dorset), 69–104.

Berghaus, Günter (1983), 'A Case of Censorship of Milton in Germany: On an Unknown Edition of the *Pro Populo Anglicano Defensio*, *MQ* 17, 61–70.

Berry, Herbert (1992), 'The Miltons and the Blackfriars Playhouse', *MP* 89, 510–14.

Birrell, T. A. (1976), *The Library of John Morris: The Reconstruction of a Seventeenth Century Collection* (London).

Blakiston, Noel, 'Milton's Birthplace', *London Topographical Record*, XIX, No. 80, 6–12 and plates.

Boyle, Robert (1744), *Works*, ed. Thomas Birch (5 vols, London)

Bradley, S.A.J. (1976), 'Ambiorix Ariovistus, Detractor of Milton's *Defensio*, Identified', *MP* 73, 382–8.

Breasted, Barbara (1971), '*Comus* and the Castlehaven Scandal', *MS* 3, 202–24.

Brown, Cedric (1985), *John Milton's Aristocratic Entertainments* (Cambridge).

Burmann, Pieter (1727), *Sylloges Epistolarum* (5 vols, Leiden).

Campbell, Gordon (1987), 'Nathaniel Tovey: Milton's Second Tutor', *MQ* 21, 81–90.

Cappelli, A., (1906), *Cronologia e calendario perpetuo* 'Manuali Hoepli' series (Milan).

Carey, John (1963), 'The Date of Milton's Italian Poems', *RES* 14, 383–6.

Chaney, Edward (1985), *The Grand Tour and the Great Rebellion* (Geneva and Turin).

Cheney, C. R. (ed.) (1945; reprinted with corrections 1981), *Handbook of Dates for Students of English History* (London).

Chifas, Eugenia (1947), 'Milton's Letter to Gill, May 20, 1628', *MLN* 62, 37–9.

Clark, Donald L. (1948), *John Milton at St Paul's School* (New York).

Clarke, Hyde (1880), *Athenæum* 2746 (12 June), 760–61.

Clavering, Rose and John Shawcross (1960), 'Anne Milton and the Milton Residences', *JEGP* 59, 680–90.

Corns, Thomas (1990), *Milton's Language* (Oxford).

Creaser, John (1984), 'Milton's *Comus*: The Irrelevance of the Castlehaven Scandal', *N&Q* 229, 307–17, reprinted in *MQ* 21 (1987), 24–34.

Darbishire, Helen (ed.) (1932), *The Early Lives of Milton* (London).

Davies, W. H. (1939), 'A Note on Milton's Annotated Copy of Gildas in the Harvard University (Widener) Library', *Papers of the British School at Rome*, 15, pp 49–51.

Di Cesare, Mario (ed.) (1991), *Milton in Italy: Contexts, Images, Contradictions* (Binghamton, NY).

Doucette, Leonard (1970), *Emery Bigot: Seventeenth-Century French Humanist* (Toronto).

Dzelzainis, Martin (1992), 'Milton's *Of True Religion* and the Earl of Castlemaine', *The SCen* 7, 53–9.

Fallon, Robert (1993), *Milton in Government* (University Park, PA).

Fatio, Guillaume (1912), 'Milton et Byron à la Villa Diodati' in *Nos Anciens et leurs Oeuvres*, ed. Jules Crosnier, pp. 21–66.

Fletcher, H. F., ed. Shawcross, John (1989), 'John Milton's Copy of Lycophron's *Alexandra* in the Library of the University of Illinois', *MQ* 23, 129–58.

Fortescue, G. K. (1908), *Catalogue of the Pamphlets ... Collected by George Thomason, 1640–1661* (2 vols, London).

Freeman, James (1984), 'Milton's Roman Connection: Giovanni Salzilli, *MS* 19, 87–104.

French, J. M. (1939), *Milton in Chancery: New Chapters in the Lives of the Poet and His Father* (New York).

French, J. M. (1942), 'Milton's Supplicats', *HLQ* 5, 349–51.

French, J. M. and Maurice Kelley, 'The Columbia Milton' *N&Q* 195, 244–6.

Galbraith, V. H. (1953), 'The *Modus Tenendi Parliamentum*', *JWCI* 16, 81–99.

Grotefend, H. (1898; 10th edition, 1960), *Taschenbuch der Zeitrechnung des deutschen Mittelalters und der Neuzeit* (Hanover).

Hammond, Paul (1981), 'Dryden's Employment by Cromwell's Government', *Transactions of the Cambridge Bibliographical Society*, 8, Part i, 130–36, plates III and IV.

Hampshire, G. (1982), 'An Unusual Bodleian Purchase in 1645', *BLR* 10, 339–48.

Hanford, J. H. (1921), 'The Chronology of Milton's Private Studies', *PMLA* 36, 251–314.

Harris, Neil (1985), 'Galileo as Symbol: The "Tuscan Artist" in *Paradise Lost*', *Annali dell'Istituto e Museo di Storia della Scienza di Firenze* 10, 3–29.

Hunter, William (1989), *The Descent of Urania: Studies in Milton 1946 to 1988*, (Lewisburg).

Inderwick, F. A. (1896–1901), *A Calendar of the Inner Temple Records* (4 vols).

Kelley, Maurice (1952), 'Additional Texts of Milton's State Papers', *MLN* 67, pp. 18–19.

Kelley, Maurice (1962), 'Milton's Dante – Della Casa – Varchi Volume', *BNYPL* 66, 499–504.

Kelley, Maurice, and Samuel Atkins (1955), 'Milton's Annotations of Aratus', *PMLA* 70, 1090–106.

Kelley, Maurice, and Samuel Atkins (1961), 'Milton's Annotations of Euripides', *JEGP* 60, 680–87.

Kelley, Maurice, and Samuel Atkins (1964), 'Milton and the Harvard Pindar', *SB* 17, 77–82.

Lindenbaum, Peter (1992), 'Milton's Contract', *Cardozo Arts and Entertainment Law Journal* 10, 439–54.

Lindenbaum, Peter (1995), 'Authors and Publishers in the Late Seventeenth Century: New Evidence on Their Relations', *Library* 17, 250–69.

MacLean, Gerald (1995), *Culture and Society in the Stuart Restoration* (Cambridge).

Masson, David (1859–1894), *The Life of John Milton* (7 vols, Cambridge and London).

Miller, Leo (1960), 'Peloni Almoni, Cosmopolites', *N&Q* 205, 424.

Miller, Leo (1970), 'Milton's State Letters: the Lünig Version', *N&Q* 215, 412–14.

Miller, Leo (1971), 'The Italian Imprimaturs in Milton's *Areopagitica*', *PBSA* 65, 345–55.

Miller, Leo (1972), 'Milton and Lassenius', *MQ* 6, 92–5.

Miller, Leo (1974a), 'Salmasius's *Responsio*: Addenda to the Milton *Life Records*', *N&Q* 219, p. 95.

Miller, Leo (1974b) 'Milton, Fichlau, Bensen and Conring: Addenda to the Life Records of John Milton', *PBSA* 68, 107–18.

Miller, Leo (1975a), 'Milton's "Areopagitica": Price 4d', *N&Q* 220, 309.

Miller, Leo (1975b), '"Milton's" (sic) *Eikon Alethine* Located', *MQ* 9, 65.

Miller, Leo (1975c), 'Milton, Salmasius and *vapulandum*: Who should be Flogged?', *MQ* 9, 70–75.

Miller, Leo (1976a), 'Milton's Portraits: An Impartial Inquiry into Their Authentication' (*MQ* Special Issue).

Miller, Leo (1976b) 'Miltoniana: Some Hitherto Unrecognised Items', *PBSA*, 107–10).

Miller, Leo (1978), 'Milton Cited in Germany, 1652: A Further Note', *MQ* 12, 28–31.

Miller, Leo (1979a), 'Milton Dines at the Jesuit College: Reconstructing the Evening of October 30, 1638', *MQ* 13, 142–6.

Miller, Leo (1979*b*), 'Milton and Vlacq', *PBSA* 73, 145–207.

Miller, Leo (1980*a*), 'Milton's Clash with Chappell: A Suggested Reconstruction', *MQ* 14, 77–87.

Miller, Leo (1980*b*), 'Milton's 1626 Obituaries Dated', *N&Q* 225, 323–4.

Miller, Leo (1981), 'Milton's *Patriis Cicutis*', *N&Q* 226, 41–2.

Miller, Leo (1982), 'Milton and Weckherlin', *MQ* 16, 1–3.

Miller, Leo (1983), 'Milton's Contemporary Reputation: A Footnote to Parker and French', *MQ* 17, 56–7.

Miller, Leo (1984), 'The Date of Christoph Arnold's Letter', *N&Q* 229, 323–4.

Miller, Leo (1985), *John Milton and the Oldenburg Safeguard* (New York).

Miller, Leo (1986*a*), 'Two Milton State Letters: New Dates and New Insights', *N&Q* 231, 461–4.

Miller, Leo (1986*b*), 'Milton's *Defensio* ordered wholesale for the States of Holland', *N&Q* 231, 33.

Miller, Leo (1987*a*), 'Milton's Conversations with Schlezer and his Letters to Brandenburg', *N&Q* 232, 321.

Miller, Leo (1987*b*), 'Before Milton was Famous: January 8, 1649–50', *MQ* 21, 1–6.

Miller, Leo (1987*c*), 'Another Milton State Paper Recovered and a Mystery Demystified', *ELN* 25, 30–31.

Miller, Leo (1988), 'The Burning of Milton's Books in 1660: Two Mysteries', *ELR* 18, 424–35.

Miller, Leo (1989*a*), 'Milton's "Oxenbridge" Boiardo Validated', *MQ* 23, 26–8.

Miller, Leo (1989*b*), 'A 1647 German Critique of *Areopagitica*', *N&Q* 234, 29–30.

Miller, Leo (1989*c*), 'Milton and Vlacq: Addenda 1644–1688', *PBSA* 83 (1989), 533–8.

Miller, Leo (1990*a*), 'On Some Verses by Alexander Gil which John Milton Read', *MQ* 24 , 22–5.

Miller, Leo (1990*b*), 'Milton in the Zollikoffer and Arnold Albums', *MQ* 24, 99–104.

Miller, Leo (1990*c*), 'The Milton/Cromwell Letter to Transylvania', *N&Q* 234, 435–42.

Miller, Leo (1990*d*), 'New Milton Texts and Data from the Aitzema Mission, 1652', *N & Q* 235, 279–88.

Miller, Leo (1992), *John Milton's Writings in the Anglo-Dutch Negotiations* (Pittsburgh).

Oras, Ants (1953), 'Metre and Chronology in Milton's "Epitaph on the Marchioness of Winchester", "L'Allegro" and "Il Penseroso"', *MQ* 198, 332–3.

Parker, W. R (1938), 'Milton and Thomas Young, 1620–1628', *MLN* 53, 399–407.

Parker, W. R. (1957), 'Milton and the News of Charles Diodati's Death', *MLN* 72, 486–8.

Parker, W. R., ed. Gordon Campbell (1996), *Milton: A Biography*, second edition (2 vols, Oxford).

Patin, Gui (1846), ed. J.-H. Reveille-Parise, *Lettres* (3 vols, Paris).

Patrick, J. Max (1950), 'The Date of Milton's *Of Prelatical Episcopacy*, *HLQ* 13, 303–11.

Phelps, W. H. (1980), 'The Date of Ben Jonson's Death', *N&Q* 225, 146–9.

Pine, John (1739), *The Tapestry Hangings of the House of Lords* (London).

Prideaux, Sir W. S. (1896), *Memorials of the Goldsmiths' Company*.

Pritchard, Allan (1980) 'Milton in Rome: According to Wood', *MQ* 14, 92–7.

Radzinowicz, Mary Ann (1978), *Toward 'Samson Agonistes': the Growth of Milton's Mind* (Princeton, NJ).

Raylor, Timothy (1993), 'New Light on Milton and Hartlib', *MQ* 27,19–31.

Roberts, Michael (1988), *Swedish Diplomats at Cromwell's Court, 1655–1656* (London).

Rosenheim, James (1978), 'An Early Appreciation of *Paradise Lost*', *MP* 75, 280–82.

Rusche, Harry (1979), 'A Reading of John Milton's Horoscope', *MQ* 13, 6–11.

Sellin, Paul (1994), 'Alexander Morus before the Hof van Holland: Some Insight into Seventeenth-Century Polemics with John Milton', *Studies in Netherlandic Culture and Literature* (Publications of the American Association for Netherlandic Studies, 7), 1–11.

Sellin, Paul (1995), 'Alexander Morus and John Milton II: Milton, Morus and Infanticide', *Contemporary Exploration in the Culture of the Low Countries* (Publications of the American Association for Netherlandic Studies, 9), 277–86.

Sellin, Paul (1996), 'Alexander Morus before the Synod of Utrecht', *HLQ* 58, 239–48.

Shawcross, John (1956), 'Milton's Sonnet 23', *N&Q* 201, 202–4.

Shawcross, John (1959), 'Notes on Milton's Amanuenses', *JEGP* 58, 29–38.

Shawcross, John (1960), 'Speculations on the Dating of the Trinity MS of Milton's Poems', *MLN* 75, 11–17.

Shawcross, John (1961), 'The Chronology of Milton's Major Poems', *PMLA* 76, 345–58.

Shawcross, John (1963*a*), 'Of Chronology and the Dates of Milton's Translation from Horace and the "New Forcers of Conscience"' *SEL* 3, 77–84.

Shawcross, John (1963*b*), 'What We Can Learn from Milton's Spelling', *HLQ* 26, 351–61.

Shawcross, John (1965*a*), 'The Date of the Separate Edition of Milton's *Epitaphium Damonis*', *SB* 18, 262–5.

Shawcross, John (1965*b*), 'The Dating of Certain Poems, Letters, and Prolusions Written by Milton', *ELN* 2, 261–6.

Shawcross, John (1966), 'Milton's *Tenure of Kings and Magistrates*: Date of Composition, Editions, and Issues', *PBSA* 60, 1–8.

Shawcross, John (1984) *Milton: A Bibliography for the Years 1624–1700* (Binghamton, NY).

Shawcross, John (1990), *Milton: A Bibliography for the Years 1624–1700. Addenda and Corrigenda* (Binghamton, NY).

Shawcross, John (1991), 'A Note on a Copy of Milton's Poems', *MQ* 25, 107–8.

Shawcross, John (1993), *John Milton: the self and the world* (Lexington, KY).

Sikes, George (?) (1662), *The Life and Death of Sir Henry Vane* (London).

Sirluck, Ernest (1961) 'Milton's Idle Right Hand', *JEGP* 60, 749–85.

Sotheby, S. L. (1861), *Ramblings in Elucidation of Milton* (London).

Steer, Francis (1968), *Scriveners' Company Common Paper 1357–1628, With a Continuation to 1678, London Record Society*, Vol. 4.

von Maltzahn, Nicholas (1991), *Milton's History of Britain: Republican Historiography in the English Revolution* (Oxford).

von Maltzahn, Nicholas (1992), 'Laureate, Republican, Calvinist: An Early Response to *Paradise Lost* (1667)', *MS* 29, 181–98.

von Maltzahn, Nicholas (1993*a*) 'Naming the Author: Some Seventeenth-Century Milton Allusions', *MQ* 27, 1–19.

von Maltzahn, Nicholas (1993*b*), 'Dating the *Digression* in Milton's *History of Britain*', *HistJ* 36, 945–56.

von Maltzahn, Nicholas (1994), 'Wood, Allam, and the Oxford Milton', *MS* 31, 155–77.

von Maltzahn, Nicholas (1995*a*), 'Samuel Butler's Milton', *SP* 92, 482–95.

von Maltzahn, Nicholas (1995*b*), 'The Whig Milton, 1667–1700', in *Milton and Republicanism*, ed. D. Armitage, A. Himy and Q. Skinner (Cambridge), pp. 229–53.

von Maltzahn, Nicholas (1995*c*), '"I admird Thee": Samuel Barrow, Doctor and Poet', *MQ* 29, 25–8.

von Maltzahn, Nicholas (1996), 'The First Reception of *Paradise Lost* (1667)', *RES* 47, 479–99.

Watson, A. T. (1867 for 1866), 'Table of Law Terms', *Appendix to the Twenty-Eighth Report of the Deputy Keeper of Public Records*, No. 12, 114–38.

Whitelocke, Bulstrode (1991), *The Diary of Bulstrode Whitelocke, 1605–1675*, ed. Ruth Spalding (London).

Whiting, George (1936), 'Milton and Lord Brooke on the Church', *MLN* 51, 161–6.

Woodhouse, A. S. P. (1949), '*Samson Agonistes* and Milton's Experience', *Transactions of the Royal Society of Canada* 43, 157–75.

Woolrych, Austin (1974), 'Milton and Richard Heath', *PQ* 53, 132–5.

Woolrych, Austin (1986), 'The Date of the *Digression* in Milton's *History of Britain*, in *For Veronica Wedgwood: These Studies in Seventeenth-Century History*, ed. R. Ollard and P. Tudor Craig (Oxford), pp. 217–46.

Woolrych, Austin (1993), 'Dating Milton's *History of Britain*', *HistJ* 36, 929–43.

Index

251